REBUILDING
A MARRIAGE
BETTER THAN NEW

CINDY BEALL

HARVEST HOUSE PUBLISHERS
EUGENE, OREGON

Cover by Lucas Art and Design, Jenison, Michigan

Cover photo © Masterfile Studios / Masterfile

REBUILDING A MARRIAGE BETTER THAN NEW
Copyright © 2016 Cindy Beall
Published by Harvest House Publishers
Eugene, Oregon 97402
www.harvesthousepublishers.com

ISBN 978-0-7369-6711-2 (pbk.)
ISBN 978-0-7369-6712-9 (eBook)

Library of Congress Cataloging-in-Publication Data
Names: Beall, Cindy, 1970-
Title: Rebuilding a marriage better than new / Cindy Beall.
Description: Eugene, Oregon : Harvest House Publishers, 2016.
Identifiers: LCCN 2015039509 | ISBN 9780736967112 (pbk.)
Subjects: LCSH: Marriage—Religious aspects—Christianity.
Classification: LCC BV835 .B3575 2016 | DDC 248.8/44—dc23 LC record available at http://lccn.loc.gov/2015039509

Printed in the United States of America

16 17 18 19 20 21 22 23 24 / BP-CD / 10 9 8 7 6 5 4 3 2

What people are saying about Cindy Beall and
Rebuilding a Marriage Better Than New

To be honest, I'm a massive Cindy Beall fan. I had the privilege of watching God restore her broken marriage and truly make it better than new. That's why I believe every married couple should read Cindy's powerful new book, *Rebuilding a Marriage Better Than New*. If your relationship needs a tune-up or a complete overhaul, read this book with an open heart and I believe God will do a new work in you.

Craig Groeschel
senior pastor of Life.Church, Edmond, Oklahoma
author of *#Struggles*

God doesn't promise improved; He promises brand new. In her book *Rebuilding a Marriage Better Than New*, Cindy takes us beyond the "ever after" and helps us find victory and hope "even after." With wisdom and encouragement born out of her own marriage story, she guides us on a path to discover God's best for our marriage. This is a must read book for all couples!

Justin and Trisha Davis
authors of *Beyond Ordinary: When a Good Marriage Just Isn't Good Enough*

Cindy Beall is basically a "hope bomb" just looking for a place to detonate! Her story provides undeniable proof that our God is a Redeemer and we have access to living HOPE in Jesus regardless of how messy, difficult, or painful our current relationships are. She's so genuine that reading her books is like having a conversation with a dear friend. My advice is to buy at least two copies because whomever you loan *Rebuilding a Marriage Better Than New* to is probably going to keep it!

Lisa Harper
author and Bible teacher

What we love about *Rebuilding a Marriage Better Than New* is that its author, Cindy Beall, isn't just giving helpful information, but she has personally lived out this message of hope for the most devastated of marriages! Cindy and Chris Beall have a beautiful testimony of partnering with God to not only see their marriage renovated but totally rebuilt and better than ever! We believe that God is going to use this book to transform families!

Joe and Lori Champion
founders of Celebration Church, Austin, TX

Cindy Beall brings to life the true meaning of hope and grace, engaging you in a practical guide to rebuild the love and relationship in your marriage that you've always dreamed of. Not only do I know this book will help you, but I know this couple and they're the real deal!

Bil Cornelius
lead pastor of Church Unlimited
author of *Today Is the Day*

The messy business of the restoration of a marriage is a worthy pursuit. However, it is a minefield of lies, fear, and pain. Breaking through to the broken heart with truth will be the only saving grace. Cindy's candid book has given leaders fighting for restoration a powerful tool. She combines her personal journey of healing along with biblical narratives and clear biblical principles to help you navigate this minefield with truth.

I recommend *Rebuilding a Marriage Better Than New* to pastors and leaders who will be a part of the fight for marriage and restoration. But mostly, it is a must read for those couples who have been devastated by infidelity. Cindy will help you walk through the journey and do more than survive; you will actually thrive.

Dr. Tim Scott
lead pastor of Grace Church, San Diego

Cindy Beall has produced a much-needed guide on how to use the tragedy of infidelity as a catalyst for creating a new and improved marriage.

Rick Reynolds
founder and president of Affair Recovery, Austin, TX

To my husband, Chris.
You are the best representation of a strong, confident man
who simultaneously walks in humility and brokenness.
Thank you for allowing me to share your darkest hour with the world.
I look forward to growing old with you.

CONTENTS

God Makes All Things New

*He who was seated on the throne said, "I am making
everything new!" Then he said, "Write this down,
for these words are trustworthy and true."*

Revelation 21:5

If God showed us a timeline of all the occurrences that would happen in our lives, we would most assuredly start hyperventilating and bargaining with Him to reroute the path ahead of us. In no way, shape, or form would we ever think we could survive such difficult circumstances. Death of a loved one, infidelity by a spouse, the loss of every material possession we own. It's more than our finite minds can even begin to fathom. And because of that, He doesn't show us. Instead, He gives us the grace we need to get through things as they come.

When you do a Google search using my name, a good amount of the results will have something to do with betrayal, infidelity, and sexual sin. Why, you ask? Because that is in my history. It's on my marriage résumé. My first book, *Healing Your Marriage When Trust Is Broken*, is about just that.

In the early part of 2002, my husband, Chris, and I had the opportunity to move to Edmond, Oklahoma, so that my husband could join the staff of Life.Church. It was truly a dream come true. He was a worship leader, and I led alongside him and had been doing so for nearly ten years. But one devastating February morning brought about a crushed heart, a wrecked marriage, and a demolished ministry for us because of my husband's infidelity and pornography addiction. My husband had been on the team for barely six weeks and could no longer live the lie he had been living for the previous few years. Within a minute, my heart went from joyful to devastated as I became keenly aware that the life I had lived with my husband was a lie. A big, fat lie. Or at least it felt that way then.

I share this part of my life with you so that you will understand where I've been. I have walked through the valley of the shadow of death and lived to talk about it…more than once. I have begged God to prevent painful situations from entering my path instead of asking Him to help me endure them…more than once. I have experienced seasons in my life where death would have been welcomed had I possessed the gumption to try…more than once. But alas, I am still on this earth because as promised in Romans 8:28, God doesn't waste one single bit of our pain. Indeed, He doesn't, friend. Indeed, He doesn't.

When something bad happens, you have three choices: you can let it define you, let it destroy you, or let it strengthen you. I don't know who first authored that statement, but I can assure you, that person has been through the wringer. You don't write that after living a life of comfort. You write it after you've walked through some dark days, years even, and lived to not only talk about it but also to encourage others because of it. On this marital hike Chris and I have been on for 14 years, there were times where our past could have destroyed us. While some may use our story to define us, we do not. We use our testimony and the power of God's renovation in our marriage to strengthen us. We don't have all the answers for marriage restoration, but we do have some tried-and-true principles and advice to offer you on your own pilgrimage.

Healing Your Marriage When Trust Is Broken was a book about healing. Many have referred to it as an emergency-room type of book. One you read to stop the bleeding and get hope and encouragement from. *Rebuilding a Marriage Better Than New* is about living. But in order to begin truly living in victory with betrayal in your marital past, you do have to walk through the appropriate valleys first.

My goal as a Christ-follower is to have my life testify to the greatness of my God. I want Him to use anything and everything to impact a lost and dying world. So that is why I tell my story and propose that you do the same. In order to help you get to that place, I've laid this book out in four sections: heal deeply, build wisely, live fully, invest generously. As you can see, the goal is to invest generously in someone's life out of our own deep aches. But we cannot invest generously into someone's life unless we first heal deeply, build wisely, and live fully.

As I've endured and flourished in my own life, I have done so by trusting in God and His perfect Word, the Bible. It is the only truth to stand on. In each chapter you will find Lie vs. Truth features that contain Scripture verses paraphrased in first person as a tool for you to combat the lies that often plague us after devastation.

I close each chapter with questions for you to further ponder and consider. I would love it if you and your spouse would walk through these. Regardless, these are meant to get you thinking deeper about your marriage and how you can learn and grow from your own experiences.

This marriage book is meant for the husband and the wife. My prayer is you will both use this as a tool to help strengthen your marriage in whatever way it needs rebuilding. I do believe that sharing about what Chris and I have endured and the victory we continue to walk in will provide hope to you and your spouse.

Hope seems to be in short supply these days. Maybe that's because we are looking to the wrong sources to find it. It is not found in a possession or a human being. It is found in the One True God. The Creator of the Universe. The First and the Last. The Beginning and the End. Our Abba. Our Heavenly Daddy.

Hope in your gracious God defines you. Your circumstance does not.

Let's seek Him like never before in our happy days and in our brutally difficult days. For He is always near and will never, ever, ever forsake us.

HEAL DEEPLY

Rebuilding from the Ground Up

At exactly 11:35 p.m. on June 29, 2013, something woke me from a deep sleep. I sat up instantly and wondered if someone was trying to break into our home. I sprung from the bed where my husband, Chris, was sleeping soundly and went to check things out. Our three boys were asleep in the theater room. There wasn't anyone or anything out of the ordinary to be seen when I peeked out onto the driveway through the service door. At that point, I was irritated and thought, *I'm going back to bed and nothing else better wake me up again tonight!*

I'm convinced that God woke me up some 25 minutes later. I heard *Wake up* in my mind. It wasn't a shout or a yell. It was a message simply, powerfully spoken to me. The clock read 12:00 a.m. on the dot. Immediately, I sat up in our bed and noticed an orange glow on the windows in the sitting area of our master bedroom. My initial thought was somebody's house was on fire. Without even gathering a coherent thought, I jumped out of bed, hurried to the laundry room, and looked out the service door again and indeed saw a fire. But the fire wasn't at *somebody's* house. No, the fire was in *my* house.

Upon seeing the flames shooting out of the attic vents down the side of our garage, I went into a full state of panic, the kind that was not going to be eased by any amount of self-talk, calming words, or even memorized Scripture. I went back to my bedroom and woke up Chris and then left him to fend for himself. My heart-beat rocketed. My mind was not entirely clear, but I had one coherent thought: my sons are getting out of this burning house.

The next events are a bit blurred. In seconds I was standing in the doorway of our theater room to wake up our three sleeping boys, lying scattered around the room. One was on the sofa, one on the oversize chair, and one on a partially deflated air mattress. I just remember flipping on the lights.

"THE HOUSE IS ON FIRE! THE HOUSE IS ON FIRE! GET UP! GET UP! GET UP!" I shouted as I tugged on their arms until the boys finally came to. I would have pulled their arms out of their sockets if I'd had to. Within a few seconds we were out the door to the backyard with our little Yorkie puppy, who thinks she's a 100-pound German shepherd, following closely behind.

Once we were outside, we came around to the side where Chris was standing and saw the flames on the corner of our garage. My first impression was that it wasn't too bad. As Chris got on his phone, he asked if I had called 911. Uh, no. No I did not. I had to get my babies out. I'm telling you, there is only one thing on a mama's mind when jeopardy is nearby.

After hanging up with the 911 operator, Chris said, "Uh, shug, you better get some clothes on, because the firefighters are on their way." I looked down and noticed that I was doing all of this running around the house and yard without being appropriately dressed. For the love. Of all nights to not sleep in my shorts it would be this one. (This is the part of the story where you are going to shake your head at me.) Because the flames were only on the side of the house, I decided to go back inside and get some shorts.

(See.)

I figured I had plenty of time to find something to wear. And if I needed more fresh air, I'd just run out the front door, grab a breath, and head back in. Easy peasy.

Sweet honey molasses, there was no fresh air to be found! The smoke smell was so rank I couldn't breathe. It was horrendous. But, I remember thinking, in my muddled mind, *My family is safe. If I don't make it back outside, at least my boys are alive.*

I ran back to my bedroom, all the while hearing the smoke alarm that had started a minute or so earlier. The power was lost by then, so it was completely dark. I grabbed my phone from the nightstand and used its flashlight feature to make my way to the closet. My crazy mind recalled that the last thing I put into the clean laundry basket was my pair of black and pink Fila running shorts. I grabbed them and started running for the back porch. By the time I reached the kitchen I remember thinking, *I'm gonna make it!*

I met up with the boys in the backyard and we proceeded to the front yard. The fire looked to be contained to one small section, so my husband decided to fight it with our water hose. As we came near him, he said, "I got this," and he continued spraying the fire, fully expecting it to diminish with each drop.

(Not even kidding.)

Unbeknownst to him, the entire attic was engulfed in flames. Like *Backdraft* the movie flames. Dark smoke was rising from all of our attic vents. Once the firefighters arrived and looked into the attic, our deepest suspicions were confirmed: Our house was truly on fire.

I didn't know what to think and couldn't have told you how I felt either. It was such a surprising moment to be standing where I was, watching what I was watching. Sadly, it was the kind of scene you swear only happens in the movies.

In one fell swoop, everything was gone. Within four hours, nearly every material possession we owned was gone. Life was normal at 11:00 p.m. on Saturday, June 29, 2013, and then some five hours later, it was completely different. Life-altering different.

I'd like to say that kind of "this can't really be happening" shock has only happened once in my life. But as I shared in the introduction, I have faced such a moment before. When Chris shared about his infidelity and addiction, I also felt half-naked, exposed, and numb with pure disbelief. And that time, like this time, I was only able to stand by helplessly as I watched the thing I believed to be my safe haven go up in flames. All I could do was say good-bye to what I had known…and pray for a way through the ashes to something new.

When Life Goes Up in Flames

Ever been here? To the place of life-altering change within a matter of hours or minutes? You're going about your day, doing your daily routine, clearly expecting to find what you normally find on that day, fully anticipating small delays in carpool lines, in grocery stores, or on expressways due to traffic, and then *bam*. Nothing is the same, and everything is different. The thought *This happens to other people* is in the forefront of your mind, and you are inching closely to the line of shock and denial. In fact, you are very close to hurdling over it and taking up residence.

You get that phone call that tells you you'll never hug the neck of someone again whom you love so dearly.

You spontaneously examine your body during your shower and feel a lump that didn't seem to be there two months ago.

You are escorted into a room to find your boss and the HR director of your company sitting at a table explaining to you your severance package.

You find a series of e-mails or text messages between your spouse and someone else indicating that something is going on that should not be going on.

Life isn't fair sometimes. Other times things happen to you of your own doing. You suffer the consequences of your actions, fully aware that you made the choice and, quite honestly, can blame no one but yourself for what is happening.

Other times, you suffer at the hand of another. Someone else's actions are causing your heartbreak. You hate them for what they've done, but even that hatred doesn't remove decades of love that you have for them.

At this stage, it is typical to want to get back to normal. To get back to the life before the lump was found, before the phone call came, before you were let go from your beloved company, before the realization came that your spouse has been cheating on you, before the house burned down. We want the old life. We want the way things were. We want to live in denial at times, or at least have the ability to make the choice to ignore our present circumstances. Our old life may not have been the most amazing life, but it certainly didn't hurt this bad.

In that moment, as much as we long for a different scenario to be our truth, we know we have to press on for ourselves and the people we care about. We have to find our way to the renewal and rebuilding that only God can provide.

Insisting on a New Foundation

Within a few weeks of the fire, Chris and I not only had decided to rebuild on our lot but had also chosen a builder and a floor plan. We wanted to get started as quickly as possible on the rebuilding of our new home so we could move back. We were blown away with how good the insurance coverage was. Our two claims adjusters told us about benefits we didn't even know we had. Most companies want to spend as little as possible. Our insurance company wanted to give us everything they possibly could. And more.

Except a new foundation.

You see, the fire shot up into the attic, and our home burned from the top down. By the time the fire was out, everything was destroyed. But the inspectors from our insurance company said the foundation *probably* wasn't damaged from the fire. There were no markings that could be seen to show significant fire damage.

Chris and I were dumbfounded. We didn't understand why they would suggest building a new home on an old foundation. While there didn't appear to be significant damage to the concrete that once held our home, we didn't know for sure. And what if the water-lines and sewer drains in the foundation were damaged? Chris and I made the decision to refuse to build something new on something old. We felt there was too much risk to build our hope and home on something possibly compromised and weakened. Thankfully, there was enough extra insurance money to cover the cost of a new foundation.

Building something new on something old. Who does that? Hurting couples do it all the time. Most of the time they do it because it's less expensive relationally and emotionally or, quite frankly, because it's an easier route…temporarily, that is.

Our culture is obsessed with taking something old and worn down and improving it. Slap a coat of fresh paint on a wall and *voilà*, you have a new look. I personally love the HGTV and DIY cable channels. I have spent hours trying to figure out which house the couple will choose after hunting for some time, and I've waited with bated breath to see how a transformed room will look. I may or may not have thought about going down to my local Home Depot or Lowe's just hoping it was the day one of the DIY guys decided to show up and crash someone's house. I have even imagined what I would say to one of those show hosts to convince them that my house should be the next one to receive their design and construction expertise. Make no mistake about it, I am a renovation junkie.

While home renovation is usually much more cost effective than building from scratch, when it comes to God, He has a tendency to tear down the old and create something new. We might be uncomfortable during the process, but why would we settle for anything less than the new thing God is trying to build in our hearts and lives?

God's Plan for Something New

Jesus often used metaphors to make a point about how we are to live our lives. In Matthew 9 Jesus answered the questions of John's disciples when they asked about fasting. In verses 16-17 He said, "No one sews a patch of unshrunk cloth on an old garment, for the patch will pull away from the garment, making the tear worse. Neither do people pour new wine into old wineskins. If they do, the skins will burst; the wine will run out and the wineskins will be ruined. No, they pour new wine into new wineskins, and both are preserved."

First of all, what's a wineskin? Today a wineskin is merely a wine bottle, but back in biblical times, they used an animal's skin, usually that of a goat, sewn together to carry their wine. When new wine was placed into new wineskins, it was not yet complete. It would continue to ferment, which would stretch the wineskin.

If we look at the original Greek language we can better understand what Jesus was speaking about when He talked of old and new. The Greek word for "old" in this passage is *palaios*, which means "antique, worn out, not recent." The Greek word for "new" is *neos*, which means "fresh." So when we try to pour new wine into old wineskins, we are trying to put something fresh into something worn out.

New wine expands and grows, so it needs a new, flexible wineskin; not an old, worn-out, brittle one that will burst open. The only thing that could be put into an old wineskin is old, fully fermented wine that is through with its aging, maturing process.

So what exactly is the new wine and old wineskin when we're taking Jesus's truth and applying it to our lives and marriages? The way I see it, the new wine is the new desires and attitudes we have and want to act on in regard to our marriage. But the old wineskin is the typical, old way we react to and with each other. We want to act differently, yet we don't. Our old ways of being and interacting cannot handle the pressure and growth that the new behaviors and goals bring. When we have new, healthy attitudes and desires (new wine) but try to achieve them by placing them into our worn patterns (old wineskin), we don't get the desired change we want. If you pour new wine into a brittle, overused wineskin, that old wineskin will burst.

God knew that we all would need this lesson on one or more occasions. We're human, so we still try to do things our way much of the time. But if you have also tried to get a new result by doing things the old, worn way or have attempted to create something new before tending to an old container or foundation, then you know how powerful this message is. If only we would remember it!

> We can't just want the change. We must make the change—inside and out.

Every married couple finds themselves hitting a wall at some point in their marriage. Some experience it far more often than others. For many couples, a crisis arises before they realize that how they build their lives and determine the things they value, the way they spend their time and money, and the way they practice virtuous dishonesty (a concept I will refer to in the next chapter) have made the wineskin old and brittle. That wineskin has to be discarded and replaced with a new one.

This doesn't mean we give up on a marriage and start looking for a new life. What it means is, we faithfully and intentionally find a new way of relating to each other, a new way of spending time together, a new way of being open with one another, and new ways of nurturing and growing our marriage.

You see, the old stuff, the old marriage, must be replaced with an entirely new structure, including a new set of values, attitudes, and behaviors. You're still the same two people in physical appearance, who hopefully still like each other and love each other. (Don't fret if you don't like or feel love for your spouse; this can return.) But the behavioral and spiritual norms have to be replaced by priorities, practices, commitments, and communication that can handle the pressure of the coming days, weeks, and months.

As difficult as this time of growth can be, it will encourage you to know these new norms will be the very things that will cause you to look back years from now and say, "I would endure it all over again in order to have the marriage that I have now."

When our life was crumbling around us years ago, Chris and I knew that our old relationship foundation had to be removed and taken away so Christ could build a new one. There were too many potential risks and flaws in the foundation where we had built our old life. Just like new wine, our lives and hopes needed a new vessel, a new foundation capable of holding them. With great intention we had to pour in new ways to relate to one another, talk to one another, minister together, raise children together, do life together.

Everything has to be given to God to be made new.

Committing to Your Relationship Rebuild

You may be asking how this works. What does that look like in everyday life? I'm glad you asked.

Maybe your marriage is really suffering. You may even be on the brink of divorce. You don't like each other and aren't even sure you want to stay together. Quite frankly, if your spouse came up and said, "I want a divorce," you'd be more relieved than you are sad. You try to live your life in a way that honors God. You pray, attend church, and read your Bible. Even though your marriage is struggling, you occasionally have thoughts like, *Maybe God will give me the marriage I've always wanted.* So you stay. And you and your spouse decide to start seeing a counselor who gives amazing, godly advice. You decide to take her suggestions and try to implement them into your marriage. Maybe you decide that you aren't going to be critical anymore about your spouse and instead try to be encouraging. Only there is still a problem. You are still clinging to some choices, habits, or even hobbies that keep you tied to the old.

For example, you hang around with the group of friends who badmouth your spouse and their own spouses because it's what all of you do. The new wine is your desire to make good changes; the old wineskin is spending time with the same group of friends who seem to lead you further away from Christ and definitely further away from a healthier marriage.

So what do you do with these friendships you've had for years, even decades? This is the hard part. You actually have to commit to working on your marriage. And you have to decide how much you are willing to sacrifice for it. How important is it to you to stay married? If these relationships do nothing to encourage you and everything to weigh you down on this new journey to save your marriage, then are they the best for you in this season?

You and your spouse could probably benefit from extended time together. Consider taking a sabbatical from outside relationships for a season so you can focus on your marriage. Not that you wouldn't talk to anyone at all, but if it was part of your routine to have dinner with friends once a week or play golf with friends every Saturday, it could be a good call to hone in on your marriage by devoting that extra time to your spouse. If your marriage is in a fragile state, you have to ask yourself just how much you are willing to let go of to make it healthy again.

Here's another example. Perhaps you have gotten so used to responding to your spouse in anger and defensiveness that neither of you wants to have a conversation, because it will almost always end in an altercation. You are tired of this way of communicating with one another and know that something has to give, because living this way is unacceptable for either of you any longer. So the desire is there. But instead of that new wine going into a new wineskin, one that is perfect for the new wine, it is sloppily poured into the old wineskin which includes hot-headed anger, a defensive tone, and several sarcastic comments. You want to make changes, but you don't. You might be able to identify with the apostle Paul, who said,

"I do not understand what I do. For what I want to do I do not do, but what I hate I do" (Romans 7:15). You're not alone. Even the godliest people struggle in this area. Don't lose heart.

Practically speaking, you have to decide not to allow your emotions and negative attitude to rise up. You can't let your emotions own your actions. When it comes to discussing things you and your spouse don't agree on, you must be willing to truly listen. Not only that, you have to be teachable and willing to recognize your own fault in the issue. If your spouse says you tend to spend too much money or that you are hardly helping with the kids, instead of getting bent out of shape, consider stopping and asking yourself if there is any truth to what he or she is saying. It is easy to become defensive when our spouse is calling us out on something we do wrong while they do wrong things too. So we ignore what they say and throw their flaws and mistakes back at them. That only breeds further conflict.

> You can't want your way into a healthy action. You have to commit to doing it.

Standing on a Foundation of Truth

You have a spiritual enemy named Satan, and he desires nothing good for you. He will trick you and oftentimes outwit you into thinking he is for you. He is not for you. At all. One of the ways you might become discouraged is by hearing and believing lies that actually feel like the truth. Our society has adopted and lives by copious numbers of great phrases, sayings, and mindsets. And it doesn't seem dangerous until we stand on those principles instead of the Word of God, the Bible. For Christians, it is our only source of absolute truth, so we must believe what it says—not society and certainly not Satan. So why is it so important to base your life, choices, marriage, and hope on truth and not deception? There are dozens of reasons but I would like to share a few with you.

The Word of God is the only constant. It has stayed the same and will stay the same. What else can make that claim? What else can be the absolute, certain foundation of truth? Nothing.

> The grass withers and the flowers fall, but the Word of our God stands forever. (Isaiah 40:8)

> Your Word, LORD, is eternal; it stands firm in the heavens. (Psalm 119:89)

Satan is a liar. Not only is he a liar, he is the father of lies (John 8:44). In order to recognize a lie, we must know the truth. We don't need to study the lies around us; we need to study God's Word. Satan is subtle and crafty. "No wonder, for Satan himself masquerades as an angel of light" (2 Corinthians 11:14). He is always malicious about his deception. He is sneaky and twists words and throws in the occasional, "Did God really say that?" Just ask Eve. Ask Jesus while you're at it. After Jesus was led into the wilderness by the Holy Spirit, Satan began tempting Him (Matthew 4). Jesus was vulnerable in every way after fasting 40 days and 40 nights. Each time Satan came at Jesus with a challenge, Jesus didn't say, "Leave me alone!" Instead, He responded by using God's truth. Satan approached Jesus two more times and Jesus responded with truth each time. Your spiritual enemy will come at you any chance he can, especially when you're vulnerable. Make sure your time in the Word is regular and strong, because when it's not, that is when our vulnerability increases.

Opinions change. Whether we listen to what society says or to what well-meaning people around us say, those opinions are not forever. I know I have changed my opinions about things over the years and I claim Christ! So even for someone like me who follows Christ, albeit imperfectly, even my suggestions, counsel, and advice, if not based upon God's perfect Word, should not be heeded. While it is wise to have godly advisers in our lives and pastors we can receive help from, we must rely first and foremost on God's Word. Allow the following scriptures to convince you:

I have hidden your word in my heart that I might not sin against you. (Psalm 119:11)

Your word is a lamp for my feet, a light on my path. (Psalm 119:105)

You are my refuge and my shield; I have put my hope in your word. (Psalm 119:114)

Knowing God's Word and reading it daily is like putting gas in the car or eating breakfast each morning. We wouldn't expect our car to drive without gasoline or our bodies to function without food. Our souls and minds need the Word of God each day so we can grow, do what we are created to do, and be effective for God.

Investing in Truth

For the past three summers I've completed a reading plan at YouVersion.com called "The Bible in 90 Days," and it is intense. A few years ago, one of the girls I mentored mentioned she was doing that plan and it took a good 45 to 60 minutes each day to complete it. My eyebrows rose, and I had to keep my jaw from dropping several inches. I was about to say, "I could never do that plan" when she said, "You know, I didn't think I could find the time for this, but then I realized I had a few hours a day to watch TV or browse Facebook. Surely I could give up one of those hours for the Word of God. So I did."

Gulp. Her words shot through me because her excuses were mine. But when the Holy Spirit truly convicts you, there is a sense of motivation and urgency. The very next morning I started the reading plan. I was actually excited about the challenge and ended up being truly moved and encouraged by reading the entire Bible in 90 days. There were books or chapters I didn't enjoy. Hello, Leviticus? But I pressed on and trusted God to do a work in me even when I didn't understand things or thought things were crazy.

Don't feel as though you have to read the Bible in 90 days. (Unless the Spirit is leading you to do so.) But if reading God's Word is not in your daily routine, implement it today. Even if it's just for five minutes. Start with reading a chapter in Proverbs a day. Or read a few psalms each day. Then as God begins to speak to you and show you things—and He will—increase your commitment and see where God takes you. Getting into God's Word will give you encouragement because it is living and breathing, and it will help you build a solid foundation on which to grow your life and your marriage.

The Lie vs. Truth feature in this book is my way of helping you stand on the promises of God from His Word even when everything around you is screaming for you to do the opposite.

After all, if we are to model Jesus and follow after Him, then this is a wonderful practice to incorporate into our lives just like Jesus did in the wilderness with the father of lies.

As a follower of Christ, you will be bombarded with lies. And the only way to stand on the truth is to know God's truth.

So what does it look like to replace a lie with the truth? Well, first of all you have to know what the Bible says. I love getting into the Word. And I love to hear what my good friends learn in the Word. My dear friend Natalie Witcher knows the Word. Not in a haughty I'm-kind-of-awesome way though. She dives into it headfirst and doesn't come up for air for a long while. We have to dig into the Scriptures to truly know what they say and begin to understand them. Friend, you will not understand every single thing about God, but you can learn more with each moment spent in God's Word. God loves to show us new things when He sees how hungry we are for His truth!

One of my favorite things to do when I'm reading God's Word is to highlight verses that state a promise. My online Bible at YouVersion.com has hundreds of verses highlighted. For example, if I am reading chapter 10 in the book of John, I might highlight verse 10, where Jesus says, "The thief comes only to steal and kill and destroy; I have come that they may have life, and have it to the full." This verse will prove effective when you hear the lie that your life is pathetic and will always be that way. Not so. The enemy wants you to believe that lie, but the truth is, Jesus came to earth so you could have a fulfilling life in Him. See how easy it is to put this concept into action?

I'll start with a particular lie that people believe every single day and the truth to combat it. *Combat* is a hefty term, but, friend, that's because we are in a spiritual war, like it or not.

LIE vs. TRUTH

Lie: I can't change. I will always be this way.

Truth: I am in Christ, and I am a new creation. The old me has gone and the new has come. (see 2 Corinthians 5:17)

This process of replacing the lie with God's truth can be draining because it is easier in the moment to believe the lie, even entertain the lie and take that lie out to dinner than it is to stop and take that thought captive. But a few seconds of doing something difficult yields a lifetime of good fruit. In fact, the more you do this, the less you have to. Your mind will be inclined to walk in the truth of God's Word as a first option instead of a last. With each lie you catch and replace with God's truth, you are taking back ground that the enemy stole. When you replace deception with God's truth, Satan is going to regret even messing with you. You are showing him who's in charge and not the other way around. You are putting him in his place.

Renewal Is a Daily Choice

Chris and I had a decision to make in the spring of 2002. Either we were going to truly change from the inside out and from the foundation up, or we were going to risk the downfall of all of our hopes. We chose to do everything in our power and embraced a whatever-it-takes mindset to become not just restored but better than new. My pastor, Craig Groeschel, says, "It's often the things that no one sees that result in the things that everyone wants."

We placed piers underneath the footings of our new marital foundation. We have an amazingly healthy marriage now because during the process of getting a new foundation in our marriage, we did things that no one will know we ever did. We sacrificed in ways that only the two of us will know about. We made choices to act honorably, respectfully, and honestly when the other wasn't around. We chose to let go of defensiveness and hear the other out when something was brought to our attention. We made many difficult choices to get where we are today. And we still have to make them. These choices weren't a one-time event where we checked certain actions off of a list. Was it difficult and is it still? Heavens, yes. It is so very challenging to deny the flesh when the flesh wants to lash back. It is a daily choice to do the things that need to be done to have what we want to have.

> I promise you this: the more you surrender your rights and needs to God, the more freedom and hope you'll find.

But you can have it. You just have to step into it. And you have to step through the pain and difficulty, through the sacrifice and discomfort that will be present on this journey.

For yourself. For your marriage. Loosen your grip on the old so that He can bring in the new. It'll be better than you ever imagined.

TO HELP YOU **HEAL DEEPLY**

1. Write down the most significant loss you've ever faced. Take some time to describe how you felt when you experienced that loss.

2. What is the progress of your healing? Do you feel God has healed you for the most part, or do you feel you are still in the thick of the pain?

3. How do you and your spouse relate to one another on a daily basis? What are your normal responses to one another? (Defensive? Sarcastic? Rude? Hateful?)

4. Recall the discussion about new wine and old wineskins. Taking some of your answers from the question above, how can you adjust those responses by turning your old behaviors into new ones?

5. What are some lies you have believed in the past? List a few of them and search Scripture to find the truth to battle the lies when they appear in your thoughts.

The Truth about the Truth

Just two months after our marriage crumbled into pieces, Chris and I were on the mend. Actually the mend began much sooner than that because our two hearts were completely willing to fight for a new marriage. During that month, there was an event at our church called "Family ID," and Chris and I signed up to attend.

Still in a vulnerable, delicate state, we didn't quite know what to expect that day. We knew the event was about finding your family vision and establishing core values, but that was all we knew. What we walked away with at the end of the day was more than we could have envisioned. During our time there, we sat and discussed what we wanted our family to be about, what we stood for, how we wanted to make a difference, and what dreams we had for our children and grandchildren. We'd been married for over nine years at this time, but with this significant speed bump in our path, it was as good a time as ever to start fresh.

By the end of our time there, we claimed our new Beall family vision statement: *From Him, through Him, and for Him*, based on Romans 11:36. In addition to the statement, we made a list of all of the values we held dear and wanted to instill in our sons:

dependability, encouragement, generosity, integrity, worship, memory making, responsibility, work ethic, honesty. Over the years we have talked about the core values with our boys and have explained why they are so vital in the development of their character.

As you can imagine, one of the most important ones to us was and is honesty. So much of our marriage was based on untruths and a blatant dishonor for the Word itself that we wanted it to be as natural to our sons as breathing. We talked about being honest in anything and everything imaginable. We did our best to answer each and every question honestly. We aimed to act honestly at all times and in all ways. To be a Beall was to be honest. In fact, our mantra around our home became *Bealls don't lie.*

After a few years, we seemed to get a handle on this new life of living honestly. Our oldest son, Noah, played regularly with another boy in our neighborhood. One particular day, we were sitting inside our home and this boy came to the front door. After hearing the doorbell, Noah said, "It's James." The look on his face said he didn't want to play with him. Chris got up from the sofa and said, "I'll tell him you're not home." Immediately Noah's eyes got wide and he said, "But, Dad, we're Bealls, and we don't lie. That's a lie."

From the mouths of babes.

Virtuous Dishonesty

Marriages need honesty. Gut-level, all-out-on-the-table honesty. Sadly but not surprisingly, it is common in life and in marriage to tell little white lies and withhold the truth. It's actually viewed as virtuous to practice that type of deception, a virtuous dishonesty, if you will. We don't want to hurt someone so we keep the truth from them. But what that really does is help that person go on living a life that is a lie, except they don't even know it.

Chris could have kept a lot of information from me when he confessed to me. He didn't have to tell me that he had been with many women. He could have just said one woman. Would that have been easier on my heart? Perhaps in the moment, but there would have always been something between us, some other level of deceit that would have kept us from growing closer. I wouldn't really have known what it was, but rest assured I would have known something was preventing healthy growth for our marriage. And don't think for a minute that Satan would not pounce all over that. He loves it when we keep secrets, even little secrets that "won't do much harm." His specialty is deceit, remember?

Sometimes we practice virtuous dishonesty because we believe we are preserving our perceived integrity and we hope that will keep life running smoothly for everyone. Only this integrity we are trying to keep to save face isn't real; it's an illusion. You know it and God most certainly knows it. Oh and don't forget, Satan knows it, too, and he will most assuredly remind you of "who you really are" at every opportunity he can find. When someone praises you for being a man or woman of integrity, of strong character, Satan is whispering in your ear, "Oh, but they don't know the real truth about you. I do." Because of that spiritual attack on your heart that no one else sees, you suffer in silence. Then you do one of two things: you live miserably or continue on in your sin, because, well, you might as well not fight it anymore. Meanwhile, God is nudging you to come clean, to make things right with Him, with yourself, and with others.

Acceptable Deception

Outwardly we have this black and white hatred for deception, but if we do an autopsy on ourselves an entire layer of acceptable deception is revealed at the same time. Typically, most people have an entire list of lies that they don't consider wrong and then a whole separate list of deceptions that are absolutely wrong. We tell half-truths and exaggerate until our story makes us look the hero. But the truth is, there is no difference in any of these. A lie is a lie. No matter how white or little it is.

We manage reality by controlling what part of the truth we are going to tell or believe. Our culture would even say that if we practice this type of deception, this virtuous dishonesty in our marriage, we are being kind to our spouse and we should be kind at all costs. That couldn't be further from the truth. What we are doing is choosing to place more importance on the feelings in the moment rather than on building a culture of honesty. When we practice this for years in our marriage and then find ourselves struggling in a big way, we tend to suffer in silence. Our emotional memory acts like muscle memory, and we continue to deceive because nothing seems more important than sparing hurt feelings in the moment. The truth should never intend to hurt; it should always be motivated by love. And if we truly want our marriages to succeed, we have to incorporate the truth at all times.

LIE vs. TRUTH

Lie: It doesn't matter if I lie sometimes as long as I don't lie all the time.

Truth: The Lord detests lying lips, but He delights in me because I am trustworthy. (see Proverbs 12:22)

Let's say you're a married man and you find yourself attracted to another woman in the office. And because you have been practicing a type of acceptable deception throughout your marriage, you don't say anything to your wife because you don't want to hurt her.

Or maybe you have a huge issue that has turned into an addiction. You don't want to share it with your husband for fear of judgment or of sending him over the edge.

These are hard situations to navigate. I mean, who wants to tell their spouse, "Hey, babe, the new receptionist at work is really hot." And what can be more vulnerable than sharing your secret that you're an all-out addict? You share it because you want to be honest, but you then have to deal with your spouse wondering what you are going to do to repair your own life. Honesty is often painful. But it is unquestionably necessary.

When Chris and I were starting over with a foundation of honesty, we couldn't just choose to be honest about some things and then be dishonest in other things. We were either honest or dishonest. Brutal, give-it-to-me-straight honesty had to weave its way into every aspect of our being. To rework this part of our lives was a battle. My heart ached when he would share with me his feelings about seeing another attractive woman. There is nothing enjoyable about that conversation.

Chris knows and readily admits that he had a stronghold of lying in his life. It was a part of how he interacted with people every day. He'd lie about big things and little things. Lying had become such a huge part of who he was, he will tell you that he didn't even realize when he was lying anymore.

I, on the other hand, have always leaned toward the honest side of things. I might have told little white lies but everyone does, so what's the big deal? I never told big lies, so that was my saving grace. At least that is the argument I used to convince myself to be okay with my dishonesty. Nevertheless, we both had to work on incorporating honesty back into our marriage, and making it the foundation.

I remember one time, about a month after Chris's confession, when he answered a question I asked him. I took his response as the truth because I assumed he was done lying. I figured his life was already pretty low, and he wouldn't keep lying. Thankfully, he didn't want to continue his lying lifestyle. How do I know? Because within a few seconds of his answering yes to my question, he stopped and said, "Actually, no. I just lied. I'm sorry." Now, the question wasn't a huge deal; it wasn't a make-or-break issue on staying together. It was something simple. But he lied. Here's a great example of how easy it is to want to pour the new wine into the old wineskin. The new habits don't always come easy, so the ongoing commitment to them is essential.

Because telling lies, believing a lie, and living a lie were the norm for him, he wanted to uproot this foundation of lying and start one of honesty. Even if it was something incredibly simple. To him, to us, it was vital that we start over with a new foundation of honesty.

So does that mean we just speak the truth at every single opportunity no matter what? Not necessarily. If your wife is sick in bed with the flu and she looks awful, you don't have to say, "Hey, babe, you look absolutely ugly." If your husband has gained 30 extra pounds, you don't have to call him "fatso" when he walks past you with a bowl of ice cream. That's absurd. Those kinds of responses are just rude.

But if we want the foundation of our marriage to be on solid, honest ground, we must not only receive grace but show it as well. My pastor, Craig Groeschel, says, "We judge other people by their actions, but we judge ourselves by our intentions." The next time your spouse comes to you to share their struggle, try looking at them the way you would look at yourself. You and I almost always give ourselves the benefit of the doubt. Let's give it to them too. They aren't trying to hurt us. They're just trying to be honest.

Seven Things

God is pretty clear in Scripture concerning how He feels about lying: "There are six things the LORD hates, seven that are detestable to him: haughty eyes, a lying tongue, hands that shed innocent blood, a heart that devises wicked schemes, feet that are quick to rush into evil, a false witness who pours out lies and a person who stirs up conflict in the community" (Proverbs 6:16-19). Out of the seven things that God detests, two of them have to do with lying. That's 29 percent! Now, I'm not a bettin' woman, but if I were, I would put all my money on the fact that we better pay close attention to what we say and make sure it is upright and honest.

Too bad Abram didn't always do that. Genesis 12 begins the story about Abram, later called Abraham. There weren't a ton of people who were actually following God at that time. Most ignored Him and continued on in their sin. There were some, however, who chose to obey God, and Abram happened to be one of them.

God called Abram to go to a land He would later show him. He promised Abram that He would make him into a great nation and give him descendants as numerous as the stars in the sky. Upon receiving God's command to "go to a land I will show you," Abram set off with his wife, Sarai, his nephew Lot, and all their possessions and servants.

Because there was a famine in the land, their travels took them down into Egypt. Before they entered Egypt, Abram said to Sarai, "I know what a beautiful woman you are. When the Egyptians see you, they will say, 'This is his wife.' Then they will kill me and will let you live. Say you are my sister, so that I will be treated well for your sake and my life will be spared because of you" (Genesis 12:11-13). Sarai did as Abram said, and when they arrived in Egypt, she was taken into Pharaoh's palace and treated well.

But Pharaoh and his household were struck by some serious diseases. That did not set well with Pharaoh, so he called Abram in and said, "What have you done to me? Why didn't you tell me she was your wife? Why did you say, 'She is my sister,' so that I took her to be my wife? Now then, here is your wife. Take her and go!" (Genesis 12:18-19). Man, that could have really turned out bad, right? Pharaoh could have killed Abram, but he didn't. Instead, he let him leave with gobs of animals and even people!

Fast-forward eight chapters to Genesis 20. You will not believe what happened next. Abraham, no longer called Abram, moved into the region of the Negev. Abimelek, the king of Gerar, noticed Sarah, previously called Sarai, and took her into his home. Now you may be saying, "Why did he take another man's wife into his home?" Funny you should ask. Because Abraham told them Sarah was his sister.

Really, Abe?

But this time Abimelek heard the truth about Sarah from God in a dream. Let the plea bargaining begin. I mean, wouldn't you start begging God to spare you for something you didn't do? I know I would. Just read what happened next: "Now Abimelek had not gone near her, so he said, 'Lord, will you destroy an innocent nation? Did he not say to me, "She is my sister" and didn't she also say, "He is my brother"? I have done this with a clear conscience and clean hands" (Genesis 20:4-5). In the morning, Sarah was returned to her brother...I mean, husband. And you will never believe this. Abimelek, who was tricked and lied to, ended up giving Abraham sheep, cattle, and slaves, and he even told him he could live wherever he wanted in the land. Unbelievable.

Because the apple doesn't fall far from the tree, Abraham's son, Isaac, did a similar thing in Genesis 26. There was a famine in the land at that time too, but instead of going down to Egypt per God's command, Isaac and his people stayed in Gerar. Some men asked Isaac if Rebekah was his wife. And get this, because she was beautiful, he told them in verse 7—wait for it—"She is my sister."

You have got to be kidding me!

If I'm being brutally honest with you, and I better be truthful, since that's what this chapter is about, this is one of my favorite stories in the Bible to poke fun at. I love the Word of God, but some of the people in the Word of God aren't the sharpest tools in the shed, if you get what I'm saying. The Word of God is perfect, but the people in the Word of God, not so much. Except Jesus, of course.

God's People but Still Sinners

Abraham and Isaac were God's people, men he called prophets. Men blessed by God Himself. Men who obeyed God and kept His commands, decrees, and instructions (Genesis 26:5). He protected them profusely. He forgave them abundantly. He loved them tremendously. Even after their sin, He did not withdraw His hand of protection, forgiveness, and love from their lives. Their actions may have proven that they acted like idiots and were fear driven, but that didn't alter the unchanging character of our Creator.

LIE vs. TRUTH

Lie: It's too late to start over and become an honest person. I've lied so much.

Truth: I will forget the former things; I will not dwell on the past. (see Isaiah 43:18)

Just like Abraham's and Isaac's actions didn't eliminate God's blessings from their lives, our actions don't eliminate our blessings either. Even when we lie. Big lies or little lies. God's love for us never fails, and He never stops believing that we will be the people He has called us to be. We are His people. And He wants more for us than humans can even imagine.

That doesn't mean that we just cheapen grace by lying, fully knowing that God will forgive us. He most certainly will forgive us and remove our transgressions from us as far as the east is from the west (Psalm 103:12). That, my friend, is a done deal. But we must still choose to be a people of truth. If we are not careful, one simple lie can turn into another. And another. And another. Before we are even aware of the web we've spun, we are living a deceitful life and can't tell what is actual and what is fabricated.

God's love for us is constant, and His forgiveness continues to be distributed no matter what we do. But His love and forgiveness don't remove consequences from our actions. God forgives me when I gossip about someone, but He won't remove the consequences my actions caused when she finds out about it. I still have to deal with the hurt feelings, broken trust, and the possibility that this relationship is forever tarnished. No, that's not God being mean; that's me getting what I deserved. At the same time, I can walk in the forgiveness He willingly disburses to all who ask.

Driven by Fear

Fear is a real struggle that most of us face at some point in our lives. While some only deal with fear occasionally, others are plagued by it. The Bible has a lot to say about this subject. If you do an online search about how many verses in the Bible discuss fear, you will find page after page. The words *fear* and *fear not* are mentioned quite a bit in the Bible.

Fear is a monster. When it enters the picture, it distorts our sense of truth and weakens our willingness to follow truth. In the midst of that fear we think our finite minds can actually come up with the best scenario. So we throw all level-headed decision making out the window and go with what our fear-driven minds suggest instead.

Abraham and Isaac were motivated by fear to tell lies. Most of us are. They were afraid they would be killed by some powerful kings because they had beautiful wives. So they lied. Even though they made off with some animals, servants, and tons of loot, their lies still ended up coming back on them.

We've all told lies at some point in our lives. I most certainly have. When I lie, it is usually because I am afraid of a particular outcome, so I choose to lie and hope my lie will cover up the truth in some way, shape, or form. It may temporarily work, but the truth will always find me out.

Battling fear can be done. But that's just it; we have to battle. And what better way to come against fear than with the truth of God's Word.

Becoming Honest

All-out honesty is not going to be accepted by all couples. I know that. I know many couples who don't want this kind of honesty in their marriage. I do hope you will choose it though. Chris and I have no option except to live this way. With what we've been through, this is the only path for us. At least that is the way we see it. And maybe that's one thing I'm most thankful for out of our story. We are honest with one another. Sometimes brutally. If you want a secure foundation built on truth, you will see a difference by choosing honesty at all costs. Even at the cost of your feelings getting hurt.

In order to begin again in the area of honesty, the biggest and most important step is to first be truthful about your need for it and how it is demonstrated in your own life. I have found that we typically lie on three levels: to ourselves, to God, and to others.

1. We lie to ourselves.

Sometimes we lie because the truth is so incredibly challenging to stomach. If you struggle with lying and you don't want to lie anymore, that's a great start. Owning your sin and confessing it to God will bring on a holy relief like you wouldn't believe. And it's commendable that you want to start again. Pay no attention to the demonic darts from the father of lies that will be coming at you left and right. When you lie, you are more like him than God. Of course he isn't going to be thrilled at this new leaf you are turning over toward becoming honest. But do it anyway.

2. We lie to God.

We can possibly get away with lying to ourselves because lies can become our reality if we believe them too long. But we can never get away with lying to God because "he knows everything" (1 John 3:20). So even though we think we are lying to God, we are not. The psalmist tells us He knows us even better than we know ourselves (Psalm 139). The most important thing for us to do here is to realize that lying to God is something that will never work.

3. We lie to others.

We have talked about virtuous dishonesty and acceptable deception. Even if it feels right in the moment, it is not.

Healing from a life of telling lies is possible. I've seen it happen with my own eyes. The Bible says that "with God all things are possible" (Matthew 19:26), and I'm fairly certain that includes lying. In order for healing to occur in our lives, we must choose to be honest with ourselves, with God, and with others. When we are honest with ourselves, we become self-aware about our flaws. Then being honest with God we simply say, "God, I know you already know this, but I have lied and it has overtaken me." Of course, healing with others takes a lot more time because our confession of lying to them exposes broken trust, and that takes such a long time to rebuild (I will visit this subject in chapter 4).

When you choose to turn over a new leaf by becoming honest, God will send His gentle conviction on you and you will be at peace.

> Guilt, from Satan, paralyzes. Conviction, from the Holy Spirit, motivates. Big difference.

Guilt is not of God. It's directly from Satan, and it virtually paralyzes you. Conviction, on the other hand, is from the Holy Spirit, and it motivates you to make a change.

God's ways are perfect. Just as He is truth and speaks truth, He wants you to be a person of truth as well. And He will stop at nothing to help you succeed in building a strong character. Don't give up.

TO HELP YOU **HEAL DEEPLY**

1. Spend the next several minutes confessing to God the lies you've told. State specific lies that come to mind quickly. For the rest, ask God to cover you with His forgiveness.

2. Think about a lie you have told. Why did you tell it? Play the scene out in your mind had you chosen to speak the truth in love.

3. Take the next several days to read what God says in the Bible about lying, being truthful, becoming a person of character, and acting uprightly and honestly. Write these verses down so that God's Word will permeate through your being. (You will want to get extra paper for this part or use your computer. It's okay to break this up into days or even a week. It will take time, but the payoff is valuable.)

4. Of the verses you wrote down, choose two or three of them to commit to memory. Write the verses out below. Use these verses as a weapon against spiritual attacks when you are tempted to believe a lie or to respond with a lie.

5. Spend some time in prayer asking God to show you when you are lying to yourself, to Him, or to others. Ask Him to make you aware before you tell a lie or convict you shortly after you lie.

It Comes with the Territory

It was a big adventure for Chris and me to move from Texas to Tennessee to begin four years of ministry at a wonderful new church. Chris was hired as both the worship and youth pastor under the leadership of our senior pastor. It was just the two of them leading. The church was portable at the time. So during the first couple of years, Chris would load all the necessary equipment and supplies for worship into his white Dodge Dakota every single Sunday morning. For 50 out of 52 weeks a year, he drove from the church office, located in an apartment complex, over to a nearby country club banquet room where we held services. It was tiresome for him, but that kind of labor is just part of the package for staff and volunteers at a portable church.

As with any new job, Chris was busy on the weekend and during the week. He spent time putting together worship sets and creating a vision for our fledgling youth ministry.

I ministered right alongside Chris. We were gradually getting to know the teenagers who were part of our church. It was a challenging task because most teenagers want to see if you are going to stick around before they start trusting you. And, of course, they wanted to make sure we were cool. Which we are, so that was a done deal.

And after living in Tennessee for six months, we got pregnant with our first son, Noah. As I expanded more each week of the pregnancy, our church was growing as well. By the time of Noah's birth, we were well on our way to having a thriving youth ministry and a strong worship team. Life was fabulous.

Noah entering our lives was a tremendous blessing, the best one ever. But children do raise the level of activity and intensity in a marriage, and we definitely felt it. I also struggled with postpartum depression for several months after Noah's birth, and I gave myself grace to feel stronger and healthier. For that reason and because Chris and I wanted me to be able to focus on our family and home, I decided to take a step back from ministry. It was a decision I do not regret in any way.

When the Lies Begin

In hindsight, Chris and I can see how we became busier and more disconnected from this point on. And more distance grew between us as his schedule intensified. Eventually, the church got him a cell phone so he could be reached when he wasn't at the office. I didn't call him often, but when I did it seemed more often than not that my call would go directly to voicemail. I would leave a message, and usually within an hour Chris would call me back and tell me he was at a ministry appointment, in a meeting, or that he just couldn't get to his phone. No big deal, I thought. He's busy. At least he called me back.

Fast-forward to 2002 when Chris confessed his infidelity to me on that unfortunate February morning. Within a matter of seconds of hearing such deplorable news, I began with the questions. Not just simple questions but questions that probably shouldn't have been asked because there were no sufficient answers. No answer would have satisfied this new, insatiable demand for truth that my heart and mind possessed.

One question I asked was about all the phone calls I'd made to him that went directly to voicemail. When hearing the question, he simply let his head fall forward and said, "I turned my phone off when I was with another woman."

LIE vs. TRUTH

Lie: I'll never be able to make it through this.

Truth: I can do this and all things through Christ who gives me strength. (see Philippians 4:13)

And there it was. That truth hit me square in the eyes and almost knocked me completely out. It felt like I'd been through 15 rounds of being beaten to a pulp. Each time I needed to reach him, sometimes for routine issues, sometimes because I truly needed him, he had shut his phone off. He was nowhere to be found. There was no way to reach him. He was inaccessible to his family. And on top of that, he deceptively labeled those times as ministry calls.

Right then and there he pledged to me that he would never turn his phone off again and would never screen my calls. He said, "I will answer every single call from you." From that day forward, he has answered nearly every call from me. If he is in a meeting, he tries to send me a quick text saying he can't talk. Only a few times have I actually been sent to his voicemail.

Why was this so essential? Because if one of my calls went to voicemail, my mind would drudge up the memories of how and why that had happened so frequently in our past. I remember the first time it happened. I called. He didn't answer. First I went to voicemail—then I went into a state of frenzy. My heart would leave the present moment and drag me right back to when Chris was acting out and being unfaithful to me. Voicemail became a trigger that took me back to a difficult time in my life.

Thankfully, Chris knew what that did to me, and he wanted to avoid adding to my pain. He knew what dark places my mind and heart would travel to if he missed my call. And I can tell you, almost always, within a minute or two, he called me back. His voice told me he knew how I was feeling and knew what his actions had caused. It didn't matter in the moment that he was being faithful and honest and pure, because the trigger had more power over the present situation than I wanted it to have.

How Pain Changes Us

The Bible is full of stories where people had to deal with consequences or results from their own actions or the actions of others. Take the story of Naomi and Ruth. There were a series of things that devastated Naomi. The first thing was that her husband, Elimelek, moved her and her sons, Mahlon and Kilion, from Bethlehem to Moab. This was a huge no-no in the Jewish culture. There was major hostility between Israel and Moab because Moab oppressed Israel. But there was a famine in Bethlehem, and Elimelek felt he had no choice.

Next thing you know, their two sons married Moabite women, Orpah and Ruth. According to God's law, Israelites (Mahlon and Kilion) were not to marry Canaanites (Orpah and Ruth). But they did, and even though Scripture doesn't allude to this, my guess is that it broke Naomi's heart.

Sometime later, Elimelek died and left Naomi a widow in Moab. Then ten years later, both of her sons died. With nothing keeping her in Moab, Naomi decided to head back to her home in Bethlehem because she heard that "the Lord had come to the aid of his people by providing food for them" (Ruth 1:6).

Naomi went through her share of grieving after losing her husband and sons. We know this because after she and Ruth traveled back to Bethlehem, people inquired and asked, "Can this be Naomi?" To which she retorted rather abruptly, "Don't call me

Naomi...Call me Mara." She wanted to be called that because "the Almighty has made my life very bitter. I went away full, but the Lord brought me back empty." She even said that "the Lord has afflicted me" and "has brought misfortune upon me" (Ruth 1:19-21). It wasn't Naomi's fault that her husband or sons died, but she was suffering because of it.

From Bitter to Better

No matter if you are in deep agony at your own hand or at the doing of someone else, pain hurts. Consequences exist even when it's not your fault. People endure the consequences at the hand of another all the time. Naomi did. Even though Elimelek, Mahlon, and Kilion weren't trying to hurt Naomi, their deaths did indeed devastate her. She was cut to her core.

I imagine that Naomi had plenty of moments of missing her husband and sons. When she would walk along the road and see a husband and wife together, she'd remember that she was no longer married. When she would be doing a "man's job," she'd remember that she had no husband or sons to do that task for her. When she would see a mother holding her son, she'd remember that she was now childless.

However, after a long turn of events, Naomi once again held a child in her arms, a grandson, Obed, which the Lord provided through Boaz and Ruth's marriage.

Did she experience sadness when she looked at the new child in her arms? Perhaps. Did it take her back to the nights of holding Mahlon and Kilion in her arms? Chances are strong it did. Did she grieve a bit because she would be helping to raise this grandson without her husband? I'm sure. While the birth of Obed was a joy for her, there were possibly some sad moments as well. But those sad moments don't minimize the sheer joy she now had after such a long season of adversity and hardship. The new life in her arms didn't replace what she lost; it was just part of the way God redeemed her suffering. Naomi exhibited longanimity, a patient endurance through hardship, better than most would in her circumstances.

Patiently enduring in challenging times is something we should work toward. It is no easy task to exhibit this virtuous trait by any means. Ever heard of road rage? Case in point. I believe patient endurance must be present on the healing journey, especially when triggers rear their ugly heads and we have to push through the difficult memories. But we often either don't want to or don't seem to have the strength to do it. It is in these moments that longanimity must rise up from a place deep within us so this fruit of God's Spirit can manifest itself in our actions.

Renewal from God comes in different ways for each of us. There is no one-size-fits-all redemption. We are all uniquely wired by God, and He knows exactly what methods will work best on our hearts as He redeems our challenging situations. But He will redeem it.

Recognizing Our Triggers

Other consequences and challenges come with the territory of betrayal and significant marriage struggles. Relationships and friendships get strained and can even end. Sometimes people lose their jobs due to marriage issues. And experiencing marriage struggles most definitely impacts what others think of you and what you think of yourself. While I can't address all the things a person can endure, I will focus on a few of them. I've walked through my own share of reminders, consequences, and challenges over the years, and I'm still standing strong. You will too.

Triggers are one of the challenges that go with betrayal in a marriage or during other difficult times in life. I lost my father when I was 19 years old. I've spent more of my life without him than I did with him. My triggers in regard to him don't come often at all. My friends Robin Storch and Christi Donaldson recently lost their fathers and they are experiencing triggers much more often due to the freshness of their loss. They walk through these moments of grief with beauty and grace.

This is a part of loss we all have to walk through, whether we want to or not. Triggers take us back to a day or an event and often to the emotions surrounding that event. Something in the present triggers us to remember something in the past: a song, a phrase, a piece of clothing, a smell. Anything can be a trigger that transports us to some other place or time. When the person who betrayed their spouse sees their spouse pained by a trigger, their first inclination is to say, "But I'm not that person anymore!" But that doesn't matter. Triggers are brutal. They totally bypass a person's healing or change and will transport you directly back to the day when you found out.

To better understand triggers, think about how a good one impacts your mind and disposition. When I drink a Sanpellegrino grapefruit Italian soda, I'm back on a grassy lawn overlooking the most majestic ocean and gorgeous Maui beach, with Chris quietly dozing next to me. It's just a drink. Consuming this tasty beverage doesn't transport me back to Maui physically (how unfortunate); yet in my mind, I am there.

Unfortunately, the triggers that linger in the wake of a crisis or loss do not leave us with such happy thoughts. But even when they are uncomfortable thoughts and emotions, triggers are a part of healing, and they come when we are headed toward healing even if it doesn't feel better than the day before. Triggers allow us to grieve. And when we grieve, we heal. Some triggers are helpful and some are counterproductive. We have to ask ourselves which is the case for us in the moment. Will addressing this trigger with my spouse help our healing or hinder it? On many occasions, we are to talk about it with our spouse and express our feelings. But sometimes, though, we need to go straight to God, because the answers to the question that keeps haunting us will never be sufficient. Only His peace will help us completely.

I'm sure you have experienced something similar. You are going about your day, doing your typical routine, driving the same roads, shopping at the same stores. No surprises, no real challenges; your mood is fairly happy. Then that song comes on the radio that was playing when you got your bad news. And you sink. Deeply. Within seconds, your heart is crushed all over again, and you are in a heap on the floor that is quickly filling up with a puddle of your own tears.

Triggers are to be expected. That doesn't lessen the impact they have on us and our minds. They distort our current reality. And our spiritual enemy always tries to use them to set us back a few steps.

Triggering More Peace Than Pain

What can you do when those triggers sneak up on you like an unexpected earthquake in the middle of Oklahoma? They will leave you spinning for a time until you can gain your composure and get back on your feet again. You can't ignore them because they will keep coming. You can't run from them because they will chase you. All you can do is just deal with them. Right there. On the spot. In the moment. Even if it's in public.

I was in Walmart and it was within the first four months of Chris's confession of infidelity. I was thrown into the past by something I saw on the shelf. It was an ingredient I had used to prepare a particular meal for Chris when we lived in Tennessee. A meal he missed because he feigned yet another "ministry appointment." My heart sank as I remembered those hurtful times when Chris's double life was happening while I was raising our son, cooking meals, and taking care of our home. While in Walmart, I could have ignored the trigger moment and acted like it didn't happen. I mean, I was in a grocery store after all with tons of people around me. But I didn't ignore it. I stepped into it. My heart literally ached, and I started to cry over what was lost. The tears didn't last long; just long enough to help me grieve this moment and push through the pain. Right in the middle of Walmart.

It didn't matter that Chris was a new person in the present. The image the trigger brings to mind does not reflect the actual reality. Things were going good with Chris. We were healing and building a new marriage. But this trigger took me back to the past. When we chase the trigger and "go there" in our minds, the memory, good or bad, is often exaggerated—the good memory is better or the bad memory is worse than the actual reality. Nevertheless, this is typical of a trigger.

What do you do when triggers arise? I suppose there are countless answers to this question. You already know what I do when they arise: *I deal with them head-on.* But allowing myself to grieve the loss of what the trigger reminds me of is just the first step. At least for me it is.

The next step is significant. After I've pushed through the grief, I declare truth to myself. I remind myself that God is working this out for my good and for His glory. I agree with myself that life isn't fair and that is okay. It's not so much about fixing something in my mind when these triggers occur; it's more about how I walk myself to a place of peace with God.

And then I always finish with a prayer, asking God to redeem my life by allowing my pain to make a difference in another's life.

The way you handle your triggers may be different. Maybe you immediately drop to your knees in prayer and allow yourself to lean back into God's everlasting arms. Or perhaps you have a picture that you love that represents this new life and healing you've found. You could be someone who loves to write, and journaling out your thoughts is your best plan of attack. Quite honestly, sometimes a good walk around a park or your neighborhood will do the trick. Whatever you need to do to propel yourself through the triggered pain is what you need to do.

If you wounded your spouse, you may feel frustrated when she experiences a trigger because it does two things: it reminds you of what you did, and it makes you feel like you haven't changed. The absolute worst thing you can do when a trigger arises is to get frustrated or mad that your spouse is still hurting. Remember, your actions caused this. But do not live in a self-loathing place. You are not a betrayer. You are a child of God who made a bad choice. You are not what you did.

LIE vs. TRUTH

Lie: I'll never be able to make it through this.

Truth: I can do this and all things through Christ who gives me strength. (see Philippians 4:13)

If you are the one who was betrayed, there will come a day when you will win the battle with triggers. It will come, and it will have no power over you. You will walk in peace and will rest in the promise that your heavenly Father will never leave you, never forsake you, and never give up on you. And He will use your life-altering story according to His plan. Keep pressing on.

Get over It, Will Ya?

Triggers are not the only thing that comes with the territory of hardships. There is also what I like to call the "get-over-it" mindset. It's often held by a person who did the offending, the person who hurt someone with their actions. Maybe you wounded your husband deeply with a significant betrayal. And while you've apologized and he has forgiven you, his eyes still show a deep sadness. His heart still aches and occasionally he voices his pain. When he does, it reminds you of what you've done and you just wish he would get over it because, well, you said you were sorry, and isn't that enough? Can't he just move on?

Not yet. I know you'd like for him to, but what he is feeling is part of the healing process. And when your get-over-it mentality shows up it actually delays his healing even more. The betrayal may have only lasted a short amount of time but unfortunately, it will take a lot more time to overcome.

When I would feel sad about Chris's betrayal, he could see it in my eyes. In the early days, the waves of grief came over me and I could barely keep my head above water. Not once did he ever say, "Why can't you just get over it?" He knew my heart was completely devastated by his actions. It wasn't my fault I was sad. I truly didn't want to live in a perpetual state of misery; it was just my reality.

I remember one particular day within a week of his confession. It was a day in which I was frequently overcome with sadness. Each time, he got sad too. He cried and apologized over and over again and begged me not to leave him. Finally, I said to him, "When I get sad like this, all I need for you to do is to hold me, tell me you're sorry that I'm hurting, and tell me you love me. That's all." So from that day forward, that is what he did.

Sadness doesn't overwhelm me anymore. It's been over 14 years. But occasionally, a thought will hit me and my heart gets a subtle sting. I tell Chris and he pulls me to him gently, wraps his strong arms around me, and says, "I'm sorry you're hurting. I love you so much." You might think he would expect me to have gotten over it after all this time. A healthy couple will tell you it's not about getting over it but about pushing through it. You know you are moving forward when triggers or anniversaries of difficult events don't break you but give you reason to pause and acknowledge healing and God's presence along the way.

Will you allow me to get in your face for a minute? If you are the one who hurt and betrayed your spouse deeply, don't expect him to get over it quickly. It won't be quick. It could take years. What may have been meaningless to you meant a shattered heart, bruised self-esteem, and a trampled-on covenant to your spouse.

One way to help you see what your spouse is walking through is to change places with him in your mind. Imagine that he cheated on or betrayed you. Maybe it was with a cherished friend. Could you get over it as quickly as you are expecting your spouse to? My guess is no. So understand that this part of the healing journey will not change as quickly as you'd like for it to. But if you expect his healing to last forever, chances are it won't. Your spouse will see that you are for him and not for yourself.

If you still have your family and a spouse who is willing to stay married, walk in humility, knowing you don't deserve to have this gift after the poor choices you have made. If you are not willing to endure this forever, then your marriage will only go so far and remain stagnant.

And if you are the one who has been wounded, don't live there. Don't keep throwing your spouse's sin back in his face at every opportunity. Don't stay in a place of misery and just expect the pain to go away. You have to do some hard things in order to heal. But you will heal by the power of God's Spirit, and you will be better because of it. Believe that.

You are both entering the most strenuous marriage therapy treatment plan of your entire lives. Overcoming marriage betrayal and serious wounding takes work, time, and a whole lot of Jesus.

D-Day Anniversary

Anniversaries are remembered days. There are good memories to remember, like birthdays, weddings, and graduations. Then there are sad memories that are also remembered, like the terrorist attacks on 9/11, the bombing at the Boston Marathon, or the death of a loved one. Remembering happy days is fun and easy and there is usually a party associated with the date. But we don't do that with sad memories. It's more of a state of mind for the day, remembering what happened on this day a year ago, five years ago, or twenty years ago.

When it comes to the anniversary of a sad date—perhaps it's your own D-Day—the best course of action is to ask the other person what she needs. Ask her what she expects, if anything. Or maybe you already know your spouse so well that you don't have to ask.

For me, I don't need Chris groveling over his past sin. I just wanted to know he remembered. Not because I want to rub his nose in his past shame. Not at all. I just want it acknowledged, because it was a big deal for us. It changed everything in our lives. It set us on a different path. It took us deeper with God. It drove us to the pit, and by the power of the Holy Spirit, we propelled through the pit and into a hopeful life.

LIE vs. TRUTH

Lie: Every time I am reminded about the past, I feel so discouraged.

Truth: I may be hard pressed on every side, but I am not crushed; I may be perplexed, but I am not in despair; I may be persecuted, but I am not abandoned; I may be struck down, but I am not destroyed. (see 2 Corinthians 4:8)

If you are reading this and you have a day when everything changed, figure out a way to remember it. I doubt it is going to be a day filled with streamers and balloons. Maybe it's a day where you tell your wife how thankful you are that she stayed and you give her some flowers. Or you tell your husband that you know your actions caused him pain, but you are beyond happy that he gave you and your marriage another chance. Remembering hard days doesn't have to be long and drawn out. It truly is the thought that counts.

Heart Adjustments

We can't control people. If we could, man, can you imagine? People would do what we want them to do, when we want them to do it, and how we want it done. Not only that, but they would have the attitude we want them to have. Mercy! It sounds amazing, doesn't it?

> When we petition God to come and change us from within, He will. We just have to do our part and sit still long enough for Him to perform a heart procedure.

Unfortunately, not only can you not control someone, you can't change them either. No amount of lectures or suggestions forced on a person will change them. They have to change from within. They have to want the change. Thankfully, God's specialty is a changed heart.

It will be anything but easy. Pain will be present. Discomfort will be close by. But a little hardship now will bring a great reward later.

What about the person whose heart needs a total bypass? His heart is so cold and callous. He thinks you're ridiculous for feeling sad about anything he did to you in the past. I mean, the past is the past. Leave it there. Although it would be wonderful if we could change people, we must focus on changing the only person we have any control over: ourselves.

You can't control how others act or how they speak to you. But you can control how you respond. You can choose to walk away from a toxic situation, and you can choose to hold your tongue and not sin in your anger.

But the most important thing you can do for the person who needs a significant heart change is to pray for them. And don't let this be your last resort after you've exhausted all of your other humanly efforts. As Christ-followers, this is our most powerful line of defense and should be our first plan of attack.

Here are a couple of verses you could pray over someone whose heart needs adjusting:

Create in me a pure heart, O God, and renew a steadfast spirit within me. (Psalm 51:10)

I will give you a new heart and put a new spirit within you; I will remove from you your heart of stone and give you a heart of flesh. (Ezekiel 36:26)

We can't change our past. We have to learn to live with it there so it doesn't make our present miserable. Nobody wants anything bad to happen in our lives. But bad things do happen. People hurt us. We hurt people.

We have to quit wishing bad things hadn't happened to us and accept that they did. When we do this, I believe we will start to experience true healing.

Praying the Scriptures over people has become something I have incorporated into my everyday life. It not only unleashes the power of God in someone's life, but it also frees you to do your part—pray—and leave the rest in God's hands. He is quite capable, my friend.

TO HELP YOU **HEAL DEEPLY**

1. Think back to some of your favorite memories in your marriage. Write down three or four of them below. What emotions come to mind?

2. Not all memories are good. Some have great amounts of pain associated with them. Share one from your marriage you want to find healing in.

3. I know certain circumstances remind you of that painful memory from the question above. How do you typically handle triggers that remind you of that situation? (Push them aside? Cry it out?)

4. In regard to anniversary dates of difficult past days, what would help you continue to heal as you approach the date? As you experience the date itself?

5. While it is vital that we heal from past wounds, we don't want to live there. Write down a verse to commit to memory to help you find victory over painful memories.

BUILD WISELY

4

Restoring Trust

Saturdays and Sundays are busy days around the Beall home. There is little rest for us on these two days even though it's the weekend. The Life.Church campus that my husband leads has seven services between Saturday evening at 5:00 and Sunday evening at 6:00.

One recent Saturday night, Chris went to dinner with Robert Wall, a pastor and mentor to campus pastors who is on our team. We've known Robert and his wife, Cindi, since we came to Oklahoma in 2002. In fact, Robert was one of the first counselors Chris met with after his confession. Robert helped Chris through some deep healing and still is a trusted adviser, wise counselor, and cherished friend to us.

That evening I knew Robert and Chris were having dinner after our 6:30 service. I didn't know when I expected Chris home, but knowing how much my husband loves a good night's sleep, I figured it would be before 10:00 p.m. At about 10:15, I was surprised he hadn't come through the door. I resisted the urge to check on Chris with a call or with the aid of technological wonders. I tease my family and they tease me about my ability to know where they at any given time of the day. Thank you, Find My Friends app. (Am I a stalker? Hardly. Perhaps. #guilty) My teenager thinks it's ludicrous that I know where he is at all times. I simply tell my family, "In case something happens to you, I want to know how to find you. Or to know when it's time to request the assistance of Raymond Redding-ton from the show *The Blacklist*. That man can find and rescue you anywhere and in just the nick of time."

I tucked my youngest son in for the night, and when I came back to my bedroom I noticed I had a voicemail. I assumed Chris had called to let me know he was heading home. I listened to the voice-mail and was surprised to hear Pastor Robert's voice. "Hey Cindy, it's Robert. I am here with Chris. I am sorry I've kept him out so late. Thanks for sharing him with me. We are about to leave the restau-rant. Hope to see you soon!"

I smiled as I listened to that familiar, kind voice. The smile came from deep in my heart because the phone call wasn't Robert's idea; it was Chris's. Chris didn't have to have Robert call me; after all, we've been on this healing road for a very long time. But after 14 years, that man is still trying to ward off any fear or mistrust I could potentially have in him. And since Chris knows that a scenario in which he is late is one Satan could use to attack my trust, he is proactive. Chris told me in 2002 that he never expected me to trust him again but would spend the rest of his life trying to earn it back. Apparently, he meant it.

When Trust Is Broken

I love that God gives us earthly relationships to bring us joy, comfort, and companionship. I could not be more thankful that we have this gift here and now as we wait for our eternal home. Yet sometimes these relationships don't go as planned. Trust is often broken, and when we lose trust in someone, it rocks us. We literally feel like we've lost our footing and have no idea where the next step is. Especially when it's someone close to us.

I'm sure you agree it would be so nice if we didn't have to ever worry about our trust being broken. But since we are all far from perfect, we will all have to deal with this issue. Yes, I mean all of us. At some point in our lives, we will break the trust of someone we love, and someone will break our trust in them. It could be done in a huge way, like betraying one's marriage vows. It could also unfold in frequent, small ways.

For example, the friend who says she will do something for you and then doesn't come through. She contacts you with a sincere apology and even has a legitimate excuse. Because you want that same grace extended to you when you make a mistake, you forgive her without hesitation. But then you see it becomes a cycle for her, a way of life. In fact, you really can't count on her to do what she says. Has she betrayed you in a devastating way? Not really. But her continued, regular, relational hiccups have chipped away at your trust in her word. You know she loves you and cares for you, but you don't trust her to be there for you when you need her.

Regardless, if losing trust is due to a huge mishap or numerous small ones, it is difficult to endure and restore—but not impossible. I know this well. I've been living it for 14 years.

Providing Assurance

I have discovered that trust is restored with humility, honor, and consistent assurance. But I also know this: providing that assurance often feels inconvenient, embarrassing, uncomfortable, annoying, and difficult.

One of the most common things I see in couples who have experienced some type of betrayal is a lack of humility. This comes into play when the offender gets frustrated that his spouse still questions, still doubts, still fears that his word isn't true. I can't tell you how many spouses I've talked to, mostly women, who have said, "He told me he is sorry and he never wants to talk about this again. He said he has changed, and I need to just believe him." In this case, the husband's attitude is the extreme opposite of what it takes to restore trust.

It is incredibly humbling and definitely awkward for Chris to have someone call me when he's out late at night. It almost seems a little absurd that I would even need that type of reassurance. And most days, I don't. But some days, I do. Chances are strong that I'm not the only spouse who needs reassurance. Yes, our reassurance must come from God, but it is vital that we also do our part to help restore what our choices may have destroyed.

Where Is Your Confidence?

Our senses are a blessing from God. They allow us to experience our world with the people we love in a plethora of ways. Our sense of touch allows us to feel how smooth our little boy's cheeks are just before he enters puberty. We have ears to hear sounds in nature and favorite harmonious chords in music. Having the ability to taste sweet, salty, and sour sends our taste buds into overdrive on any given day. We have a nose, albeit often one bigger than we'd like, that makes the world come alive by bringing in smells that jar our memories and cause our stomachs to rumble. Our eyes take in beauty that can't be explained, whether it's waves crashing on a shore or the sight of a bride on her wedding day.

While it is terrific having all these senses, we often put our confidence in the things they allow us to experience instead of in God.

We lean on our spouses. Understandably so. But we go too far when we place our full trust in them. And while it is important to be trusting and to have people in our lives whom we can trust, people are not a replacement for God.

I recognize this is a difficult line to draw, the line between knowing you can trust people and placing our full confidence in them. We so want to be able to say, "I have complete trust in my husband" or "I know my mother will never let me down." But those statements are setting us up to be disappointed. (I will discuss this issue later in the chapter.)

God's Word is chock-full of verses that talk about trusting God and putting our complete confidence in Him. Here are some of my favorites:

> In you, LORD my God, I put my trust. (Psalm 25:1)
>
> When I am afraid, I put my trust in you. (Psalm 56:3)
>
> Trust in him at all times, you people; pour out your hearts to him, for God is our refuge. (Psalm 62:8)
>
> It is better to take refuge in the LORD than to trust in humans. (Psalm 118:8)
>
> Your kingdom is an everlasting kingdom, and your dominion endures through all generations. The LORD is trustworthy in all he promises and faithful in all he does. (Psalm 145:13)
>
> Trust in the LORD with all your heart and lean not on your own understanding; in all your ways submit to him, and he will make your paths straight. (Proverbs 3:5-6)
>
> "Blessed is the one who trusts in the LORD, whose confidence is in him. They will be like a tree planted by the water that sends out its roots by the stream. It does not fear when heat comes; its leaves are always green. It has no worries in a year of drought and never fails to bear fruit." The heart is deceitful above all things and beyond cure. Who can understand it? (Jeremiah 17:7-9)

One of my favorite parts of the Bible where a person trusted God wholeheartedly is the story of Mary, the mother of Jesus. Imagine the scene with me from Luke, chapter 1. Mary is pledged to be married to a great guy named Joseph. The Bible refers to Mary as a virgin, which was absolutely essential in the Hebrew culture, especially when a girl was pledged to be married to a descendant of King David.

The angel Gabriel came to see Mary in Nazareth. Scripture says that Mary was troubled at what Gabriel told her and she wondered why he came to visit. And rightly so. He told her she was highly favored and that God was with her. He knew she was nervous about his presence and what he'd said, so he spoke again to her: "Do not be afraid, Mary; you have found favor with God. You will conceive and give birth to a son, and you are to call him Jesus. He will be great and will be called the Son of the Most High. The Lord God will give him the throne of his father David, and he will reign over Jacob's descendants forever; his kingdom will never end" (Luke 1:30-33).

Upon hearing this, Mary asked, "How will this be...since I am a virgin?" (verse 34). Now Mary had just heard the most shocking and alarming news of her young life, and she asked only one question. I'm pretty sure my jaw would have been on the floor when he said I would conceive and give birth to a son while I'm still a virgin. But to hear that the Holy Spirit would come on me and that my child would be the Son of God? The Messiah? The promised Savior of the world? I would have surely passed out or at least have come up with a long list of questions and requests that demanded explanation. But Mary humbly asked that one question, to which the angel replied, "The Holy Spirit will come on you, and the power of the Most High will overshadow you. So the holy one to be born will be called the Son of God" (verse 35).

Mary did not use that moment either to break out her list of questions. She simply said, "I am the Lord's servant...May your word to me be fulfilled" (verse 38).

Wow. Such trust this young girl had in her Lord. And she had to have known the ridicule she would receive from everyone who knew her. She had to be anxious about what Joseph would say and do when he found out she was expecting a child that wasn't his. He would be heartbroken, humiliated, and everything in his human nature would compel him to dump her on the spot. Thankfully, an angel of the Lord appeared to him in a dream and told him not to be afraid and to take Mary as his wife, because the son she would birth would save His people from their sins (Matthew 1:20-21).

LIE vs. TRUTH

Lie: I've got this. My way is the best way.

Truth: God's way is perfect: The Lord's word is flawless; he shields me because I take refuge in him. (see Psalm 18:30)

Even with the comfort of an angel, Mary and Joseph still had so many unknown obstacles on the road ahead; yet they still trusted God. And that, my friend, is confidence in the Lord.

Obstacles on Our Path

I don't know what you have walked through in your life or what you will walk through. I would like to tell you that all of your hard days are behind you and that nothing but pleasant days are ahead. But I'd be making promises I don't have the right to make because I cannot predict the future. Yes, I have wisdom gleaned from my past experiences that gives me a glimpse into possible outcomes, but I don't know for certain what will happen. Only One does. And He deserves all our trust.

The kind of trust Mary placed in God is beyond what most of us can fathom. She was not perfect, so my guess is, she probably struggled with fear occasionally. Can you imagine going about your life telling people you are a virgin pregnant with the Messiah? You can almost see the eye rolls and hear the "yeah right" comments that would follow that proclamation.

Just as the obstacles on Mary's path seem insurmountable, sometimes ours do too. I remember the day of Chris's confession and feeling the weight of my new reality upon me. Upon us. How in the world were we to find our way back to healing when devastation was camped out on our doorstep? Once I decided not to divorce Chris, how was I ever supposed to trust him again? That order was incredibly tall and seemed absolutely unreasonable. So because I could not trust my husband's actions or words, I decided to trust my God.

And you can too. Jesus Christ is the same yesterday, today, and forever (Hebrews 13:8). He has always been faithful and trustworthy, and that means He is still faithful and trustworthy today. If He can deliver Mary through her circumstances, He can deliver you through yours. All you have to do is trust Him.

In God We Trust

As I mentioned earlier, there is a difference between trusting people and placing our full confidence in them instead of God. Scripture never says to trust humans fully, but we are commanded to trust God fully. He is the only One deserving of that.

We can place some trust in some people. Someone you have years of experience with. Someone you know incredibly well. Someone who has been by your side on more than one occasion. Someone who is always there, through thick and thin. I have people like that in my life, and I'm sure you do too.

My brother, David, is one of those people. When I talked to him on the morning after my house burned, he said, "I can be there in four hours." And he would have been, except I had no door for him to walk through, or no chair for him to sit on, or no bed for him to sleep in. He didn't care. He said, "I can just come and hug you for a little bit." David would drop everything to come to my aid. He has earned my trust.

But I also know he's not perfect. He makes mistakes. I make mistakes. Everyone does. How we deal with others' mistakes, big or small, is on us. Do we say, "Well, I will never believe or trust them again," or will we choose to accept their status as human and not expect them to act perfect like God? We are going to make mistakes and poor choices, and don't we want that same grace extended to us? So for me, understanding the line we draw when trusting people is tied to understanding our daily need for grace.

We are imperfect and will make mistakes regularly. It's wise to just expect that. Now, I don't mean you should walk around like Negative Nelly and expect everyone you meet to do you wrong. I'm simply saying we need to not be shocked when someone does something wrong. It is inevitable.

It surprises me every time someone says, "I can't believe they did that!" Now, I get that there are some actions that truly do surprise us (I have lived through a few), but when someone lies to you or isn't up-front about a situation, does that really surprise you? It doesn't surprise me because I still lie. Yep, I told a lie the other day when someone at a store asked me a question. I flat-out lied. Right to her face. And it wasn't even a "necessary" lie. I didn't know the person, and I certainly didn't need to lie to her. But I did. I was convicted immediately by the Holy Spirit. I knew I had just lied, so I confessed and repented immediately to God.

So how do we deal with the shock of people letting us down and breaking our trust? One way I believe we can trust humans is by realizing they will let us down. I know that sounds strange, but bear with me on this. I know Chris will let me down. I know he will break my trust again in some way. I don't believe it will be the way it was when our marriage almost ended, but it could be. I think we can trust humans by recognizing they will fail us. What will help us to continue trusting them is how well they come through it. When someone breaks your trust, are they genuinely apologetic? Do they see the error of their ways? Did they just have a short lapse in judgment?

And what about us? How well we respond to our own failures, I believe, determines how trustworthy we can be. If we ignore our failures and act like they are not a big deal, then restoring trust in us is going to be a difficult task. But if we are self-aware enough to deal with our own shortcomings in a healthy way and are willing to make amends, we will understand and embrace our need for grace and mercy. In turn, we will be more ready and willing to show grace and mercy to others.

Restoring Trust

I personally believe that everyone will break the trust of someone at some point in their lives. Whether it is a small spark of distrust, like a white lie, or a major four-alarm fire, like the one that eradicated trust in my marriage. The flare of broken trust will burn at some point in our lives. How do we restore trust? Together we will explore some keys to rebuilding trust that Chris and I have found valuable along our road. The fruit of hardship is this opportunity to share our story of God's healing and to glorify His wisdom.

Embrace Mutual Brokenness

The defensiveness that comes from pointing the finger has more to do with the person pointing than with the person being pointed at. It illustrates the pointer's unwillingness to address his or her own issues.

When we embrace mutual brokenness, we embrace this truth: we all need God's grace. The apostle Paul said, "All have sinned and fall short of the glory of God" (Romans 3:23). This verse is not just for some people. It says *all,* and the last time I checked, *all* means all. Whether we've sinned and broken our marriage vows or we continue to battle the demon of gossip, all of us have sinned. Acceptance of our mutual brokenness means we are profoundly aware of our own depravity.

> One of the greatest barriers to healing, restoring, and building trust is a posture of blame.

Jesus dealt with this head-on when He said, "Why do you look at the speck of sawdust in your brother's eye and pay no attention to the plank in your own eye? How can you say to your brother, 'Let me take the speck out of your eye' when all the time there is a plank in your own eye?" (Matthew 7:3-4).

Jesus didn't merely tell us to stop focusing on the other person's sawdust; He told us to figure out what is blocking our vision, our life: "You hypocrite, first take the plank out of your own eye, and then you will see clearly to remove the speck from your brother's eye" (Matthew 7:5). The point is, don't focus on what someone else needs to change; focus on what you need to change. Focus on what obstacle you have in your life in regard to truth and trust. Because we all have a plank of some sort to remove before we have clarity and discernment to offer another person assistance.

> Our power to help others overcome their brokenness is directly tied to our willingness to deal with our own.

I have been faithful to my husband for all of our 23 years of marriage. But on our marital, healing journey, as I sought God and dove headfirst into His Word, He began to show me ways where I contributed to the mess of our marriage. One was the fact that I was an enabler with Chris. I was so fearful of my security and our reputation as pastors that I chose not to say anything to Chris when I knew things were off. Now, I didn't know they were as off as they were, but I knew something was wrong. I don't take responsibility for his actions because they were his actions. But I wonder how things would have been different had I confronted him when my spirit was telling me that things weren't right. Would an uncomfortable altercation with my husband that led to professional counseling have stopped us where we were so that healing could begin before infidelity occurred? I don't know. But I was at least willing to see what contributions I'd made to the detriment of my marriage.

It takes two to make a marriage work and two to make it fail.

Remain Patient in the Healing

Healing does not happen overnight, so the path to rebuilding trust requires a willingness to wait and a willingness to endure the discomfort of moving forward without guarantees. This spiritual patience reinforces the commitment of "I'm in this" for the long haul. When my husband meets with men who have broken their marriage vows and in turn have crushed the hearts of their wives, he asks, "How many years are you willing to endure her hurt for the chance, not the guarantee, to rebuild trust?" He then goes on to say that if their answer is not *forever*, then they lack perspective of what they deserve in light of the opportunity they have been given. And that will, in some way or another, impede the ability to restore trust. What took a few minutes to break will take a long time to rebuild. And it's not that it will take a lifetime, but if it does, we need to be okay with that. The question "When are you going to get over this?" can never come out of your mouth. Nor can the statement, "I just can't do this anymore."

Scripture says, "Let us not become weary in doing good, for at the proper time we will reap a harvest if we do not give up" (Galatians 6:9). All too often couples give up too soon. Sometimes it's only one person, sometimes it's both. And I get it. The pain is too great and you think you can't take one more painful step, especially if you are the only one taking steps. You cannot carry the load for both of you.

Becoming weary on a road like this is par for the course. It is tiresome and grueling. But Paul exhorts us not to become weary while doing good. Keep doing the right thing, even without seeing positive results, because at the proper time you will see a harvest, a great marriage, if you don't throw in the towel. Growing weary is easy to do when you focus on the hardships in front of you.

We need to raise our eyes and look farther out. We need to recognize that these momentary struggles are just that, momentary.

And we should never make a permanent decision when our emotions are heightened.

Keep putting your feet down on the path, one foot in front of the other, all the while keeping your eyes up and focused on what you want to see in the end, not on the difficulties you face now. That is the remedy for not growing weary in doing good.

Walk in the Holy Spirit

The last ingredient vital to restoring trust requires us to quit walking in our own power and strength, which is difficult for most of us. Walking in the Holy Spirit, however, is the only way true, lasting healing will emerge. God's Word tells us to "be filled with the Spirit" (Ephesians 5:18). We must be empowered by the Holy Spirit, the God in us is whom we place our trust in.

How do we grow and strengthen our spirit? We feed it. When we feed the spirit, the flesh will starve. But the converse is true as well. When we feed the flesh, the spirit will starve. If we nurture our spirit within, we will have an awareness of God's leading. At any given time in our walk with Christ, we have all felt like our flesh was in control and there was no solution. Untrue. While focusing on our flesh is definitely defeating, focusing on our spirit will bring us life in God's power. This intentional growth leads us to walk by the Holy Spirit.

What does it look like in our daily lives to walk by the Holy Spirit? Well, we make choices, decisions, and priorities by first asking, "Is this going to propel me closer to God or further away from Him?"

I was born and raised in my home state of Texas even though Oklahoma is the state I now call home. Because of that, I love country music. And not just today's country music; I love the country music that my daddy used to sing: Charley Pride, Kenny Rogers, George Jones, Merle Haggard to name a few. And while there is nothing inherently wrong with country music, sometimes if I listen to it for too long it doesn't really benefit me. In fact, it takes me to a place where my thoughts are not on the Lord. So I listen to worship music or contemporary Christian music more than I do any other kind of music. Music has power for most people and especially for me. Because it does, I make sure I don't let it control me and let my flesh become stronger than my spirit.

LIE vs. TRUTH

Lie: I can trust my family and close friends to never let me down.

Truth: It is better for me to take refuge in God than to trust in humans. (see Psalm 118:8)

Maybe you love to read books or watch TV. You can finish a novel in less than 24 hours if you push everything else aside. Or you binge-watch a television series on Netflix, and before you know it, it's 9:00 p.m. and you've almost finished an entire season of said show. Yet that whole day you did not pick up the Bible once. This isn't to make you feel guilty for not reading it or to make you think God loves you any less. Remember, guilt is from our spiritual enemy, and God loves you the same no matter your actions. But what has reading that novel or watching that series done to your spirit? Not much. In fact, it has fed your flesh. Again, no judgment from me because I have been known to watch one or seven shows on Netflix in a day. The bottom line here: instead of feeding our spirit with the truth of God's Word, we often choose to feed it with entertainment.

Walking in the Spirit and being filled with the Spirit happens when we make room for the Spirit to reside in us. We have to be willing to let God show us what clutter needs to be removed from our lives so He can fill us back up. If we store all the clutter, the fleshly desires, impure motives, and our own agendas in us, there is little room for the Spirit to occupy. Salvation and the sealing of the Holy Spirit are done at once. But walking in the Spirit is an ongoing action and commitment.

These three key actions I have suggested for you are not the only ones for restoring truth. You may come up with more, and I'm certain other people have as well. Chris and I have just found that these three have played the biggest role in our marriage restoration. I pray you will incorporate them into your journey as well.

Absolute Trust

After 14 years, I have grown to trust my husband again. When he is allowing the Spirit of God to live through him and lead him, I trust him. It doesn't mean I think he would never mess up again. It just means that I know the character of God and when I see Chris yielding to His leadership, I trust Chris. So, I guess you could say that I trust the Jesus in him.

As much as Chris and I have both grown in the trust area, I do not trust him fully, nor does he trust me fully. That honor is for God alone. The human heart is deceitful. It is. That is why the Lord warns, "Above all else, guard your heart, for everything you do flows from it" (Proverbs 4:23).

Only One has the place of absolute trust in my life. There is only One who will never fail me or let me down. There is only One who can comfort me completely and guide me perfectly. There is only One who will never leave me or forsake me.

People are imperfect. God is not.

People will fail me. God will not.

People will abandon me. God will not.

Blessed are those—you, me, us—who trust in the Lord and have made the Lord their—your, my, our—hope and confidence.

TO HELP YOU **BUILD WISELY**

1. Write down one way your spouse or someone else close to you has broken your trust. If it's not a huge act of betrayal share how frequent small acts have diminished your trust in this person.

2. On a scale from 1 to 10, how difficult is it for you to truly trust God? (1 = easy; 10 = difficult) Why do you think it is easy or difficult for you?

3. Considering we all have our own "planks," what would you say is your plank in regard to your marriage? What steps do you need to take today to help remove your plank so you can be a benefit to your spouse? (If you feel overwhelmed at the amount of planks you have, relax. Just choose one or two to focus on for now.)

4. We explored three keys to restoring trust: embrace mutual brokenness, remain patient in the healing, and walk in the Holy Spirit. Which of these are present in your marriage? Which one is missing?

5. Create a list of things you do each day that feed your flesh and another list of what you do to feed your spirit. It typically takes 21 days to form a habit, so spend that much time feeding your spirit and focusing on new ways to do so. After those three weeks, evaluate where you are and any progress you've made.

5

Expectation Management

During the summer of 2010, I was preparing for a new season in my life. My youngest son, Seth Joseph, was about to start first grade, and that meant, come mid-August, both of my boys would be in school all day long. (And all the moms raised their hands and shouted, "Hallelujah!")

But about one month into school, God started stirring within me some change. Change that would give a facelift to the Beall family forever. I was settling into my weekly routine of lengthy studies of the Word of God, shopping, lunches with friends and girls I mentor, and then an afternoon making sure that groceries were purchased for the delicious meals I was going to prepare at night. All would be accomplished before I went to the carpool line at 3:30. My family would see how amazing I was, and they would rise up and call me blessed, because I was the Proverbs 31 woman. Somebody find me some land to buy.

But this change came at me before I knew it was coming. What change, you might ask? Homeschooling.

Dear Jesus, no. Please no. They are just fine in school. Our schools are good, and they've had such amazing teachers, and they've made some good friends and…and…and. I couldn't even make the excuse that I didn't know enough or have enough training because, hello, I did. I taught four years in both public and private schools. I had experience.

And then the strangest thing happened one night in the middle of my pity party with God. I prayed, *God, if this is what's best for our family, then I will do it. But would You please change my heart?*

I fell asleep that night and woke up with a new calling and purpose. My heart was changed. I was borderline excited about this new journey of homeschooling my sons.

Now fast-forward several weeks to our first official week at home as a homeschooling family. My good friend Deleise Klaassen encouraged me to spend a lot of time reading to my boys. I loved reading to my kids, but finding a book to read aloud to them could pose a bit of a challenge because of the five years that separated them. I eventually chose the true classic *Charlotte's Web* by E.B. White.

I spent the next few weeks reading it aloud to them. Noah, our then 11-year-old son, was completely immersed in the story, listening intently and putting the words I read into pictures in his mind. Our six-year-old, Seth, on the other hand, had to stay busy while I read. He either colored or built with his LEGO blocks. Being a kinesthetic learner, he listens best when he's moving, even doing something else.

Or so I thought.

I got to the end of the book, where Wilbur and Charlotte are at the fair. Everyone in attendance is expecting another word to be spun in a web by Wilbur. That's why they even came to the fair, after all. Charlotte knew her trip to the fair was a one-way trip. She would literally give up her life for Wilbur's.

I came to the part where Charlotte did indeed die. I read the words, "Charlotte died." And with both curiosity and confusion in his mind, Seth looked up and asked, "Who's Charlotte?"

Let the Good Times Roll

Expectations. We all have them. And because we have them, we all typically experience disappointment. Because what we expect doesn't always line up with reality. My friend Kim Heinecke says, "The key to happiness is expectation management." The girl knows what she is talking about.

What has it been for you? Did you have lofty dreams of how your marriage would be? Surely you would have sex every day, because your wife couldn't keep her hands off you during the time you dated. You practically had to push her away and take a cold shower after every date! You just knew you'd be the couple who really did have the best sex life ever. But you're not having sex every day. In fact, you're not even having sex once a week! You have so many IOUs from your wife that you've lost count.

Maybe you dreamed that your knight in shining armor would romance you like the actors do on soap operas. I mean, he wooed you when he was pursuing you and was always the most thoughtful boyfriend in the world. He bought you flowers and gifts. He wrote notes declaring his never-ending love for you. He opened doors for you and always wanted you to be happy. You imagined he would take you in his arms at just the right time and not get defensive when you bring up things that frustrate you. He would always understand you and always know when you need to be held without you having to tell him. He would know what you need before it even came to your lips. He could practically read your mind! But now he looks at you like you're crazy when you cry for no apparent reason. When you tell him you need to be held, he gives a big huff because you are interrupting the NBA Finals, but he halfheartedly hugs you anyway. He gets defensive when you want to "talk" and make your marriage better, because to him what you're really saying is, "Hey buddy, you know that whole knight-in-shining-armor dude? Well, you're really sucking at it."

I expected our homeschooling journey to be amazing from day one. I expected that my sons would love to learn and be completely excited about our lessons. That they would say, "Let's learn about this, Mom," and "Let's go learn on a field trip, Mom." Then we'd be off, and before I knew it they'd be practically teaching themselves. I dreamed they'd get up, give each other hugs, like I'd heard other homeschooling families did, and we'd all pray together after our family devotion. I envisioned my older son lending a hand to his younger brother as they learned to make their own sandwiches. I pictured reading time in the afternoons where they listened intently to every word I said, as they laughed when they were supposed to laugh and felt sadness where that was necessary as well. I pictured car rides where they'd laugh and learn because all around us was a world with opportunities to teach us. I wanted our family to live out the phrase "Life is school," shared with me by my dear friend Robin Meadows. Yes, this was going to be glorious.

Instead, my youngest didn't remember Charlotte; they woke up with grouchy attitudes on most mornings; they didn't want the breakfast I made for them; they couldn't believe I expected them to get dressed and brush their teeth; they rolled their eyes when I told them it was time for math; and they'd be in a fight, complete with tears and yelling, before 10:00 in the morning.

Let the good times roll.

If You Had Been Here

When reading the Bible, you'll find many stories where people expected things to happen a certain way, but it didn't. Just because the Bible is the perfect, inspired Word of God doesn't mean the people in the Bible were perfect and didn't struggle just like you and I do. God's Word, ways, thoughts, and plans are perfect; humans are far from it. Because of this, it makes sense that the people in the Bible acted in ways and thought thoughts just like you and I do every day.

In Luke 15, Jesus told the parable of the prodigal son. The father had expectations of his sons and how they would live. His older son followed the plan, but his younger son did not. When the younger son left with his inheritance, the father was hurt. The younger son had expectations that this life he chose apart from his family would provide him everything he wanted and needed. But he spent everything his father had given him and ended up feeding pigs for a living. When the younger son came home and repented, the older son was angry and expected that his father would teach him a lesson. When that didn't happen, he was disappointed. The father and both of his sons had expectations that caused them disappointment.

LIE vs. TRUTH

Lie: What if all this work I do for my marriage doesn't pay off?

Truth: Some trust in chariots and some in horses, but I trust in the name of the LORD our God. (see Psalm 20:7)

In the Old Testament book of Hosea, the Lord spoke to Hosea and told him to marry a promiscuous woman and have children with her. Not only that, but the Lord told Hosea what names to give these children, and these names did not have great meanings. Hosea obeyed God, but my guess is that marrying a prostitute wasn't really what he had envisioned for his life. And having to name your children Jezreel, after the massacre of Jezreel, Lo-Ruhamah, which means "not loved," and Lo-Ammi, which means "not my people," were names probably not on the top of the list from the book of baby names.

I suppose the passage of Scripture that jumps out at me the most when we are talking about expectations can be found in John 11. The chapter starts by telling us that a man named Lazarus was sick. Lazarus had two sisters, Mary and Martha, and the three of them were close to Jesus. In fact, when the sisters sent word to Jesus about Lazarus's illness, they referred to their brother as "the one you love."

Upon hearing the news that Lazarus was sick, Jesus stated in verse 4 that Lazarus's sickness would not end in death and that this sickness was for God's glory so that God's Son would be glorified through it. Now, you might think that Jesus would pick up immediately and go to Lazarus. But He didn't go to Lazarus right then, even though Lazarus needed him to. Jesus waited two full days before leaving. Two full days. After those two days passed, he headed toward Lazarus.

When Jesus arrived two days later, Lazarus had been in the tomb for four days. The sisters heard that Jesus had arrived, and only Martha went out to meet him; Mary stayed home (verse 20). Immediately, Martha told Jesus that had He been there, Lazarus wouldn't have died. Although she was clearly upset that Jesus didn't come in time, she still believed He had the power to heal her brother. She then went on to say, "I know that even now God will give you whatever you ask" (verse 21). Still another statement of her profound faith in Jesus, the Messiah, her Teacher.

After her conversation with Jesus, Martha went to her sister, Mary, and told her Jesus was looking for her. Mary got up quickly to go to Jesus, and when she got to him she fell at His feet. Just like her sister, Mary was also full of faith that Jesus could do anything, and she cried out, "Lord, if you had been here, my brother would not have died" (verse 32). Seeing her tears, Jesus was moved and asked to be taken to where Lazarus was laid. And then the most amazing, compassionate, profound two words in the entire Bible revealed the humanity of our Savior: "Jesus wept" (John 11:35).

I picture Jesus in true, human form right here. Weeping like you and I weep when we are in pain. Not a simple cry where we can somehow manage to gain our composure after a few seconds. No, it's the kind of grief where our faces contort and we start the ugly cry; our noses start to run profusely, and our eyes become bloodshot from the tears streaming down our faces. In that moment, my Jesus, your Jesus grieved over something He could have prevented and ultimately would repair with a three-word command: "Lazarus, come out!" (verse 43). With that, Lazarus came out of the tomb, his body covered in linen strips. Upon Lazarus's resurrection, Jesus said, "Take off the grave clothes and let him go" (verse 44).

Good vs. Great

Oh the expectations are abundant in this passage in John 11. The sisters had the expectation that Jesus would come be with them and see their brother, so they sent word to let Him know. They had the expectation that Jesus would come quickly because they knew Jesus loved their brother. They had the expectation that He would heal their brother and that Lazarus would not die. Even the people had the expectation that since He healed a blind guy He would most certainly be able to keep Lazarus from dying (verse 37). None of those expectations was met, and disappointment arose.

One of the problems with all of the expectations in this story is that they were unspoken. When Mary and Martha sent word to Jesus about their brother, they didn't include a request for Him to come. They assumed that when He found out about Lazarus He would come. They also assumed that He would get there quickly and spare the life of their brother. The people assumed that Jesus would heal Lazarus because, after all, He made a blind guy see, so they knew He could do it, so surely He would. Assumptions are expectations that will bring disappointment. We have to clearly communicate in order to avoid the disappointment that our unmet expectations bring.

Another problem with the expectations in this story is that they wanted something good, but what they got was something great. Since we know the outcome of the story, we know that while they did have expectations that went unmet at first, they eventually were met. Why? Because what they expected was Jesus to heal their brother. And although He didn't meet that expectation and heal their brother, they still got their brother back. That is what they wanted in the first place. This desire for their brother to be healed from his illness was something good. What they got was something great. The ability to not only have their brother back from the dead but to experience the glory of God through the One they had come to love deeply and follow wholeheartedly was something they were not expecting. They did not see this coming.

I think it's safe to say that our human expectations pale in comparison to God's plans. Even on our best day, we can't come up with a better plan than God's. Even on the day where everything around us is going great, when we are feeling it and we have that "this is it" idea, those days still fall short of God's best.

But you see, there is this thing called pain. It is almost always involved when God moves in great ways. The friends and family members of Lazarus grieved for him for four days. Two of those days Jesus stayed put, and two of those days He traveled. Jesus could have healed Lazarus the moment He heard of his illness and none of that pain would have happened. He could have done it with just a thought in His perfect head, and the tears Mary and Martha cried would have never left their tear ducts. He was fully God and had the power to do so. But He didn't. I believe that healing Lazarus would have been a good thing. A very good thing. But raising him from the dead to display the glory of God and allow the people to see just how incredible our God is was a great thing.

> The distance between good and great is usually measured in tears. It's painful.

Why Can't He Just Read My Mind?

We fall into this expectation trap in our relationships all the time. We expect someone to do something for us at a specific time or in a specific setting. Sometimes we expect them to do it because they said they would. Other times we place expectations on them because they play a certain role in our lives and, well, they should just know. We do it within our careers when we expect a boss or a coworker to say a certain thing. We do it with our children by expecting them to act a particular way. We most certainly do it in our marriages, when we expect our imperfect spouses to act perfectly. That last sentence sounds a bit absurd, doesn't it? Yet it happens all the time. We expect perfection from an imperfect human. No wonder we're disappointed.

For the first several years of our marriage, Chris and I did not communicate well. He did his best with me, but I wanted him to just know how I felt and what I needed. I didn't want to have to tell him when I walked in the door that I'd had a hard day teaching. I wanted him to be aware, see the signs on my face and in my body language, and then rush over to greet me at the door. Then I'd expect him to gently wrap his arm around me and say, "Let's go eat some Mexican food. Will that make you feel better?"

Instead, what would typically happen is that I would walk in the door, distraught from teaching 24 third graders who may or may not have obeyed that day, and get frustrated when I'd have to tell him how I was feeling. I didn't want to have to tell him I was ready to quit. I didn't want to ask him to take me out to dinner. He should have known all of this, right? We're married, for crying out loud. Doesn't he know what I'm thinking and feeling?

I so wanted the romance in that moment. The romance that we just knew each other so intimately that words were unnecessary. That romance rarely came. Because, newsflash, my husband is not a mind reader. I know, I know; crazy as it sounds, he cannot guess what I'm thinking on any given day. Yes, the signs were all there and he should have just known because he's my husband, but he just didn't. Sure, he probably saw that I wasn't in the best mood, but to come in, sweep me away to Taco Cabana for fajitas and tell me it would all be okay wasn't him, even though I wholeheartedly expected him to act that way. The problem is, I never told him.

From Disappointment to Encouragement

I have found four transformative ways to help you go from disappointment to encouragement in your marriage when it comes to expectations.

1. Let your spouse off the hook. You have placed expectations on your spouse that he or she will never be able to meet. You are expecting them to meet your every need and desire. You want them to be perfect and never let you down. This is completely unrealistic. Flip the scenario. Would you like for your spouse to expect perfection from you? Would you want him to expect you to meet each and every need he has? You will not have the perfect marriage with no problems. It does not exist. But great marriages with healthy people do.

2. When you do have realistic expectations, tell your spouse. Don't expect him to read your mind and just know what you need. Body language and facial expressions often do tell us what someone is feeling, but it doesn't always. I can't tell you how many times Chris asked me in the past if something was wrong, and in order to string things along and find out how much he really wanted to know, I would simply say, "I'm fine." And you and I both know I wasn't fine. I just wanted him to fight for what was inside me because it was romantic. It's much more romantic to know that your spouse really cares and isn't just asking because he thinks he has to. Talk to your spouse about what you expect and what you need.

3. Surrender your expectations for your life, your marriage, your family, and your future to God. Like I said, we expect and desire good things in our lives. There is nothing wrong with that. But we hold on to those ideals, often with white knuckles, and we don't want to let them go. Though all along, God is saying, "Trust me

with your dreams. I have something so much better than what you are holding on to." God gives His best to us. Doesn't it make sense to turn over our dreams to him?

4. Become a student of your spouse. Study them. Get to know them better than you think you do. Learn how they think. And learn what their needs are and how they feel loved.

Typically, in every marriage there is a giver and a taker. One spouse is usually more giving than the other, and one typically receives more than the other. I know, I know, that is rather harsh, but if you truly do an inventory on your marriage, you will probably see that is true. Becoming a student of your spouse in order to know how to love them well will take a dying-to-self attitude. This will be a challenge, especially for those spouses who happen to be the takers in the marriage. But you can't just blame the takers. The givers are more comfortable giving so they don't say anything. They have to learn to receive as well. Both people have to learn new behaviors.

I know that some will say, "My spouse is just a servant. He loves to serve me." And that may be so. But I happen to know that always giving and never receiving leads to burnout and resentment. A healthy marriage is one where both give and both receive. Allow me to next suggest a way to study your spouse by learning how they are wired to receive so you can more lovingly give.

The Five Love Languages

Gary Chapman wrote a book called *The 5 Love Languages*. I cannot speak enough great things about this book. It quite frankly saved our marriage right around year six. Allow me to explain.

In his book Dr. Chapman introduces five different love languages: words of affirmation, acts of service, quality time, receiving gifts, and physical touch.[1] According to Dr. Chapman, you have a primary love language, and you feel loved when someone loves you in that way.

My primary love language has been quality time, though in the past few years I've found that I also enjoy words of affirmation and physical touch. (I tell my husband I like all the love languages and that he needs to get busy.) My husband's primary love language is acts of service. We know this now but didn't for the first several years of our marriage. When you don't know how your spouse receives love, then he may not understand your attempt to show him love. If you don't know what each other's love languages are, it is as if you are speaking Chinese and your spouse is speaking Spanish.

LIE vs. TRUTH

Lie: I'll never have a good life.

Truth: Christ came that I might have life, and have it to the full. (see John 10:10)

For years, in the summer Chris would come home from work early about once a week to mow the yard. He spent a long time on it each week, edging and weed-eating it just perfectly. Then he would walk in the house with a big, cheesy grin and say to me, "Shug, I just mowed the yard for you." I'd always give him a look clearly showing I didn't care nor was I impressed. (Nice wife.) And it would make him feel bad. He was trying to show me love by doing something for me. But that isn't the way I received it. I did not see his act of service as loving me, but he was showing his love to me doing that act of service. He was trying to show me love the way he receives love. I, on the other hand, would rather go grocery shopping together, take a walk in the neighborhood, or sit on the couch and talk about our days. So I would try to do that with him and think I was being a good wife. He tolerated it. Just like him, I was trying to love him the way I wanted to receive love.

When we read *The 5 Love Languages* we were astounded! It made total sense to us. Once we understood the concept, we both worked hard to try to show our love for each other in unique ways. It actually became a fun thing to do. We both looked for creative ways to love each other the way we received love. I would have his favorite drink ready for him when he came home from work or complete an errand for him that he was going to have to do on his day off. He would wake up on his day off and say, "Babe, I thought we could go to the grocery store together after we go out to lunch." Come on baby, light my fire. You can push my grocery cart anytime.

What if our expectations for our marriage are nothing compared to what God desires for our marriage? What you think would be an amazing marriage may not be God's definition of amazing. What if, in order to get that dream marriage, you have to go through an exorbitant amount of pain to get it? Would you want it? What if letting our spouse off the hook and removing unrealistic expectations make it easier for God to show us His expectations for our marriage?

We want to be happy and enjoy life, which is good. God wants us to follow Him and be holy, which is great. We want to have a comfortable life and career that will make a good living, which is good. God wants us to surrender our dreams to Him so He can show us what a dream really is, which is great. Expectations in and of themselves are not bad. But we do have to manage them and be realistic about them. We can't expect a fairy tale life in this world because this place is not our home. We were never meant for it. But we can both pursue Christ, and in that pursuit we'll find the abundant life He promised us (John 10:10). Abundance is found in Christ. His is the plan where true joy is found.

TO HELP YOU **BUILD WISELY**

1. Think about a time recently when you were extremely disappointed. What event or action led to that?

2. In regard to your marriage, what expectations did you have of your spouse before you got married? Make a list of three or four and tell which ones are met and unmet.

3. When you find that your expectations aren't met, is it usually because they are unrealistic, unspoken, or both? Take some time to really examine what is behind the disappointment you feel in your marriage by analyzing your expectations.

4. What is your love language? What is your spouse's love language? List three ways you can show love to your spouse the way they receive it. Commit to do those each day. (If you haven't read Gary Chapman's *The 5 Love Languages*, read it. You won't be sorry.)

5. Spend some time praying with your spouse now. If you can't now, wait until the kids are in bed or you have some time alone. Seek God together and surrender your old habits and expectations in your marriage and ask God to give you His desires.

6

Living as a Victor or Victim

My fifth grade school year was a rough one for me. Not only was I taller than almost every kid in school, I also had become quite chubby. Being a food lover and not very active at that time, the pounds added up. I struggled with feeling insecure about my appearance, my intellect, and my ability to get a boyfriend. None of the boys wanted to "go with me" and my mediocre grades were just that. Thankfully, I did have a lot of good friends who seemed to think I was a nice friend too. Until one Monday morning.

It must have happened on the playground when I wasn't around because the moment I walked into my fifth grade classroom at Northside Elementary in Georgetown, Texas, none of my friends would talk to me. In fact, they wouldn't even look at me. All because *she* told them not to.

I'll call her Beth. We'd been "friends" since I moved to Georgetown two years before. And by "friends," I really mean she was nice to me when she wanted to be and casually bullied me the rest of the time. But her harassment had never gone this far. Later that fateful day, I spoke to a friend on the phone who revealed that Beth had told everyone in my class to stop talking to me or she would beat them up. And she could have. Not only was she my height, she was bigger than me and had an even bigger attitude to go with her physical stature. All the kids were scared of her. Heck, the teachers might have been scared of her.

For six painful weeks, nobody would talk to me at the lunch table. Nobody would willingly be my partner in PE. Nobody would play against me at tetherball during recess. Nobody invited me over for a sleepover on Friday night. Even with crowds of people around me at school, I was virtually alone. Or at least it felt that way.

Until the day Reese Parker decided to talk to me at lunch. He was a small boy, much shorter than me. But his character was much larger than anyone else's, because he ignored the command from a girl bully. We were a regular duo during those weeks. I didn't have a crush on him, and he certainly didn't have a crush on me. We were just two kids who became friends, and we remained friends throughout our school years.

I'll never know if someone talked to Beth or forced her to quit bullying me, but one day I came to school and my friends were my friends again. I had lots of friends to talk to at lunch, on the playground, and on the bus. Life was back to normal for me. And I was relieved.

Teaching Others about Our Worth

It stinks being mistreated, doesn't it? To be the brunt of someone's joke or to be picked on persistently by someone hurts to the core. It could happen to us as adults at work, at home, or even at church. The mistreatment could come in the form of name-calling or disrespect. It might be something more serious, like physical, emotional, or sexual abuse.

If my mother has told me once, she's told me a thousand times, "Dr. Phil says you teach people how to treat you." In fact, it is his Life Law #8. Here is what he says about that:

You either teach people to treat you with dignity and respect, or you don't. This means you are partly responsible for the mistreatment that you get at the hands of someone else. You shape others' behavior when you teach them what they can get away with and what they cannot.

If the people in your life treat you in an undesirable way, figure out what you are doing to reinforce, elicit, or allow that treatment. Identify the payoffs you may be giving someone in response to any negative behavior. For example, when people are aggressive, bossy, or controlling—and then get their way—you have rewarded them for unacceptable behavior.

Because you are accountable, you can declare the relationship "reopened for negotiation" at any time you choose, and for as long as you choose. Even a pattern of relating that is 30 years old can be redefined. Before you reopen the negotiation, you must commit to do so from a position of strength and power, not fear and self-doubt.[2]

For real, Dr. Phil? You mean to tell me I am partly responsible for how Beth treated me during those miserable six weeks in fifth grade? That somehow I could have prevented that mistreatment in some way? I mean, she was the hateful one; not me. I was voted best friend of my senior class in 1989. Not her. I don't have a mean bone in my body! I'm nice. People e-mail and text me all the time. People like me. They've always liked me!

But I do believe he's accurate. While I may not have egged her on to treat me poorly or instigated a fight with her, my unwillingness to stand up for myself allowed her to treat me poorly. I did not confront her or risk bodily injury by standing up to her. She acted out hatefully, and I cowered down to her harassment. So yeah, I'm partly to blame for what happened to me in fifth grade back in 1981. Oh, to know then what I know now.

I'd like to tell you that after fifth grade I no longer allowed people to treat me poorly. But as the old adage goes, "Old habits die hard." Indeed, they do. I could list many different instances where I allowed people to mistreat me, but that would bore you. Maybe there weren't any physical altercations with people, unless you count my brothers punching me in the bicep, but there were plenty of instances where I was knocked around verbally, emotionally, and mentally.

In addition to being nice, the biggest reason I never stood up for myself was because I was a people pleaser, an approval addict. I wanted everyone to like me, and at the time, I was willing to do whatever I could to make sure everyone did. I wanted peace at all costs with any relationship I had. If I stood up to someone, I risked losing them as a friend. And at the time, I was just not capable of doing that.

LIE vs. TRUTH

Lie: I will never find freedom from this.

Truth: Now the Lord is the Spirit, and where the Spirit of the Lord is, there is my freedom. (see 2 Corinthians 3:17)

Perhaps you are a people pleaser with your spouse. You allow yourself to be mistreated, even if it's in a small way, so that peace reigns. You don't stand up for yourself and allow yourself to be beaten down. This, my friend, cannot be blamed on your spouse. Sure, they may tend to act more rudely than you do, but you have to decide how you will be treated. In my own marriage, Chris and I have been rude, ugly, and harsh with each other. And both of us have said to each other, "Hey, I'm not going to be treated or talked to disrespectfully like this. When you want to talk in a more respectful tone, I'll listen."

Being a nice person or a people pleaser doesn't mean you can't stand up for yourself. I have learned this in such an incredibly hard way. Most people pleasers don't stand up for themselves because they don't want people to stop liking them. So they allow certain things to be said of them and to them without taking a stand for themselves. But in order to show people how to treat us, we must be willing to make changes concerning what we allow.

"I Know a Guy"

There are victims in this world, true victims. People who have been attacked, injured, robbed, or even murdered. Quite honestly, my guess is, we could all don the label "victim" at some point in our lives. Sometimes you know a victim when you see one, but sometimes you don't.

Take my dear friend Amy Newberry, for example. Her childhood was rough. Not rough like she couldn't get the jeans she wanted for the first day of school rough. I'm talking, the girl didn't know if she would be fed on any given day or abused on another or have a blanket to cover up with on the random couch that would serve as her bed. She was a victim of horrible things that a child should never have to endure.

Her parents divorced when she was nine, and after that she moved into a domestic women's shelter with her mother. Two years later, the Department of Human Services (DHS) got involved, and she was placed in foster care. At the age of 14, she ran away from her foster family and stayed on the streets, occasionally visiting her grandmother's home over the following 18 months.

Eventually, things turned around for Amy, and she was invited into an amazing home just shy of her 16th birthday. A little over two years later, she became the very first adult to be adopted in the state of Oklahoma. Today, she is a wife and mother to four children and is surrounded by numerous loving friends and family members. She has used her story to impact thousands of lives in the greater Oklahoma City metro area.

If you meet Amy today, you would never know that was in her past. In fact, there is nothing in her demeanor or vocabulary that lends itself to a woe-is-me or feel-sorry-for-me attitude. Unless you catch her joking about her days on the street, you'd never imagine she has experienced the things she has. I laugh every time she says, "I know a guy," when she is willing to come to the aid of her tribe in any way. Someone who keeps living like a victim has a victim mentality. That is not Amy Newberry.

Dr. Judith Orloff, assistant clinical professor of psychiatry at UCLA and author of *Emotional Freedom*, described what this can look like:

> The victim grates on you with a poor-me attitude, and is allergic to taking responsibility for their actions. People are always against them, the reason for their unhappiness. They portray themselves as unfortunates who demand rescuing, and they will make you into their therapist."[3]

Basically, having a victim mentality means that you blame everyone else for all that is happening to you, and you take no responsibility for anything. It's never your fault.

Wow. I do not want to be that person ever. Do you? But sometimes we are, because it doesn't hurt as bad to shift blame away from ourselves or even away from someone we love. Now, I am in no way saying that my friend Amy could do much about her circumstances. She was a child, after all. But had she embraced the victim mindset, she easily could have used her difficult past as an excuse to make poor choices in her present. She chose to be a victor instead.

From Prisoner to Pharaoh's Right-Hand Man

If anyone had a right to play the victim card it was Joseph. He was Jacob's favored son, even though he had 11 brothers. I'm guessing that Joseph had a hunch he was his daddy's favorite because he paraded around in a colorful robe that his father gave him. Scripture tells us that his brothers were jealous of him (Genesis 37:11).

Sometime later the brothers were tending to their father's flocks and Jacob sent Joseph to make sure everything was going well. When they saw him coming, they were more than annoyed at his presence. So much so that they began to plot his death. When he arrived, they stripped the robe from him and threw him into an empty cistern.

With Joseph in the cistern, they decide to sit down to eat their meal. (Makes sense.) After a time, a caravan of Ishmaelites came by. The brothers relented and decided not to kill their father's beloved son. Instead, they did something far more gracious in their own eyes; they sold him as a slave to the Ishmaelites. Upon hearing the news, their father was distraught and mourned for his son, whom he assumed was dead. Meanwhile, Joseph was sold to Potiphar, one of Pharaoh's officials in Egypt.

This unfortunate move to Egypt didn't start out too bad. Well, except for the betrayal and mistreatment by his brothers when they sold him. Joseph wasn't mistreated, beaten, or forced to do hard labor but instead lived in the house of his Egyptian master, Potiphar (Genesis 39). The Lord was with Joseph and gave him success in everything he did. So much success that he found favor in his master's eyes and received his trust. But here's where the problems ensued.

Not only did Potiphar like Joseph, but Potiphar's wife did too. Uh oh. Apparently Joseph's muscles and rugged good looks caught her attention. But Joseph's character was strong, and even though I imagine he was tempted, he denied her every sexual advance. You know that does only one thing to the pursuer: it makes them want to pursue their desired object even more. One time she grabbed his cloak as he ran away from her advance. With his cloak in her hand, she yelled for help and then told the most elaborate scheme about Joseph's making an advance at her. As you can figure, Potiphar did not take that news lightly. In fact, Scripture says he burned with anger and put Joseph in prison.

Joseph was granted favor in the eyes of the prison warden. He was put in charge of all the prisoners and was made responsible for all that was done there. The Lord granted Joseph success in whatever he did (verse 23). Yet he was still in prison. Even though he wasn't mistreated there, he was still imprisoned wrongly and unfairly. Life wasn't fair for Joseph.

The next chapter tells us that the pharaoh's cupbearer and baker were put in prison as well. The day after they arrived in prison, they had dreams they didn't understand. God gave Joseph the ability to interpret those dreams. Hopeful that this interpretation would be his ticket to get out of jail, he made a request to the cupbearer, asking him to remember Joseph and mention him to Pharaoh (Genesis 40:14-15).

The cupbearer was restored to his position as cupbearer, but he did not remember Joseph. For two full years Joseph remained in prison. That is the opposite of fair.

But then one day Pharaoh had a dream that troubled him, and nobody could interpret it. At that time, the cupbearer remembered Joseph. He told Pharaoh the entire story, and immediately Pharaoh sent for Joseph.

Once he had been cleaned up, shaven, and given different clothes, Joseph was brought before Pharaoh. Pharaoh requested that Joseph interpret his dream, to which Joseph replied, "I cannot do it...but God will give Pharaoh the answer he desires" (Genesis 41:16).

Sure enough, after hearing Pharaoh's dream Joseph was able to interpret it. Not only did Joseph interpret it, but he then made a suggestion as to how Pharaoh should handle the information.

Immediately, Pharaoh put Joseph in charge of his palace and all his people. The only person greater than Joseph was Pharaoh himself. Joseph started the day as a 30-year-old prisoner in a dungeon and finished the day as second in command to the king of Egypt. What a day!

Many years later, his brothers went to Egypt during the famine to buy food. When his brothers arrived, Joseph immediately recognized them, but they didn't recognize him. After a series of events, all his brothers ended up in Egypt dining with Joseph. Joseph managed to hold his emotions together while he was around his brothers, but finally he made himself known to them, and in doing so he wept so loudly that the Egyptians heard him. When he told them who he was, his first question to them was, "Is my father still living?" (Genesis 45:3). Clearly shocked at his announcement, his brothers couldn't answer him because they were scared to death.

Here's the amazing part about this story that encompasses two decades of Joseph's life. He could have blamed his brothers for selling him to that Ishmaelite caravan all those years ago and would have been justified at being mad at them because their cruel action caused him so much suffering. But he was not. Instead, he showed a tremendous amount of perspective by telling them not to be angry with themselves. He told them it was God who sent him ahead to "preserve for you a remnant on earth" and get prepared before the famine struck (Genesis 45:5-8).

In time, all of Joseph's brothers, their families, and his father arrived in Egypt. Joseph went to Pharaoh and told him that his family was there. Pharaoh told Joseph to settle his family in the best part of the land and to put any of them in charge of his flocks that Joseph deemed worthy. Joseph also provided all their households with food.

The Big Picture We Can't See

Did you catch all that? Joseph told them not to be mad at themselves for what they did to him all those years ago, because there was a purpose for what had happened to him. To make sure they understood that God had a purpose in his pain, Joseph said not once, not twice, but three times that God sent him there. And then his family waltzed right into Egypt, got the best land, and got all of their food provided for them from their estranged brother. Joseph could have played the "why me" card and lived as a victim because of what was done to him, and nobody would have blamed him or expected anything otherwise. But he did not play the victim card. He showered them with grace instead.

The most common thing I hear from people, women especially, when they meet me after reading my book or hearing our story is, "I could never do what you did." That phrase always makes me smile because I would have said the same thing to me!

Now, I'm not congratulating myself for a job well done. Not at all. If you only knew our behind-the-scenes healing journey you would know better. I'm just saying, my story is my story, and I've lived with it being my story for over 14 years. I'm used to it. So when I meet people when I'm traveling and they ask the typical "business or pleasure?" question, I say, "I'm an author and speaker." Of course, they ask what my books are about, and when I tell them the name of my first book, *Healing Your Marriage When Trust Is Broken*, and then follow it up with, "My marriage was on the brink of divorce due to my husband's unfaithfulness and pornography addiction," they either keep talking to me because they are curious or they stop talking, look the other way, and spend the rest of the flight feeling oddly uncomfortable. People are surprised that there is not some element of resentfulness in me. I've been known to tell a woman my story over lunch and then say, "Did you want key lime pie or a brownie for dessert?"

Being married brings its own set of challenges. Even without infidelity or some other type of betrayal, it's hard work to have a healthy, strong marriage. Sometimes our wounds are so deep and so comfortable at the same time that we just stay in a place of self-pity, which turns into a victim mentality. We say things like, "Well, if she hadn't done that, then I wouldn't have done this," or "If he would be a better husband, I would be a better wife." We cannot hold off on making healthy choices because of someone else's poor treatment of us.

Next to Christ, Joseph is the best example of pushing through a difficult set of circumstances until he sees the purpose in it. He was able to see past his own pain to a bigger picture. And even when we can't see how in the world God can use something terrible in our lives, He still can. And not only can He use them, He will use them. Just step up, shake the dust off your feet, and allow Him to do it.

I Know a God

You may be thinking my advice is nice and inspirational, but you don't know exactly what to do, and you need practical hands and feet added to this whole "not living like a victim" perspective. I hear you. And I'm thrilled you are wondering about how to make this real in your life.

Amy's good-humored reference to the tough guys she knows who can intervene on any troubled friend's behalf invites this discussion: Who is our protector? Who looks out for the weak, the hurt, the needy? Who carries the burden of justice so victims can become victors? Well, I know a God.

God is the basis for our transformation from victim to victor. Yes, you've been hurt, and yes, you didn't deserve it, but He is bigger than your pain. Not only that, there can be purpose in it. I have found a couple of things that have helped me ensure that the victim mindset is gone and the mindset of a victor stays. We'll take some time to discover how to choose forgiveness and how to believe that God can use anything for good.

Choose Forgiveness

First of all, the most important step toward living like a victor rather than a victim is choosing forgiveness. Everyone wants forgiveness. We want it from our best friend when she finds out we said something rude about her behind her back. We want it from our children when we apologize to them for the umpteenth time for blowing our temper. We want it from our employers when we don't meet a deadline or we consistently show up late for work. We want it from our spouses when we have said words in anger and bruised their heart. But we are far less generous handing over forgiveness when a wrong has been done to us. We can't believe people would hurt us the way they did. Surely they meant to and were planning and scheming all along to make us miserable. Or were they?

Think about a time when you know you hurt your spouse in the past. Did you mean to hurt her? Did you sit down and plan out your mistake so she would be hurt? My guess is you did not. We don't always mean to hurt our spouses when we hurt them. Sometimes we do, but mostly it's because we made a poor choice and didn't operate wisely. Maybe we assumed we would never do such a thing and ended up doing it because our flesh is stronger than we gave it credit for. Now turn that around. Display empathy right now and try to put yourself in your spouse's shoes. Do you think she planned this out? Do you think she woke up that morning and planned to break your heart? Again, I'm guessing that wasn't the case.

Now, I recognize that there are times when people may have planned it all out. I know there are some people who are just flat-out mean and selfish. Even still, forgiveness is the vital element in choosing not to live like a victim despite all you've endured. You may say, "Cindy, I don't think he deserves my forgiveness for what he did to me." Do you really want to say that? After all, the apostle Paul exhorts us to "be kind and compassionate to one another, forgiving each other, just as in Christ God forgave you" (Ephesians 4:32).

I've run into people who think their sin is less sinful than someone else's. People have literally told me they have a hard time forgiving because *they* don't do bad things. Oh mercy. Yes, honey, you do. Just because you don't think gossip isn't that bad doesn't mean it isn't. Its consequences may not be as extreme as, say, murder or infidelity, but it's still sin.

LIE vs. TRUTH

Lie: It seems that everyone is out to get me.

Truth: God is for me so who can be against me? (see Romans 8:31)

I believe what will help us understand forgiveness is to first understand how much we need Jesus to forgive us. God is 100 percent perfect. But since you and I are imperfect we must be less than 100 percent. Let's say you are, on your very best day, at 73 percent. (That's not bad, my friend. Good job.) And because I'm nice, I'll take a lower number like 48 percent. Now, you are higher than me. I will give you that. But you still need 27 percent to get to God. I, on the other hand, need 52 percent. Both of us are less perfect than God. The only One who can make up that percentage is Christ, and He did that on the cross for us. Don't you see, my friend? He made up the difference for both of us! Even if you were at 99 percent, you still need Christ's sacrifice and the forgiveness of God like everyone else.

I truly believe forgiveness brings freedom. Show me a miserable person, and I will show you someone who is bitter and has chosen not to forgive. And it is a choice. It is a difficult one, but it can be done. Jesus said, "Love your enemies and pray for those who persecute you" (Matthew 5:44). Do you want to help yourself be a forgiving person? Pray for people you don't like. Pray for people who make you mad. Pray for people who annoy you. Because there is a chance you are that annoying person to someone else. Just sayin'.

Choosing to forgive people for hurting you is a choice you will spend the rest of your life making. This fallen and broken world we live in is filled with fallen and broken people who hurt others. And those fallen and broken people are you and me.

As you take this journey toward living a victorious life, not victimhood, remember that Christ loves you and He came for you. He urges you, "Come to me, all you who are weary and burdened, and I will give you rest. Take my yoke upon you and learn from me, for I am gentle and humble in heart, and you will find rest for your souls. For my yoke is easy and my burden is light" (Matthew 11:28-30).

God Can Use Anything for Good

A second element to consider that will help you become a victor is to understand that what may have been meant for evil in your life can be used by God for good. I will dive into this more in chapter 11 when I talk about God using anything and everything. Because He will! I've seen Him use the most awful circumstances for a bigger, broader purpose that you and I can't see. Joseph didn't see what purpose there was in what happened to him. He was sold into slavery by his brothers, taken away from his family, and wrongly imprisoned. Joseph had to wait many, many years to see what God was doing. That's all terrible stuff! But God knew exactly what He was doing. There was a famine coming and Joseph's wisdom would literally save millions of people.

There is purpose in your pain. There is a bigger picture. And once you have healed from the immense pain, ask God to show you what it is. Whether someone put you through the pain or you brought it on yourself, your pain can be redeemed.

I've already discussed that God's ways are higher than ours, and even on our best day the plan we come up with will pale in comparison to His. I think it's wise to compare our limited vision to God's perfect line of sight:

- We see adversity on every side, but God sees an advantage.

- We see a barrier upon our path, but God sees a break-through in our future.

- We see a detour sign, but God is showing us His direction.

- We see a predicament, but God is saying, "No, child, that's progress."

- We see an obstacle, but God sees an opportunity.

- We see a roadblock, but God is showing us His roadmap.

- We see a setback, but God is telling us this is His setup for something great.

I know life stinks sometimes. I know it so well. I feel for you wherever you are in your marriage. You may be in a marriage with someone who is just not willing to do their part. Or maybe you are divorced and didn't want to be and you are suffering immensely while your spouse seems to be doing fine. Friend, just because something has knocked you down, kicked you around, and made you prefer death does not mean you succumb to it. You get right back up and take a stand. You let Satan know that what he intended for evil, God will use for good. He wants to and He will, but you have to let Him. You can't wallow in a sea of self-pity and expect God to do the great things He wants to do in your life. It just doesn't work that way.

> Put away the victim mentality and choose instead to use an awful circumstance as a step stool to see a bright future.

I can't promise a certain outcome for you or that there will be little pain and discomfort. What I can promise you is, in the midst of your pain and struggles, if you will allow God to heal you from the inside out, He will take this mess you've found yourself in and turn it into a ministry for you.

Someone is being abused right now and she will need your

presence in her life one day because you've been there. Someone is about to get the news that his child has died, and he will need you to walk the road with him because you've been there. Someone's spouse is choosing to leave her this week, and she will need support from you because you've been there.

I firmly believe God will use your victories and victorious attitude to glorify His name and to share His power with others.

TO HELP YOU **BUILD WISELY**

1. Write down a time in your life when you have been mistreated. Think about the incident and how it made you feel.

2. According to Dr. Phil McGraw, we teach people how to treat us. How do people typically treat you? What would you say you've done or allowed to happen that has made people treat you this way?

3. Do you typically take responsibility for your actions, or do you shift the blame to someone or something else? If you are a blame shifter, why do you do that?

4. Think about what situation you wrote down in the first question. How could you see God using this in someone else's life?

5. Do you consider yourself to be a forgiving person? Why or why not? Write down two or three things you will commit to doing in order to become someone who forgives others (memorize Scripture to combat the lie, pray for people you don't like, etc.).

LIVE FULLY

A New You

I dreamed of being a tap dancer when I was a child. And even at age 45, I can still locate that dream in the depths of my heart when I watch musicals with tap dancing in them. I do not exaggerate when I tell you I've seen the musical *Singin' in the Rain* at least 25 times. And it makes me want to put on my tap shoes every time.

I started taking tap lessons at the age of five when I was in kindergarten. We lived in Frisco, Texas, where my mother taught elementary school and my father was the high school principal. To say we were known in the town would be accurate. It was small back in the 1970s. It most certainly didn't have the stores and hotels it does today. I mean, there is an IKEA there, people. IKEA!

Now, I was no Bill "Bojangles" Robinson or Vera Ellen, but I had some talent. And after a year of weekly lessons, I was ready for my first recital. Picture it with me, if you will: Our entire class was standing on the gymnasium stage. The curtain was pulled so the audience couldn't see our adorable fuchsia leotards, white tutus and tights, and black tap shoes adorned with cute bows. Our teacher was backstage with us and made sure we were all in place like the Rockettes. Because I come from a family of tall genes, I was front and center on the line of tap dancers. And rightly so. I was born for this, this tap dancing career. My legs were long and my family members were athletes. I got this. Give me my space, people.

The time had come. The curtain opened, revealing all of my fans; I mean, the friends and family members who came to see our show. My heart started beating faster with each passing second, but that was typical for performers. Several of my friends began waving at their parents and giggling with the girls next to them in line. Not me. I was focused. I was ready for this. Born for this. The music started, but instead of showing my newfound talent that would have made tap legend Eleanor Powell proud, I froze. Completely froze. And not only did I freeze, but I placed my hands over my face, expecting that to make the audience disappear. And they did disappear from my sight. I just didn't disappear from theirs.

(Did I mention I was front and center? Right, good. You know that piece of information. Wonderful.)

I don't think I need to tell you, I pulled out of tap dancing lessons after that year. I mean, my schedule was tight since I would be going into first grade and all. It just seemed like the right thing to do.

Please. For the love, Cindy.

I'm sure if you think back in your own life you can remember your own version of a tap dancing recital fiasco. There are many reasons why we have versions of ourselves that haunt us. Maybe people still call you an annoying nickname that was bestowed on you after that one thing you did way back when. Or perhaps you made a professional or personal mistake that nobody will let you forget or live down. Maybe your misstep was so big that it rocked your marriage. It's possible that you broke your marriage vows, like my husband did, and now, that is the title that plagues you. Once a cheater, always a cheater. But in your heart, you don't want to live by that title. You want to be the most amazing, faithful wife or husband there is. Yet what you did still follows you. And you don't know how to get rid of it.

Today, I am no longer that shy girl who covered her face. Would you believe I get on stages regularly now and speak to people? I used to lead worship and sing on stage with my husband in front of packed-out auditoriums. That is all Christ.

> It is amazing what the power of God can do in a life when we allow Him to transform us from the inside out. And that begins with our identity in Christ. We have to know who we are.

Whatever negative reputation you've built or been given does not have to stay with you. What you did or who people thought you were in the past is not who you are. It was what you did. Big difference, my friend. It's not easy to shed our past identities, especially when they are based on mistakes. But when God gets a hold of us, He helps us shed and change those identities by His power. No matter what happened in your past, know that we serve a God who is all about forgiveness, second chances, new lives, or even new names.

The Gift of a New Name

God's desire to change lives with second chances is beautifully illustrated in His relationships with different people throughout Scripture. In the New Testament, the apostle Peter is mentioned more than any of the other disciples in God's Word. He did some amazing things in Jesus's name, but he also did the unthinkable: He denied knowing Jesus. And he did that on the night Jesus was arrested. Jesus told Peter that before the rooster crowed three times he would disown Him. And he did (Luke 22:54-62). Peter had been named Simon until Jesus gave him a new name, Cephas, which is translated Peter (John 1:42). In Aramaic, the name Peter means "stone." This name change possibly shows the major role Peter would play in establishing the church. After his denial of Jesus, Peter spent the rest of his life preaching the gospel.

Also in the New Testament we read how Saul, meaning "asked

for" or "prayed for," eventually went by Paul, meaning "small" or "little." Many people assume that God changed Saul's name. Scripture doesn't support that: "Then Saul, who was also called Paul, was filled with the Holy Spirit" (Acts 13:9). From that point forward in the Bible, he is called Paul, except when referred to in the past and how he persecuted the church. We don't know for sure why he decided to go by Paul. It could be that he knew his name, Saul, was associated with hatred and violence, and he no longer wanted people to know him that way.

LIE vs. TRUTH

Lie: I feel so much shame for what I've done.

Truth: Therefore, there is now no condemnation for me because I am in Christ Jesus. (see Romans 8:1)

Because of God's promise to Abraham to become a father of many nations, God changed Abram's and Sarai's names (Genesis 17). Abram, meaning "high father," became Abraham, meaning "father of multitude." Abraham's wife, Sarai, became Sarah. Sarai means "my princess," and Sarah means "mother of nations." God changed Jacob's name, meaning "supplanter," to Israel, meaning "having power with God." Scripture says, "Your name will no longer be Jacob, but Israel, because you have struggled with God and with humans and have overcome" (Genesis 32:28).

Many scholars have asked why God changed the names of a handful of people in the Bible, but we will never really know. But each time a change is noted, it seems that God chose a name to match the calling that was ahead of the person. He was arming them with the identity they would need to live out their second chance.

Claiming a New Identity

Chris's confession changed our entire lives. Not only was our marriage in shambles, but our own identities dissolved because we had allowed them to get wrapped up in what we did instead of who we were. Although I did not betray Chris or forsake my marital vows, I still had my own concerns to address.

Chris spent the first 18 months of our healing journey working at a local home-improvement warehouse. No longer did he have people telling him what a great worship leader he was or what a great pastor he was. He simply helped people find lumber and load it into their vehicles. In the past, he allowed his occupation to give him a good reputation, but now he had to learn to rest in who he was in Christ. Nothing more.

Even though he had faith, every single morning he awoke to reminders of what he had done. God chose not to remember Chris's sin, but Chris still did. He fought that battle for some time on his morning commute. He spent part of his drive listening to praise and worship music and part of it in prayer. And right before he walked into work, while it was still dark outside, he sat in our 1995 Geo Prism and spoke these truths to himself:

I am God's child (John 1:12).

I am a friend of Jesus Christ (John 15:15).

I have been bought with a price and I belong to God (1 Corinthians 6:19-20).

I have been chosen by God and adopted as His child (Ephesians 1:3-8).

I have been redeemed and forgiven of all my sins (Colossians 1:13-14).

I am free from condemnation (Romans 8:1-2).

I am hidden with Christ in God (Colossians 3:1-4).

I am a citizen of heaven (Philippians 3:20).

I am God's temple (1 Corinthians 3:16).

I am God's workmanship (Ephesians 2:10).[4]

Every single morning the truth from those scriptures and many more flooded my husband's mind and eventually sank into his heart.

He didn't believe what he spoke at first, but within a matter of weeks he began to live it. He didn't try to change his actions and then hope he became a better person. He went to the heart of it and allowed God to show him who he really was first. When Chris began to believe it, his actions changed to glorify God more. He walked with Holy Spirit confidence in a humble manner because his mind knew the truth and believed it. He didn't have confidence in himself but in the One who created him, loved him, died for him, and forgave him.

When I look into the eyes of the man I married in 1993, I do not see the same man. He is a new man. His name may not have changed, but everything else did.

You Are Not What You Do

The human mind and heart struggle with the expansive inclusiveness of God's forgiveness. We tend to make mental lists of reasons why God (or anyone) could surely *not* forgive. We can't quite fathom how God could look upon us sinners with love. But in the story of David we get to witness just how God does love that way and how God sees us beyond what we do.

You are probably already quite familiar with David's encounter with Bathsheba presented in 2 Samuel 11. She was the wife of Uriah, who was off at war fighting for Israel, while his king, David, was at home. David saw Bathsheba bathing on a rooftop and ended up calling for her. When she was brought to him, he slept with her. Sometime later, she told him she was pregnant.

David needed to cover his tracks somehow so he formed an elaborate scheme. At first he brought Uriah home from the war, hoping he would spend the night with his wife and then later believe he had conceived the child with her. But Uriah did not sleep with his wife. He would not. There was no way he was going to enjoy himself while his friends were still fighting a battle. With that plan foiled, David moved on to a more drastic solution: he decided to get rid of Uriah. He actually sent a note to the commander, Joab, to place

Uriah on the front lines and then have the men withdraw so that Uriah would be struck down and die.

That was the guy who, years before, God had called "a man after his own heart" (1 Samuel 13:14). David, an adulterer and murderer, was a man after God's own heart. How can that be? You see, God said this about David before David did those heinous actions.

A few chapters later we read that King David's son Solomon became king after him. Called the wisest person who ever lived, Solomon followed God wholeheartedly but eventually fell away because his wives led him astray. All 700 of them! (I know.)

Scripture says that Solomon did evil in God's eyes and did not follow the Lord completely like his father, David, did (1 Kings 11:4, 6,34,38). Here God is praising the faithfulness of David. Here is this man who made some really poor choices with harsh consequences, and God still says David followed Him completely. I believe this is such a beautiful example of how God sees us as His children and not as our actions. David made some poor choices, yes, but he still had a heart that loved God and followed after Him desperately, and God saw David's heart.

How is it that David did what he did and could still be labeled obedient and faithful? I think it works like this: David repented. Truly and honestly repented. With the help of the prophet Nathan, David recognized his sin and turned from it. The forgiveness David received from God literally removed his sin as far as the east is from the west, and God, in His infinite wisdom and majesty, chose to remember it no more. And when "we confess our sins, he is faithful and just and will forgive us our sins and purify us from all unrighteousness" (1 John 1:9).

All of it.

Christians can embrace and believe this story about David because it's in the Bible and we know the Bible is the inspired Word of God. But when this story plays out in contemporary lives, like Chris's and mine and many others, people are hesitant to believe a change has really occurred. Let's be honest, we have all looked at a certain gloomy situation and thought, *They'll never change.* We not only think that about others, we often think it about ourselves.

For a long time, my husband walked in shame for what he did to the name of Christ. To me. To our children. To our family and friends. You don't live a double life like he did and not have some residue hanging around on the new life you're trying to find. As difficult as it was, Chris chose to believe what God spoke over him instead of what others, including himself, said about him. This was a brutal process for him that took months upon months. But he learned that the more he spoke those truths over himself, the more he believed it.

One thing I had to push through and come out on top of was walking differently despite what other people thought about me. Now I didn't cheat on my husband, but I was the woman who took back her cheating husband. That says something pretty strong, most would say. Most people would say that move was weak and that I didn't have enough strength to walk away from a doomed marriage. And while I see that some people may not have the strength to walk away from a marriage they should walk away from, I knew I was to stay. And let me tell you, it took every ounce of strength I had to stay and choose to forgive a man who cut me to the core with his actions. While many still feel sorry for me because I stayed and didn't start over, I know that my choice to stay was God's best. One I do not regret.

So whether you have been unfaithful or not, whether you have betrayed your spouse in another way or not, and no matter how bad our actions are, nothing can separate us from God's love for us (Romans 8:35-39). And nothing we do changes who we are in Christ.

Remembering Who You Are

The apostle Paul said to "set your mind on things above, not on earthly things" (Colossians 3:2). I believe this is the key to finding our identity in Christ. And by *find*, I really mean realize, own, and adopt, because the identity has always been there.

LIE vs. TRUTH

Lie: God won't forgive me for what I've done.

Truth: If I confess my sin, God is faithful and just and will forgive my sin and cleanse me from all unrighteousness. (see 1 John 1:9)

I recognize that most of us have done some things we are not proud of and are maybe even embarrassed or humiliated because of them. But always remember, what we do is not who we are. We are children of God, free from condemnation and citizens of heaven. Why? Because of Christ's sacrifice for us. God sees us through His perfect Son. He chooses not to see all our past sin. But we are humans, and we know what we've done. Because of that, we focus on that and forget who we are.

One of the most profound ways I have seen this play out is when people go from shame to gratitude. People often don't know how to make this adjustment. We are so used to being ashamed of ourselves for what we've done or what's been done to us, and we can't imagine not living with that frame of mind. Not only do we struggle with this, but people around us will tell us how ashamed we should be. But what would it look like if, instead of wallowing in that miserable place of shame, we decided to live with a grateful heart? What if, instead of feeling bad for what we've done and asking God to forgive us *again*, we said, "Thank you, God, for forgiving me and showing me who I am"? God has forgiven us and shown us mercy like we never could have imagined! Friend, we just have to receive it, believe it, and step into it!

You may be wondering how this is possible. Maybe you think

I'm crazy for even suggesting it. Well, if I told you that a man who was addicted to pornography and committed multiple acts of infidelity on his wife is now being used by God to impact one of the most influential churches in America, would you believe it? That is my husband. This way of living is possible.

I want to give you a couple of weapons in your arsenal when the attacks come. Because honestly, most of the shame we feel heaped upon us isn't usually from people. Sometimes it is, but most of the time it's from our spiritual enemy. Remember, he wants no good thing for you, so you have to submit to the Lord, resist the devil, and he will flee (James 4:7).

1. Encourage yourself with the truth. During a time when King David was greatly distressed, "David found strength in the LORD his God" (1 Samuel 30:6). When the enemy's lies or people's judgmental looks weigh down on you, remind yourself of who you are in Christ. The list my husband used is a great tool to help you get through the dark days ahead. I love to pull up favorite verses on the YouVersion Bible app, take screenshots, and then quickly refer back to those favorites when I am struggling. You have to remind yourself of who you are in Christ.

2. Be aware of what you let into your mind. Distractions pop up everywhere. Technology sits at our fingertips. We have access to anything we could ever want. We can watch anything or listen to anything. That makes us extremely vulnerable. Consider limiting what you let fill your mind.

When Chris and I were in the early stage of our healing journey, we did that. Our antenna could get only a few TV channels. We didn't watch a lot of movies because of their content. We listened mostly to worship music. We spent time together as a family and then just the two of us. We limited how much time we spent with people unless it was our mentors. This was vital for us in those early days. I believe it helped both of us truly understand our identity in

Christ because that's where our minds were set. They were not set on earthly things.

Give yourself some time. Do not feel defeated if you don't get this down immediately. Take it day by day. And celebrate small victories. Just realize that you have to choose not to live in a broken, beaten-down place of self-hatred because of your past. Instead, you must rest in who you are in Christ despite what you once did. You may have done things that have caused great relational chasms, but don't let that be an excuse to continue to walk along the same path.

> Start fresh. You are not what you have done.

A New Marriage

God wants to give you a new marriage. But that new marriage can't happen without a new husband and a new wife. Both of you have to participate. "But, Cindy, I didn't do anything wrong. It was my husband's fault." I'm going to disagree with you here and say it takes two to make a marriage work and two to make a marriage fail. You have to be willing to let God work on you from the inside out. That means both of you, even if you think you didn't do anything wrong.

You have to believe your marriage can receive a new identity. You may have been known for being short-tempered or impatient. Maybe it's time to exhibit forbearance toward those around you. You may have been known for not putting in much effort to make any changes. Perhaps you have to get up and start making an effort. Let me tell you, when you change and believe who you are in Christ, your marriage will change. It will be better than you thought possible. It will be beyond your wildest dreams.

Getting a new marriage starts with getting a new you.

TO HELP YOU **LIVE FULLY**

1. Similar to Cindy's tap dancing experience, what experiences from your past have left a label on you?

2. How have you allowed those experiences to stagnate you in your life?

3. Do you ever find yourself thinking you'll always be this way? If so, what steps do you need to take today to begin to change that?

4. Find two or three scriptures you can speak aloud for encouragement. Write them down and post them where you can see them regularly. Speak them to yourself daily. Or take pictures of different verses with your phone and then thumb through them regularly to encourage yourself with the truth.

5. Are there practices in your life or relationships that need to be removed as you learn to set your mind on things above? Make a list of some action steps you will take today to begin this process.

6. Here is the complete list of "Who I Am in Christ" statements from *The Bondage Breaker*® by Neil T. Anderson[5]. Read these daily to reinforce and embrace your identity in Christ.

I am accepted...

I am God's child. (John 1:12)

As a disciple, I am a friend of Jesus Christ. (John 15:15)

I have been justified. (Romans 5:1)

I am united with the Lord, and I am one with Him in spirit.
(1 Corinthians 6:17)

I have been bought with a price and I belong to God.
(1 Corinthians 6:19-20)

I am a member of Christ's body. (1 Corinthians 12:27)

I have been chosen by God and adopted as His child.
(Ephesians 1:3-8)

I have been redeemed and forgiven of all my sins.
(Colossians 1:13-14)

I am complete in Christ. (Colossians 2:9-10)

I have direct access to the throne of grace through Jesus Christ.
(Hebrews 4:14-16)

I am secure...

I am free from condemnation. (Romans 8:1-2)

I am assured that God works for my good in all circumstances.
(Romans 8:28)

I am free from any condemnation brought against me and I
cannot be separated from the love of God. (Romans 8:31-39)

I have been established, anointed, and sealed by God.
(2 Corinthians 1:21-22)

I am hidden with Christ in God. (Colossians 3:1-4)

I am confident that God will complete the good work He
started in me. (Philippians 1:6)

I am a citizen of heaven. (Philippians 3:20)

I have not been given a spirit of fear but of power, love, and a
sound mind. (2 Timothy 1:7)

I am born of God and the evil one cannot touch me.
(1 John 5:18)

I am significant...

I am a branch of Jesus Christ, the true vine, and a channel of
His life. (John 15:5)

I have been chosen and appointed to bear fruit. (John 15:16)

I am God's temple. (1 Corinthians 3:16)

I am a minister of reconciliation for God.
(2 Corinthians 5:17-21)

I am seated with Jesus Christ in the heavenly realm.
(Ephesians 2:6)

I am God's workmanship. (Ephesians 2:10)

I may approach God with freedom and confidence.
(Ephesians 3:12)

I can do all things through Christ, who strengthens me.
(Philippians 4:13)

8

Do the Hard Things

I needed to hear from God stat. My world had caved in all around me, and I felt like I was in a deep abyss searching for any amount of guidance I could find. The consequences of my husband's actions were being hurled at me with a force that knocked my breath and hope away. I had a decision to make. And I worried that if I took too long to make it I would waste more of my life than I felt had already been wasted by the so-called man of my dreams.

The decision? Whether or not to get a divorce. The thought of being divorced was more than I could fathom. But staying with a man who had repeatedly broken my heart and my trust was also unimaginable.

Yet I kept moving forward toward reconciliation even though there was very little in me that believed it to be possible. Yes, people around me were telling me to have faith, and while I knew they were right, my heart didn't seem to get the memo. My faith walk hit a fork in the road: either I believed what I said I believed my entire life or I didn't. Because I was unsure, I decided to go toward the path of believing God, because the alternative seemed too hopeless to bear. I read and reread the verses in the Bible that say God does the impossible. And I personally had seen a few impossible scenarios in my life unfold toward the possible. I held on to these assurances as uncertainty threatened to drag me deeper into the abyss.

Even though I had allowed divorce to enter my list of options, I still pursued God and pleaded with Him daily to show me His path. I knew that though God hates divorce, He allows it in my situation, according to Matthew 19. Still, just because I had the right to divorce didn't mean I had to. And that's where I was stranded. That was the huge, life-changing choice I had to make, and I desperately needed to hear from God to make it.

Seeking a Word from God

I lived in an ongoing state of confusion for those few weeks and was thankful to receive amazing, godly advice from others. I had wise people surrounding me and praying for me. I had the support of my pastor, his wife, our mentors, our family, and our ministry team. They didn't kick us to the curb; they embraced us, wept with us, and prayed for us.

But I needed a word from God.

Not an audible, bust-through-the-heavens kind of voice, but a still, small voice that gently and persistently told my heart that He was near and He had a plan for my mess of a life. Have you ever been there? On your knees and pleading for the powerful whisper that would let you know without a doubt that God was speaking?

I wanted a word from His Word to stand on. I had been on this journey with God long enough to know that everything around me would fade, wither, and go away (Isaiah 40:8), but God's Word would hold strong and never diminish. So for three weeks my prayer was, *God, I need a word.*

I became so desperate to hear from God that I took off for my home state of Texas to get a new perspective. My oldest son, Noah, and I spent some time with my mom before I headed down to San Antonio to see another friend. I planned to stay Friday night through Sunday morning because I wanted to attend my friend's church before returning to my mom's house. But when I got to my friend's place I learned that her pastor was out of town and would not be leading the service. To say I was discouraged would be putting it mildly. I loved her pastor and found myself thinking that he would be the one to give me what I needed to hear. I almost chose not to attend because of this news. But then I decided to go. And I am so glad that I did.

On that day, Sunday, March 10, 2002, He delivered that word. Not once, but twice on the same day by two different people who did not know each other or know me. The word, you ask? Habakkuk 2:3: "The revelation awaits an appointed time; it speaks of the end and will not prove false. Though it linger, wait for it; it will certainly come and will not delay."

Now you might be wondering why in the world God spoke to me through a minor prophet named Habakkuk. Most people don't know this book in the Bible, and when they get to it they certainly can't pronounce it. Why not Jeremiah or Isaiah? Or why didn't He show me something through the apostle Paul? Not only that, but how did He speak through that verse? Well, I will explain it to you, but it may not make much sense.

You see, this was God's specific word to me at this time in my life for my situation. I believe that with all my heart. And upon hearing Him speak through His Word, I felt as if God was standing right behind me with one hand on my shoulder and the other pointing out into a future that was muddied to me but profoundly clear to Him. It was as if He was saying, *I know you don't see the road ahead or how I can make this better. But I can, and I will.* The final part of that divine interaction with the Creator of the Universe rested in His concluding question: *Do you trust Me?*

And there it was. The question that haunted me and thrilled me at the same time. The faithful part in me wanted to shout a huge, loud YES! But the fearful part of me knew if I said yes then that truly meant trusting God and staying in a broken marriage, since trusting my husband was not an option. I spent the next several hours that Sunday afternoon wrestling with God over that.

> I trusted God with my salvation, but did I really trust Him with my life here on earth?

This would literally mean walking in blind trust for the rest of my life, because even though my husband confessed his sin, repented of his sin, and wanted freedom from the bondage that tied him up for two decades, he could fall. I knew in my heart that he didn't want to cheat on me again, but that didn't mean he wasn't capable of doing it. He most certainly was. We all are, actually.

My friend and one of the women who shared the word with me had just finished praying over me before I headed back to my mom's house. When they were finished, I sat there silently before the Lord and simply said, *Lord, I trust You.*

And immediately the peace of God that passes all understanding (Philippians 4:7) did just that. I do not understand what happened in the spiritual realm when I said that. I cannot describe to you what covered me in that moment. I cannot fathom the transformation that was occurring the second I tapped out of my wrestling match with God. All I know is, I was hopeless and scared one minute and completely at peace and trusting the next. It was as if God then said, *Thank you, Cindy. I've got this.*

No Looking Back

This chapter is about releasing your investment in the flesh so you can be empowered in the battle by God and guided toward His ways. Doing the hard things takes determination and faith. We must have a foundation of faith in God and His power if we ever expect to do the hard things in life. God's Word says, "Without faith it is impossible to please God, because anyone who comes to him must believe that he exists and that he rewards those who earnestly seek him" (Hebrews 11:6).

It took faith for me to trust God when so many options and even some people were shouting, "Run, Cindy, run! Don't look back. Do not pass go! Do not collect your $200! This is your 'get out of jail free' card. Take it!" The challenge I faced to ultimately relinquish any power I thought I had was seemingly impossible. And it was most definitely exhausting. Yet all along I sensed that if I ran away from trusting God after receiving His assurances in His Word, I would always be looking back. But when we are called to run *toward* God, there's no looking back.

LIE vs. TRUTH

Lie: It doesn't really matter what I think about as long as I don't do it.

Truth: Finally, [insert your name], whatever is true, whatever is noble, whatever is right, whatever is pure, whatever is lovely, whatever is admirable—if anything is excellent or praiseworthy—think about such things. (see Philippians 4:8)

I mustered up every bit of faith I could that Sunday afternoon to voice those four, powerful words to God: Lord, I trust You. It took such effort to release my life to Him that you would've thought I was preparing for a competition. And I suppose I was. While the competition was not going to be of a physical nature, it would most certainly exhaust me in the coming months and years. Just because God had given me a word to stand on and I surrendered to Him did not mean that God would remove every difficult circumstance that would cross our paths. No, there were brutal days ahead that would make me desire death over living. When the days came when

I wondered if Chris had cheated again, the fleshly part of me was trying to find anything physical to grasp onto. Yet I knew that a human or anything tangible would not satisfy my fretful heart. So I had no other option but to lean on God and allow Him to carry me. One of the most difficult things to do is to stop *doing* and start *relying* on the promises of God.

My story is not your story, and your story is not someone else's story. However, we are all called to have faith, for without it, pleasing God is like trying to grasp the wind. If you are in a marriage where your spouse was unfaithful and he has chosen not to work on the marriage, God may release you. Or He may call you to stay and fight even if you're the only one fighting. I have seen it happen both ways. So this is not about me telling you to do what I did and stay in your marriage at all costs. Only you can make that decision, because you have to live with your decision and the ramifications of that decision.

I do believe, however, that it is vital that you seek God and ask Him for His guidance. Whether you stay or go, it will be difficult. Marriage is the most refining tool God uses to sharpen us and remove the parts of us that need extracting. And then we have children. Mercy.

Is your faith in God dwindling when it comes to your marriage? Do you look at the situation before you and wonder how anything good can come from it? I get that. I was there. The problem with keeping faith in God these days is that we have so many other things in our society to place our faith in. I believe this is why we please God when we have faith in the unseen when so many seen things around us are vying for our attention and devotion.

> We are not responsible for the results of our faith. We are just responsible for *having* faith!

Jesus spoke about having "faith as small as a mustard seed" (Matthew 17:20). Did you know that the mustard seed is the smallest seed but produces the largest garden plant? What a strange concept that something so small can produce something so big. It doesn't take a lot of faith to please God. When we offer our mustard seed of faith, God brings about the biggest result from that small contribution.

Sin, Rescue, Worship, Repeat

The pattern in the book of Judges is simple and a bit predictable. God's people, the Israelites, started doubting God and turned to false idols, which is a clear rebellion of the first commandment. That was always followed by some ruthless ruler's gruesome oppression that would last years, even decades. Then they would cry out to God and He would send a deliverer or judge and their repentance would turn them back to God. Within a matter of time, the people would fall back into sin by worshipping false idols and repeating this sin-rescue-worship-sin cycle over and over and over again. Same story, different day.

Even though all sorts of junk occurred in this book of Judges—lots of commandment breaking, rebelling against a perfect God, and bloviating about how they should have stayed in Egypt and lived as slaves—some really amazing people stood out and followed God.

Gideon is one such example of a man who, despite doubting his ability, eventually trusted God to do what He said He would do: deliver the Midianites into their hands. And we can clearly see that this domination was truly of God because Gideon was only allowed 300 men after weaning the amount down from 22,000, a remarkable story that shows God's majestic muscles in spite of such formidable obstacles.

But I think the story of Deborah in Judges 4 is one of the most important ones to illustrate what I want to say to you right now. This story shows leadership, cowardice, doubt, courage, mercy, belief, deliverance, and dare I say it, gumption. All sorts of different emotions come to the surface in this chapter.

The story begins with "Again the Israelites did evil in the eyes of the LORD" (Judges 4:1). Surprise, surprise. They were then sold into the hands of Jabin and were cruelly oppressed by him for 20 years. (What? You're not serious.) Enter Deborah, the judge of Israel. (Right on schedule.) She heard from the Lord and told this to Barak, one of the Hebrew men:

> She sent for Barak son of Abinoam from Kedesh in Naphtali and said to him, "The LORD, the God of Israel, commands you: 'Go, take with you ten thousand men of Naphtali and Zebulun and lead them up to Mount Tabor. I will lead Sisera, the commander of Jabin's army, with his chariots and his troops to the Kishon River and give him into your hands.'" (Judges 4:6-7)

Apparently hearing this command from God via Deborah wasn't enough. Sadly, it isn't always easy to believe that God has spoken to us and told us what to do. And Barak was scared. So scared, in fact, that he begged Deborah to go with him. Okay, so maybe he didn't beg, but I do sense a hint of grovel in his actions: "Barak said to her, 'If you go with me, I will go; but if you don't go with me, I won't go'" (verse 8).

Wow. Yeah, he was scared. I don't blame him, honestly. The king, Jabin, tyrant if you will, had oppressed them for one-fifth of a century, and now Barak, a young, insecure Hebrew man without the combat training he assumed Sisera had, was expected to defeat him. Pretty tall order, if you ask me.

Although Deborah agreed to Barak's request, I can sense annoyance in her voice and possibly an eye roll in her reply back to Barak:

> "Certainly I will go with you," said Deborah. "But because of the course you are taking, the honor will not be yours, for the LORD will deliver Sisera into the hands of a woman." So Deborah went with Barak to Kedesh. There Barak summoned Zebulun and Naphtali, and ten

thousand men went up under his command. Deborah
also went up with him. (verses 9-10)

Now this isn't my way of standing up for or against the feminist
movement. While I am in complete belief that women are equal to
men and should be treated as such, I do not like the man bashing
that oftentimes comes with the territory. I cringe when I see commercials or movies that allow a woman to be a complete jerk to a
man and belittle him.

But y'all...a woman!

A woman would get the credit and honor of delivering God's
people from the control of Jabin. I like that. It is pretty cool that
a woman was leading Israel and then in turn became the strength
behind the commander God chose to lead His people into a life of
freedom.

While I do like the part about her being the backbone of strength
when Barak and the army kicked some Canaanite booty, my favorite part is where Deborah says:

> "Go! This is the day the LORD has given Sisera into your
> hands. Has not the LORD gone ahead of you?" So Barak
> went down Mount Tabor, with ten thousand men fol-
> lowing him. (verse 14)

Has not the Lord gone ahead of you?

There it is. The most assuring verse in the chapter, perhaps in
the whole Word of God. No wonder you need not look back when
you trust and follow the Lord. The Lord has gone ahead of you. He
is leading the way forward from whatever pain, betrayal, or battle
you have encountered. He has already started on this journey that
He expects you to follow. He already has the necessary supplies and
equipment you'll need for this voyage. He is already there in your
tomorrow, in your future.

You just have to go and follow.

God did indeed allow Barak's army to defeat Jabin's army. There were advancements and reroutings, people pursuing and people fleeing. And the final blow to kill off Sisera after he snuck away to hide was committed by another woman, Jael, Heber's wife. (You rock, Jael.) It was definitely your action-packed, modern-day movie, had there been motion pictures back in the time of the Judges. Perhaps Barak, once he walked in courage despite the fears that initially plagued him, would have been akin to Jason Bourne and Jack Bauer rolled into one. Boy, would that have been a sight for this mom of boys who is a lover of all things action and adventure.

After Sisera's death and the deliverance of God's people "God subdued Jabin king of Canaan before the Israelites" (verse 23).

God did it. All of it.

Deborah knew it. Barak knew it. God most certainly knew it. It was God who subdued Jabin, king of Canaan. And once they were delivered by God Almighty, they sang His praises (Judges 5). They did it on that very day.

When God Goes Before Us

God delivered the Israelites from under the burden of such a dictatorial, heavy-handed, overbearing bully by using two unsuspecting individuals. He spoke to Deborah. She gave the message to Barak. Barak and his army went out to the battle that God had already engaged in by going out before them.

But they still had to do their part.

They still had to take the first step and engage in the battle. They still had to fight, and fight hard. God wasn't going to subdue Jabin's army with a snap of His sovereign fingers, even though He could easily have done so. He wasn't going to strike them all down with a plague and let Barak enjoy an easily found victory. No, He would deliver them, but they had to participate.

The fear that comes from self-doubt and insecurity is real. At times it is scary to be expected to take steps on an unfamiliar road, let alone have no earthly idea where it's leading. I guarantee you,

Barak took his first step with trepidation. Few things frighten me more than stepping out in faith, not completely sure if and when God will show up and deliver. I think our minds start this series of questions like, "What if I heard God wrong?" "What if I really should have gone this way instead of the way I'm going?" "What if what I thought I heard was just indigestion from the burrito I had for lunch?"

But when God goes before us, we have Him to trust, not just our fickle human minds or preferences. We are walking in a way made for us. How do we know God has gone before us? Because He is already in our tomorrow waiting for us. But we still have to do our part in the deliverance aspect of our lives. It takes work, hard work to go forth and do what we know we are to do every day. And we must do it every day if we want to walk in a continual state of deliverance.

You may be wondering what deliverance I'm talking about since you are not at war like Barak was. Well, the deliverance I am referring to is deliverance from ourselves. We get in the way of so much that God wants to do. We want what we want when we want it in the manner we want it. And oftentimes, we will not stop until that desire is sated.

The Prison of Pornography

Let's just jump right in and illustrate the statement above. Our flesh is hungry and usually doesn't stop until it gets fed. Many of you reading this either struggle with pornography, or you have suffered because your spouse struggles with this. Pornography has always been thought to be a man's struggle. That's not the case anymore. Women viewing pornography has increased tremendously over the last decade. Covenant Eyes is a company devoted to Internet accountability and filtering. Our family uses this for accountability purposes. According to their website, there are some pretty alarming statistics that you should be aware of:

> The porn industry generates $13 billion each year in the United States.
>
> 1 in 5 mobile searches are for pornography.
>
> 64% of Christian men and 15% of Christian women say they watch porn at least once a month.
>
> 9 out of 10 boys and 6 out of 10 girls are exposed to pornography before age 18.
>
> 71% of teens hide online behavior from their parents.
>
> 67% of young men and 49% of young women say viewing porn is an acceptable way to express one's sexuality. [6]

Copious amounts of pornography statistics can be found online. It is a dangerous beast that strips us, the viewers, of our dignity and purity and also stunts our marriage relationships. Countless excuses are given by men and women about viewing porn: "Yeah, I watch porn, but I'm not really hurting anyone. I mean, I'm not exactly cheating on my wife or anything." Friend, that's what my husband said in the beginning. Sin grows. And this sin is a beast that must be fed. What enticed you a few months ago will not satisfy you today. You will have to keep feeding this monster, and before you know it the monster will own you.

Chris and I have taken some pretty drastic steps when it comes to pornography. But even then, the very savvy can still find ways around it. We have a filter on our computers and smart phones. If a search for porn is attempted, it is immediately blocked. We check movies for sexual content. A great source is PluggedInOnline.com.

We have open communication with our sons. Yes, it can mean an uncomfortable conversation, but we do it anyway. My husband was completely steeped in and held captive by pornography for 22 years. We do not want our sons to experience the same. And if they ever share something they've seen or done, we will not panic. While this grotesque sin is a challenge to find freedom from, it is possible.

My husband is living proof. So we persevere through the challenging things now, believing it will prevent our sons a lifetime of bondage.

Just like Deborah and Barak, with whatever battle you face just step out in faith and trust and begin the fight to do the right thing. God will be there waiting for you.

Fighting For, Not Against

As you choose to take the narrow, more difficult path of right choices, you may be wondering, what does that really mean, and how does it work? It means you choose to do what is right in God's eyes even when your flesh is begging for the opposite. Making these choices to honor God and deny the flesh will be some of the hardest choices you'll ever make.

Maybe you're like my friend Elizabeth Ziegler and have been consistent with a workout routine and healthy diet for years and years. If so, then you already know how to make difficult, go-against-the-flesh choices. And it truly works when you ask God to give you strength so you can overcome yourself. You see, when we gratify the desires of our sinful nature, we are not obeying God. The sinful nature desires what is contrary to the Spirit of God. They are actually in conflict with one another (Galatians 5:16-18). To help you truly grasp this concept, I'm going to share an example with you that Chris and I have incorporated into our daily lives.

In order to have a healthy marriage, many key components must be present, including mutual respect, admiration, and submission. And on a good, easy day that may not be a difficult task. But what about the days where you are not getting along and are experiencing conflict? Because, friend, you know those days come. Instead of hoping they don't, prepare ahead of time for when they do. Every couple will experience conflict at some point in their marriage. Don't think something is wrong with you as a couple when you don't see eye to eye on an issue. Some couples may have more conflict than others. But there is still going to be some amount of tension, stress, and stress factors in addition to irritations. We are imperfect humans trying to cohabitate and raise children together. Of course there will be issues to wade through.

Chris and I have chosen to fight for each other, not against each other. When we choose to fight for each other, we choose to honor our spouse. Regardless of how either of us may be acting in the moment or for the last month. Are we perfect at this? Of course not. But we don't go into this with a mindset that says I will *try* to honor you. We have adopted the mindset that says I *will* honor you. Then when we fail, because we will at some point, we apologize and start again. Each day is a new opportunity to step into and live fully in a marriage that is envisioned.

It seems that married couples love to dredge up old stuff and throw it in each other's faces during times of disagreement. Not only that, we love to prove our point, get our spouse to see that we are right, and win the whole thing. Proving our point doesn't count for anything if we've left our spouse emotionally and verbally beaten on the side of the road. If our spouse loses, the marriage loses. And that means we lose too.

When Chris and I have an argument, we never allow it to get out of control like it used to. In fact, since 2002 I can only remember two fights that we let things spiral downward. Now, are we just amazingly kind people who have great self-control? Hardly. This desire to fight for each other and not against comes after fighting against each other for the entire first decade we were together. With everything we have been through, there are too many petty things that just aren't worth a fight. So we let them go.

One thing Chris and I have learned to do is focus on the here and now. If he brings up something I said or did that hurt him, I don't say, "Yeah, well, you really hurt me when you cheated on me, and you don't have a right to get mad about what I just said to you!" Look, he repented and I forgave him. We have moved through that part of our lives and have found a healthy, current reality. I cannot dredge up the past just because my present becomes uncomfortable when a conflict has surfaced.

When you add infidelity or another type of betrayal to the marriage mix, you typically face even more conflict. We must learn to fight for our marriages after betrayal and embrace the value of marriage even after things have fallen apart. When there has been deep pain in our marriage because of betrayal, it is so tempting to go back to that and bring it up, even if the current struggle has nothing to do with our past. If we have a fight, then clearly it's because of what we've been through. If we don't communicate well, surely it's because of what my spouse did to me. If we are having a tough season, then it's got to be because our marriage fell apart years ago. Sure, our past can contribute to our present conflict, but sometimes I think couples jump to blame that way too often. It's become a crutch to lean on so we don't have to take responsibility for the here and now.

LIE vs. TRUTH

Lie: It's too hard to walk through the hard times.

Truth: When I pass through the waters, God will be with me; and when I pass through the rivers, they will not sweep over me. When I walk through the fire, I will not be burned; the flames will not set me ablaze. (see Isaiah 43:2)

There may have been significant damage done to your marriage. But maybe this conflict you are experiencing now is just because you're a couple who has a conflict. Nothing more. Plenty of couples have far more conflict than Chris and I do, but they haven't endured infidelity. So current conflict can't always be blamed on what happened in our past. We have to push through that and focus on the present circumstances and how our actions are affecting our marriage now.

In those early years of our marriage we were for ourselves, not our marriage. We have been down that road, know where it leads, and aren't interested in visiting it again. So we do the hard thing. We look inside ourselves and ask if there is truth to our spouse's concerns or accusations. We empathize for each other and apologize to each other. And sometimes we just have to graciously agree to disagree. Either we are for our marriage or we are not. We cannot expect a better-than-new marriage to surface after betrayal if we are still vying to win an argument and put our spouse down.

> We choose to battle against our own flesh during a fight instead of battling our spouse's.

We must continue rebuilding our marriage with future conflict in mind. It will arise again. You will do something to offend your spouse and vice versa. Do not let the wounds of betrayal keep you in a blame cycle with your spouse. It will be tempting to stop the pursuit of a healthier marriage, but don't let that stop you from rebuilding a healthy outlook when it comes to conflict.

What Nobody Wants to Mention

Do you want to honor your marriage relationship and be faithful? Then prepare yourself ahead of time, because you will find other people attractive. I know some of you are shaking your heads and saying, "Cindy, I only find my husband (or my wife) attractive. No one else." Please. There are over seven billion people on the planet. You think you'll just be attracted to one person? I highly doubt that. Your spouse is not the last person you'll find attractive. Just because we fall in love and get married does not mean we won't notice a good looking person crossing our path. And some of those attractive people might even make our heart skip a beat. That, my friend, is called chemistry. It is not love. There will always be others who catch our eye. We are humans, not robots. We notice gorgeous people. We notice well-built physiques. We notice dreamy eyes and adorable dimples. People we find attractive will be everywhere. But recognizing that and preparing for it ahead of time will help us deny our flesh when that first flirtatious comment or inappropriately long stare happens.

Doing what the sinful nature desires would be to vacate your marriage because you "finally found your soul mate" or because you may not find your spouse attractive anymore. But stopping and recognizing this is just one of many attractive or tempting people who will cross your path and staying committed to your spouse is doing the hard thing. Your flesh wants to indulge itself with this person. But God has called you to a higher standard and commands you to honor Him and your marriage vows. Do the hard thing and walk away.

Marriage is wonderful. It's about love and romance and that tingly feeling you get when he walks right past you and gently touches your arm or when she walks into a room looking fabulous and you have a hard time concentrating on the conversation you were having. Yes, it's all those things, and those things are fun and they feel good. But it's mostly commitment. Chris and I have a healthy marriage and friendship now. We have chosen to honor our commitment to God and to each other by doing things that are difficult to do. But as we have done the hard things in life and made choices that honor God, we are drawn to keep working in that direction. When we do hard things that feel contrary to the flesh, we are usually doing the right things.

Keep Your Focus Upward

"Anything worth having takes work," is something I say often. Are you willing to work hard and do what is more difficult in order to achieve your goals? Are you willing to honor God and obey Him even when it's the more challenging option? Are you willing to stay committed to God when everything around you is telling you to walk away from the things that test you?

Denying our flesh is a tremendous struggle. No one said doing the hard thing was going to be easy. Heck, it's called the hard thing for a reason! We don't want to do it. Ever. Especially when we see something we want. But God is already ahead of your struggle. He's already there and waiting for you to call out to Him. He's waiting to deliver you when you draw upon His strength and choose to deny your flesh. And let me promise you something, you will need His power to help you say no and do the hard things. In fact, you cannot succeed without it.

Choosing to walk the narrow path will be quite an ordeal at first. But over time it will be much easier to do because you will depend on God as your strength. It will be like a magnet pulling you in. When we focus on what we are missing out on, we will want to follow that path. We go toward what we focus on. So heed Paul's wise exhortation, "Set your minds on things above, not on earthly things" (Colossians 3:2). Keeping your mind focused above earthly things will ensure that you keep your eyes on the elevated horizon of God's righteous path.

TO HELP YOU **LIVE FULLY**

1. This chapter discusses the battle of trusting God in the midst of devastating and frightening circumstances. Describe a situation you've faced where you chose to rest in your faith in God and not on the things or people of this world.

2. On a scale from 1 to 10, what is your faith level in God? In the areas that are low, try to pinpoint why that is the case. In these areas, rate your faith level: marriage, children, work, school, etc.

3. Think of a time when you didn't do the hard thing and instead chose an easier route? How did it turn out? What do you think would have happened had you done the hard thing in the first place?

4. How well do you and your spouse fight for each other instead of against each other? Take some time to really analyze your own actions.

5. Has God shown you a step to take? What is stopping you from taking it? What do you need to do today to move in the direction God is leading? List a few action steps.

9

Find Your Porch

Fruit lights. Chris and I wanted fruit lights. Can you imagine the joy in our new marriage when we both realized we knew what fruit lights were? I mean, Jesus was the center and He brought us together, but fruit lights? That's like the cherry on top. Seriously, our marriage was destined to last forever with this newfound discovery.

You may be asking what fruit lights are. If you have ever spent any amount of time at a campground, then you will know what I am referring to. But if your travels took you to beaches or other continents or bustling cities, or if your idea of camping is staying at a Hilton near dozens of restaurant choices, you will have no idea what fruit lights are.

But we both did. And we wanted them badly. Badly, I tell you.

Fruit lights are amazing. They're fun and colorful. They are plastic, multicolored stringed lights in the shape of fruit like oranges, grapes, and bananas. They provide lighting for an area, but not too much, and definitely not too little. Similar to the little bear and his porridge, fruit lights are juuuuuuust right. They say, "Hey, you're on vacation. Enjoy yourself. Have a Fanta orange soda. Eat some Double Stuff Oreos." They are a party waiting to happen.

We spent the better part of 1993 looking for fruit lights. We'd searched the greater San Antonio and Austin areas for what we were certain would improve our struggling marriage. United and on a mission, we went to every RV store we could locate and visited every outdoor or camping equipment retailer we could find. We called around to stores in other towns, and when we asked, "Do you have fruit lights?" we received all sorts of responses. Lots of long pauses, plenty of "What type of lights?" and a whole slew of people handing us off to another sales associate.

Then a day came. Oh, happy day and glory to God in the highest! There was an RV store that wasn't close to us, but it was worth the Saturday afternoon drive. It was worth the risk, quite frankly. Where the fruit lights lead us, we will follow. We'll go find them, find them, anywhere.

But they didn't have fruit lights. They had owl lights. That long search with disappointing dead ends led us to owl lights? Owl lights! Well, that's fine. They still did the trick. They still provided the ambient lighting. They still adorned the front porch of our duplex on Mill Street in San Marcos, Texas.

Mercy, they did. We are not proud of this fact, but we cannot lie. We got home from that store, and Chris attached them to the porch overhang so all the world could see. And just so we could see them every day, we sat on our six-dollar lawn chairs on the porch so we could drink our sweet tea together and visit every evening (#youmightbearedneck).

This was the beginning of porch time.

What's Your Porch Experience?

Chris and I have logged many hours on porches. In fact, every single house we have lived in had either a front porch or back porch. We didn't really care as long as we had our place. We did choose to leave the owl lights in a box once we purchased our first home because we didn't live on 160 acres like my friend Jennifer Edmunson does. And we didn't figure the HOA would appreciate them.

Our front porch experiences mattered. It wasn't about the porch or those lights, but it was about having a safe, comfortable place to be together to talk up a storm or sit in silence. It didn't matter what we did as long as we were connecting, because finding your porch is about connecting with each other as a couple.

LIE vs. TRUTH

Lie: I don't know if my marriage will ever be what I dream it will be.

Truth: Now to Him who is able to do immeasurably more than all I can ask or imagine, according to His power that is at work within me. (see Ephesians 3:20)

If you think back to the days when you first met, you wanted to be together all the time. When you were together, you probably had a hard time keeping your hands off each other. *Ahem.* But many couples allowed this feeling to diminish with the addition of major events and responsibilities, including careers, buying a home, losing loved ones, having children, difficult medical diagnoses, vacations, aging parents, community involvement, participating in outside activities, even church activities, and you name it. A mix of milestones, blessings, and hard realities can and will shift our focus away from our marriage relationship. Before we know it, we are roommates, strangers even, and the only thing that shows we're married is our wedding ring. We don't act like a married couple and hardly make any time to better our marriage. This is breeding ground for betrayal, and it is a setup for failure in healing after a betrayal.

You may not have a porch or live in an area where sitting outside is even doable. And the thought of sitting out where your neighbors might stare at you could be the least safe place you can think of. But think about where your porch experience might take place, and then figure out when you can make that happen.

We all live by different schedules and careers and family demands. Maybe you cope with physical or financial conditions that limit you from activities or getaways. But whatever your circumstance, find a place and a time that works for you to connect and rebuild as a couple.

So what's your porch experience? Maybe you enjoy walking together in the cool evenings several times a week. That's your porch. Maybe you go on a date every Friday night. That's your porch. Maybe you don't have the funds to go out, so you put the kids to bed early and then have a date in your bedroom. That's your porch. There is no right way to spend time together. It's just important that you and your spouse schedule regular alone time together. Without your children.

Whatever your porch is, keep on connecting in that way. If you don't have a porch yet, find it. I don't want to sound melodramatic, but when I say your marriage depends on it, it does.

Believe in Marriage Again

At one time, being married meant something. It meant commitment and forever. When people said their marriage vows and concluded with "'til death do us part," they meant it.

In our society, marriage often means "We'll try this out" or "I'll stay with you as long as it works for me" or "I will stick around until you get fat." Of course, not all marriages are like that, but by the look of our divorce rates, even among Christians, it seems like this perspective has become the most popular.

I think it's pretty clear how God feels about marriage. Even though the apostle Paul said in 1 Corinthians 7 that it's better to stay single and not get married, the Bible is laced with verses that tell us just how vital the marriage relationship is. Here are a handful of those scriptures in the NIV translation:

> Therefore, what God has joined together, let no one separate. (Mark 10:9)

> Wives, submit yourselves to your own husbands as you do to the Lord. (Ephesians 5:22)

> Husbands, love your wives, just as Christ loved the church and gave himself up for her. (Ephesians 5:25)

> Marriage should be honored by all, and the marriage bed kept pure, for God will judge the adulterer and all the sexually immoral. (Hebrews 13:4)

What God has joined together, let no one separate? Marriage should be honored by all? Wives, submit as if submitting to the Lord? Husbands, love your wives and be willing to give your lives for her? Yeah, I'd say that means marriage is important to God, so we should treat it as the valuable covenant it is.

Please know that in no way am I condemning anyone for experiencing a divorce. Sometimes getting a divorce is the better option. If your husband is abusive and you fear for your life, it's wise to remove yourself from that situation. If your wife leaves you and your children for another man, moving on is a choice you should consider making.

> God's grace doesn't remove consequences, but it does remove condemnation.

What if you have chosen divorce in your past and now regret it? Never fear, God's grace covers all sin when we confess and repent of it. Regardless of your past situation, if you are married right now, God wants you to fight for your marriage.

Never Give Up

I am certainly no expert in the marriage field. I have no official training other than my experience in leading alongside my husband in ministry for over 20 years and being married for 23 years. There are no initials following my last name to state how smart or educated I am. But, Chris and I have found some valuable tools that have helped us tremendously in strengthening our marriage. These ideas might at first appear simple, but as you incorporate them into your marriage you will realize that they are the ways to be in the fight for your marriage. Tending to the needs of you and your spouse is the way you stand up against potential betrayal, and you prepare for and walk forward in life as a united couple.

Pray together. I know, I know, that's so cliché and expected for Christians. Stay with me, please. Don't be intimidated by this. Praying is simply speaking to and listening to God. During our prayer times, we pour out our hearts to God. We can even tell Him how upset we are about something in our current situation. Praying is such an intimate thing to do, which is why few Christian couples actually do it together. (And you can't count praying before a meal!) The thought of praying aloud while our spouse is listening scares many of us. We wonder if they will use our confession of some struggle as ammunition against us in a future fight or, worse, make fun of us in a social setting for having that struggle. I understand those fears. We want to believe our spouse will hold us up and keep our frail hearts safe. I recognize the fear, but if you set your hearts on Christ and seek Him, praying together can be a beautiful thing.

Prayer was not a part of our regular commitment to our marriage until our pastor, Craig Groeschel, did a five-part marriage sermon series called From This Day Forward.[7] (He and his wife, Amy, later released a book with that title that is a wonderful read!) In the first sermon, he gave us five things to do in our marriage to make it stronger: seek God, fight fair, have fun, stay pure, and never give up. Well, Chris and I went through the list together and realized we were pretty good at all of them. We had just finished patting ourselves on the back when Pastor Craig said, "The best advice I can give you is to pray together every day." *Gulp*.

That is something we did not do. Now, that's funny considering we are in full-time ministry leading the largest campus of Life. Church. But it was the truth. We prayed together when situations were intense, and we certainly prayed for other people. But praying together was not in our daily routine. Instead, during most of our years together, I was met with a husband who didn't really want to pray with me. In fact, he confessed to me that when we were lying in bed at night all those years, he would act like he was asleep and lay real still so I would not ask him to pray. Because the last thing he needed from his self-righteous wife was another lecture on how we needed to pray together. All it did was remind him of how much he wasn't doing as a husband. I became quite good at letting him know, unfortunately.

That means we were married for 19 years before we became faithful at praying together. Nineteen years! I find myself wondering what could have been different if we had spent more time going to God together.

Praying was not a part of our routine, but it is now. That sermon series in 2012 changed everything. And I can tell you that in nearly four years we have only missed mornings due to one of us traveling or having an early meeting. The difference it has made in our spiritual lives and in our marriage can't be calculated. It's been such a rich time for us. Sometimes we pray quick prayers and don't really have a ton to say. Sometimes they are longer and more detailed with the cries of our hearts. Regardless, we are praying together.

Talk about everything and talk about nothing. Sometimes in marriages it seems that only the heavy topics are discussed. We will go on and on about our marriage issues and struggles with our kids. No wonder we want to avoid conversation with our spouse. If all we talk about are burdens that weigh us down, we are missing the gift of connecting without tension now and then. Chris and I have found that talking about nothing is sometimes therapeutic. When we take walks at night or are out to dinner, we talk about the weather or how we can keep our Yorkie from peeing on the carpet or how much we like our pool vacuum. All of our conversations as married couples don't have to be heavy. They can just be nothing sometimes.

It's important that both of you talk and both of you listen. I know that one of you may talk more than the other. That's fine, but you can't have a relationship when just one person talks. If you are the talker, take some of those words you are drowning your spouse with and talk to God. Part of looking to Christ to meet our needs is not feeling like we have to address every single, itty-bitty issue that arises in our marriage. If your husband has had a hard week and seems distant, just give him space. He may not be able to communicate with you how he is feeling at that moment.

LIE vs. TRUTH

Lie: I don't have anything in common with my spouse. We will never find anything to do together.

Truth: With God, all things are possible in my life. (see Matthew 19:26)

I experience this with Chris especially when his role as a pastor is placing him under added emotional pressure. When he is ministering to a family who has lost a loved one unexpectedly, I know he is overwhelmed. So I back off and just try to make his life easier. I wait for him to come to me to talk. Trust me, it works. And when I have something to share, I know I have only a short window of communication time with Chris. The man is amazing in so many ways, but when I'm sharing my heart with him, I can see his eyes start to glaze over and his stare moves off into the distance. I know I have limited time so I get to the point. Then when he talks, I listen. I do my best not to interrupt, because people who interrupt are self-centered and thinking about what they'll say next rather than what the other is saying right then.

One of the more challenging things to wade through as a couple who has endured infidelity or another significant betrayal is knowing when to bring up something about that time in your life. It's easy to talk about the "nothings" in life because they're not a big deal, but when we have to talk about that thing that happened in our marriage that still sometimes causes us pain, we want to run from it. I know there are times when you may not want to talk or listen, but for the sake of your marriage, talk and listen. Share your heart, both of you. And when both of you are sharing what is going on and you don't allow your defenses to reign, you will begin to see an environment of respect, admiration, and honor develop between you. Friend, just because you are still hurting does not mean there is unforgiveness in your heart. Contrary to public opinion, pain does not equal unforgiveness. Can it? Sure. But not always. It just means that the pain was deep and real and that you need more healing when some trigger arises or some fear overwhelms you. Talk about it, but don't dwell on it.

Commit to doing shared activities. Chris and I are so very different in our personalities and the way we process things. He's a visionary, and I see things as they are. He's a thinker, and I am a feeler. But we have many things in common when it comes to what we enjoy doing. We both actually enjoy home renovation and working around the house. It's productive and therapeutic for us because we see a finished product and don't usually see that in full-time ministry.

Many years ago, we remodeled our kitchen and breakfast area, which included my handy husband tearing down some unwanted cabinets and ripping out some carpet. When all was said and done, we had tiled our kitchen, painted the existing cabinets, added new hardware, and repainted the rooms. Yes, there were stressful moments that occurred, but for the most part we really enjoyed spending that time together. It works for us. Your idea of doing home remodeling may be hiring a contractor to do the work. But maybe you enjoy biking or golfing. Perhaps you enjoy traveling together, even if it's just a day trip to a local city. Whatever it is, finding shared activities has proven to be vital for our marriage, and I guarantee you will benefit from it as well.

I'm well aware we are all walking through different seasons in life. And I know it may be a challenge to have an extra five minutes, because children are crying or there is something else on the calendar. The bottom line is, you have to make time for each other. Chris and I have time together on our back porch every morning and sometimes every evening. We can pick up and go run an errand and tell the kids we'll be back in a couple of hours. We have the ability to go out to dinner alone anytime we want to. We can do that because our sons are 17, 14, and 12. They still need us, but they don't need us like a two-year-old does. So give yourself some grace to find out how to make your marriage stronger. Some of you have the funds to hire a babysitter every week and just need to make it a priority. Men, date your wife and open the car door for her on a date. Ladies, build up your man and thank him for working hard for the family and loving you. Your season will change before you know it. Before I know it, Chris and I will be empty nesters. I think about how much sweeter that stage of our relationship will be because we chose to fight for our marriage by committing to these simple actions.

In our busy lives it can be a challenge to make time to invest in our marriages. We all have the time, but we just have to choose to use that time to make our marriages stronger and last until death parts us. It's that important.

Let your last waking moments together be enjoyable. If fights and hurt feelings are a relational disease, you are most apt to catch them at night. Our relational immune system is weakest in the evenings. But as couples, the only time we tend to talk about heavy things is at night. The problem with this is, our lenses are skewed. We are viewing life after having worked all day or maybe having a rough day with our children. Then we go to bed and decide, "Yeah, this is a great time to talk about how awful my marriage is." I know that evenings may be your only kid-free time, but just beware of the danger in that.

Chris and I rarely discuss heavy issues after 9:00 p.m. It's just not wise on either of our parts. So we make an effort to discuss things in the mornings so we have the day to work through them if we need it.

I know it's a challenge to stick to this guideline. Man, do I know. Especially when you have young children who need your attention all day. When they are finally tucked in for the night, you can't wait to talk to your spouse about everything that is going on in that head of yours. Sometimes it's good stuff to discuss, but sometimes it's not. And when we talk about those things that are more difficult, our defenses rise and we make no progress. In fact, we take steps backward. Closing your day together in peace will help you both reconnect after even the longest of days.

You started out as a couple and you will leave this earth as a couple. Next to our relationship with Christ, the marriage relationship is the most significant relationship we have. We must pursue health in it at all times. Even when it's challenging. Even when we don't want to. Even when we feel like giving up. Pray together. Talk to each other. Do things together.

And don't give up.

TO HELP YOU **LIVE FULLY**

1. How often do you and your spouse spend quality time together? How often do you get away without your children? Consider how to make time together a priority in your lives.

2. What is your ideal way to relax? What is your ideal vacation? Do you and your spouse have similar ideas of relaxation and vacationing? Have one of your front-porch conversations be about these questions.

3. Do you and your spouse pray together? Why or why not? If both of you are willing, consider making a commitment to pray together every day starting today. If your spouse is not interested in praying with you, pray on your own and trust God to bring a changed heart.

4. Make a list of things you enjoy doing. Circle the ones you both enjoy and would like to do together.

5. Benjamin Franklin said, "If you fail to plan, you are planning to fail." Spend some time creating a plan for how you will make time for each other, pray together, and share activities. Once you make a plan, stick with it.

INVEST GENEROUSLY

10

Refined in God's Timing

When we had spent the better part of four hours watching our home and all our material possessions be destroyed by fire, it was hard to believe in restoration. The damage was horrific, and we assumed that everything was completely gone. But much to our surprise, firefighters gradually began bringing a few items out of the house that had not burned. Two acoustic guitars with burn marks on their cases. The Bible from Seth's bedside table. A few jackets in the entry closet. Family picture frames from the hallway. Two original pieces of artwork drawn by my maternal grandmother I never met. Other than those few items, most possessions were either burned by the fire or severely damaged with smoke and 120,000 gallons of water, including my 75-year-old heirloom piano. This blessed piece did not burn but was submerged in the life-saving water that eventually put out the fire. This was the piano I grew up playing. This was the piano my mother grew up playing. To lose this piece was heartbreaking.

All of my photo albums and scrapbooks were gone. The few things I had left from my dad, who died 26 years ago, were destroyed. Christmas ornaments that the boys made when they were young.

Journals I had written throughout my adult life. My yearbooks and letter jacket from high school. Anything and almost every material possession and keepsake from 43 years of life…gone.

The shell of our burned home stood on our street for five and a half weeks after the fire. I'm certain our neighbors were tired of the view and the lingering smoke smell that was apparent the moment you went outside. Inside the home there was broken glass, burned beams, charred pieces of furniture, mildewed bedding, and singed articles of clothing everywhere. Next to the metal frame that once had sofa cushions on it was a scorched basket that held remnants of yarn from an afghan I'd been crocheting for months. Don't ask me how that didn't burn up in the heat of the flames, when the table next to it was nothing but ashes.

Only a few items here and there were salvageable, because our dear friends Bill and Julie Dinkines spent the better part of the first three weeks digging through the soggy ashes to return to us anything we would find meaningful. They scoured the garage floor looking for our old photo albums that housed pictures of our childhoods, the dating years, the married years without children, and the early years of our first son's life before the digital age arrived. They managed to salvage about 20 percent of them, which to this day are still some of my favorite pictures, burn marks, water stains, and all. They found the seven-foot piece of pine recording the measurements of our boys' heights. It didn't burn up even though it was near where the fire started. It currently leans against our living room wall, and it doesn't even bother me that there are marks all over it from fallen embers. In fact, I rather like that part the best. We were beyond grateful for those acts of kindness toward a family who had little left of the material possessions and keepsakes they held dear.

The night before demolition was to happen, we went out to the house and walked around in the debris one last time. It was strange to come out to the awful site of our home but to somehow feel comfortable there. It just seemed like the thing to do that night: to go and bid adieu to the place where we had some great memories with our family. Every time we were there, I had a bit of hope that I'd find the diamond necklace my dad gave my mom on their 25th anniversary or that I would find something that belonged to my sons that I'd stored in the attic. Because even though I knew I'd lost everything, I didn't know exactly what I lost until I couldn't find it.

Walking through the debris that night, I cried. I was heartbroken to close a chapter of our life that brought immeasurable joy but equally excited for the new chapter about to come. Regardless of how bad it would hurt, the next day it would all be gone. Any material remnant from my old pre-fire life would just be a distant memory in my mind.

But the demolition was what needed to happen, regardless of how emotionally taxing it would be. It was time to step into something new that God had for us.

Discovered Hope in the Rebuilding

Once the rebuilding phase started, we were able to embrace the new beginning. It actually became an enjoyable process. We would drive out to the house nearly every day to see the progress, just to be out there. Even if nothing was different from the day before. Everything was the same—the view, the yard, the neighbors—yet everything was different. The house we were building did not resemble the house we lost at all. We started over completely.

It was fun looking through floor plans and figuring out what we wanted. We figured that if we were getting to rebuild then we would build what we really wanted. We spent hours on home-decorating websites looking at kitchens and bathrooms. We looked at hundreds of rooms to see what paint colors worked best and would give us the look we desired. We compared styles and weeded out the ones that seemed worn out and overused. We picked out furniture, I, bedding, just about everything during those months.

But before that part of the process could ever have begun, we had to remove the old. And we had to be brave enough to move on. Stepping into that new thing often feels scary. We fear the unknown. We have no idea what to expect on our new path. Quite frankly, we just want things to get back to normal. We'd found a level of comfort in the old. We knew what to expect. We knew what it would feel like. And because we just didn't know what the new would look like, we weren't sure we wanted to go there. We didn't know if venturing out of our safety zone would be a wise move.

Our old marriage wasn't that great, but we knew what to expect. We had an idea of what would happen from day to day even though it was far from healthy. And if we're really honest, we don't want to be that couple who has gone through something devastating or difficult. We don't want to be the people who people feel sorry for. We want to walk tall with our chins up, not in arrogance but in confidence.

And for some reason, we think that walking through our own fiery trial will somehow keep us from experiencing abundance in our lives. Friend, it will not. There is hope in the rebuilding, and there is so much good ahead.

I believe that walking through the valley of the shadow of death will help you view the beauty and experience the greatness from the top of the mountain.

Refine Us, Lord

I have the honor of calling Justin and Trisha Davis my friends. Trisha and I connected back in 2010. Since that time, we have served in ministry together through Leading and Loving It, a ministry to pastors' wives and to women in ministry. We are kindred in spirit and have a deep love and admiration for each other. In addition to each of us having three sons, we also have something else in common. Justin and Trisha endured their own hell on earth in 2005.

Justin and Trisha planted a church and loved ministry together. But Trisha's heart was trampled with Justin's confession of infidelity with her best friend a few years later. Without the guarantee of a transformed marriage, they both decided to push through their pain and grief with hope that something miraculous would happen. The years were long, but the days felt even longer. This season almost took them out, they will tell you.

Then God showed Himself to be faithful.

Justin and Trisha did their part by making hard choices and trusting in their God. They pursued Jesus relentlessly and knew their very lives depended on Him. They laid everything out on the table and allowed God to use them as He saw fit. In 2009, they moved to Nashville, Tennessee so Justin could join the Cross Point Church staff.

But this wasn't where it stopped. They also founded RefineUs ministry and travel around the country speaking at churches

> God is doing an important work in us so He can continue to do a work through us. We must trust God's timing and prep work. Because in due time there will be a harvest, not only in our own lives but in the lives of others because of the work in us.

and conferences about what God did and continues to do in their marriage journey. They use their story of failure, loss, and transformation to assist individuals, couples, churches, pastors, pastors' wives, and church planters toward having a healthy marriage and family. They believe that if you want a healthy ministry, you need a healthy marriage first.

And that's not all. The Davises became authors when their first book, *Beyond Ordinary: When a Good Marriage Isn't Good Enough*, released in 2012. On that dark day in 2005, if you had asked Justin or Trisha if they thought God would do this, they would have laughed or cried uncontrollably. Not because God isn't able, but because they didn't think they were able. But apparently, God wasn't kidding when He said nothing is impossible with Him. Talk about God blowing their minds with all He had in store.

Most recently, after ministering to thousands upon thousands of people, Justin and Trisha moved back to Indianapolis, Indiana, the place where their lives fell apart 11 years before. It wasn't to reflect on the pain of loss or the devastation of a marriage uprooted. No, they returned to that place to plant a new church called Hope City Church.

Yes, God's timing is perfect.

God has redeemed their loss and made them whole again. And now He is going to redeem the city that once held such tragic memories in their lives and in their marriage. I, for one, cannot wait to see all that transpires.

Perfect Timing, Perfect Peace

The power of God's perfect timing is a power we can believe in and rest in. I can't find a better illustration to share from the Bible than the account of Jesus's ministry. The Bible tells us little about His growing up years. According to Luke 2 we know He was born in Bethlehem, was taken shortly after to the temple to be consecrated, and was left behind at the temple courts at age 12. The last thing in the chapter that is said of Him is, "Jesus grew in wisdom and stature, and in favor with God and man" (Luke 2:52).

Fast-forward 18 years and you'll find John the Baptist preaching, baptizing, and preparing the way for Jesus, the Messiah. During that time, Jesus came forward and was baptized too. Luke said, "Jesus himself was about thirty years old when he began his ministry" (Luke 3:23). Right after that, Jesus was led into the wilderness by the Holy Spirit where He was tempted by the devil for 40 days and did not eat anything during that time. (What a way to jump into ministry!)

I don't know about you, but my finite mind wonders what else happened in His life. What happened in His teen years? Because He was 100 percent perfect, He was a terrific, obedient, even-tempered teenager, which is a total oxymoron in today's society. He didn't dishonor his parents. He was the perfect big brother to His younger, imperfect siblings. He didn't stay out past curfew. He worked hard. He did everything right.

LIE vs. TRUTH

Lie: I'm not smart enough. I wouldn't know where to start.

Truth: If I lack wisdom, I should ask God, who gives generously without finding fault, and it will be given to me. (see James 1:5)

I also wonder about the timing of how late His ministry began. Not trying to brag, but I'm an excellent time manager, and I would have had Jesus in ministry way before age 30. I mean, it just makes sense, right? At age 12 He was keeping up with all the temple scholars, so why not let Him begin His ministry sooner? He had the power to heal people, so why not let Him start healing sooner? I don't know why God chose to wait until Jesus was 30, but He did. It just wasn't time yet.

Timing is crucial. Most babies are born when they are ready to depart their mother's womb. Plants emerge from the ground at just the right time in their growing season. Leaves die and fall from trees when cooler temperatures arrive.

I don't know exactly what was happening in Jesus's life during those years before His ministry began. Scripture doesn't give us much detail, except that He grew up and gained wisdom and favor with God and man. While I will never know or understand why Jesus's earthly ministry didn't start until He was 30 years old, I do believe God had a specific purpose in the waiting.

I believe God had a specific purpose for me in the writing of my first book. I knew within the first year of our marriage disaster I would write a book. That was in 2002. But my book did not get picked up by a publisher until 2010. That's eight years of waiting.

Eight years of wondering if I'd heard God incorrectly. Eight years of writing and rewriting chapters, hoping I would say what needed to be said to hurting couples all over the world.

And as hard as that waiting period was, it was the right amount of time. God was already using our story prior to my book release. We were mentoring couples along their own journeys. We were doing our part to share our story to help distribute hope to an often hopeless situation. But there was still a long period of waiting before He allowed us, and even commissioned us, to make His name great by our story.

The period of time spent waiting for God can be brutal. But it's transformative. Ask the Davises or anyone who has been through the fire. We often want to move out of that waiting period before it's time. We figure that if we quote a few verses that will slap a spiritual Band-Aid on our profound wound. But that incomplete response won't hold up when the winds shift and the waves get higher. We must trust His perfect timing. It is where our peace lies.

North Winds and South Winds

In *My Utmost for His Highest* Oswald Chambers wrote:

> Huge waves that would frighten an ordinary swimmer produce a tremendous thrill for the surfer who has ridden them. Let's apply that to our own circumstances. The things we try to avoid and fight against—tribulation, suffering, and persecution—are the very things that produce abundant joy in us. "We are more than conquerors through Him" "in all these things"; not in spite of them, but in the midst of them. A saint doesn't know the joy of the Lord in spite of tribulation, but because of it. Paul said, "I am exceedingly joyful in all our tribulation" (2 Corinthians 7:4).[8]

In life, there are good times and bad times. That's nothing new to you. You've been through your share of each, I'm certain. Many years ago God spoke to Chris and me about seasons in our lives. We gave a name to the good, easy times and a different name to the more turbulent times. We call the easier times "south-wind seasons" and the harder times "north-wind seasons."

Living in the southern part of the United States we know how pleasant a south wind can be on a scorching hot day. In these south-wind seasons, relationships are typically strong. There is a lot of rest and reflection on how truly blessed we all are. We feel close to God. We often stand on the mountaintop and genuinely enjoy the view. Everything just feels right in this season. It's a necessary season that provides a rest from the previous season and gears us up for the next.

North-wind seasons are often full of hard, difficult days. When north winds come in the winter, they are bitter cold. It can be a mild temperature outside, but when a 40 miles-per-hour wind out of the north cuts right through you, you can feel like you're in North Dakota. It seems like every day is an effort. Relationships can be strained and take just about everything you have to make it through the day without a fight. You wonder if your prayers are making it past the ceiling. You may have even wondered where God is in the midst of your pain and trials.

South-wind seasons are enjoyable and provide a sense of peace for us. And they are necessary. They allow us to breathe, to rest, to rejuvenate. And we need that. But don't mistake these seasons for the times where you truly grow. The growth typically comes during the north-wind seasons.

Plants don't bloom until they've successfully struggled and eventually pushed through the soil. This is the season where we are in the valley, where it's lush and full of life. The only thing is, we don't realize the beauty of this season until we make the treacherous climb to the mountaintop. Once we are there, we start a new south-wind season, where we see the beauty of the valley as well as the steep climb we took to get there.

I don't know what season you are in right now, but I encourage you to embrace it. If you are living easy right now in a south-wind season and even find yourself with some mental, emotional, and physical margin, don't try to fill it. You need this rest. But if your circumstances are challenging right now, push through them, not around them. Keep praying, keep worshipping, keep seeking God, and keep reading the Word even when you don't feel like it. And when you do that, I am confident you will experience true joy. Not in spite of your trials, as Paul mentioned, but in the midst of them.

> You may be praying that God will calm your storm. What He may choose to do instead is calm you.

Where Are You in the Journey?

Let's get practical for a minute. The difficult seasons are not ones we welcome. But they are the seasons that offer us new healing and growth. When we try to sidestep parts of the journey, we hinder the healing. There is no benefit in that choice. The pain will be there until you work through it.

Contrary to public opinion, time does not heal all wounds. Time, in and of itself, can't heal our pain. But when we use time appropriately, it can be beneficial to us. I've watched people grieve over something two decades after a loss just like it was the day they experienced their loss. Time did nothing for that wound because perhaps the person did not push through the grief to find healing. Grief is necessary for healing, but we often don't want to invite it in to do its cleansing work. While there is no way to know for certain when it's time for you to step into a new season of helping others, Chris and I have a few questions for you to consider as you analyze where you are on your journey.

The first question you should ask is, *Who has my ear?* Who speaks into your life to where you listen? What godly influences are in your life? Is it your pastor? Is it a mentor? Is it a family member who can be unbiased about your situation? It is important to have people we admire and respect in our lives. Those who are willing to challenge us, push us, and protect us according to God's Word.

When Chris and I left full-time ministry to heal our marriage, we had no thought of ever returning to it. We just wanted our marriage healed. But over the coming months, God began to show us we would be back on a church staff one day. Well, that one day seemed to take forever. In fact, there were times during the first several months that we wanted to say, "We're ready! Coach, put us back in!" But our mentors, Jim and Beth Kuykendall, were so wise to help us see we were getting ahead of ourselves. We trusted them to see things we couldn't see. Our emotions were still heightened, and we still had so much healing to do before God brought us back. Because we loved and respected Jim and Beth, we listened to what they had to say. They led us because we really couldn't lead ourselves effectively for that early season of healing. And they still speak into our lives today even though the Oklahoma-Texas state line separates us.

LIE vs. TRUTH

Lie: I'm afraid to do this.

Truth: For the Spirit God gave us does not make me timid, but gives me power, love and self-discipline. (2 Timothy 1:7)

It is very important that you have wise counsel speaking into your life. Even if it can't be a one-on-one situation, join a small group where you can gain the wisdom from more couples than just yourselves.

The second question should be *Is our marriage ready to handle spiritual attack?* Clearly, your marriage has endured some pretty difficult challenges. Even if you haven't specifically experienced infidelity, the fact that you're reading this book tells me you have plenty of other challenges.

When we put ourselves in a place to minister out of our own past (or current) pain, we are placing ourselves in the line of fire of Satan's arrows. Listen, he does not like the fact that you are still married and didn't get a divorce. He does not like the fact that God is healing you. And he definitely does not want you to help others stay married. He wants division and broken families. So as you pray about whether or not you are ready to begin this next season, also ask yourselves if your marriage can handle more attack. If you are not sure, then just keep on the healing path and get stronger. As you do this, eventually you will be able to ask yourself that question and then say, "Yes, we are ready!"

While this isn't the last question you should ask yourself, it's the last one I'm going to suggest: *Have you healed enough?* I use the word *enough* because the healing road back from marriage betrayal doesn't come overnight. You don't have to heal completely to help someone, but you do want to heal enough so you aren't crying incessantly or talking about your story too frequently while you are helping someone through their own pain. And you have to be honest about where you stand.

> Acknowledge and embrace where you are so you can get to where you want to go.

My mentor, Beth, says, "You know you've healed from a situation when you can look back on it and it's a fact." I believe I am there in my own healing. I think I've been there for probably the last seven years. That doesn't mean I was crying every day and hurting for seven years. Not at all. I just mean that for some time now, my healing has been as complete as it can be this side of heaven. During the first seven years, I experienced tremendous healing. In the early years, it was still difficult to go a week without remembering what happened and how it marked us. As our healing continued and we earnestly pressed into Jesus, the speed of our healing increased. And as I mentioned earlier, we used time to help us.

Your Time Will Come

There will come a time when God will place a burden on your heart to share what you've gone through in your own life. Maybe you've watched a loved one suffer and die from cancer. Maybe you've walked a stormy road with your teenager or adult child for years on end. Maybe you have been burned time and again by family members. Or maybe your marriage hit a brick wall because of infidelity like mine did. Whatever your situation, God can and will use it.

What would happen if you took all that you've been through in your life and offered assistance to someone else in their own misery? What would happen if you decided to step out of your comfortable place and chose vulnerability by sharing something from your past? What would happen if you chose to allow God to redeem your suffering by providing a godly presence in the life of someone else? I will tell you what will happen. There will be more stories like Justin's and Trisha's in the world. There will be more stories like Chris's and mine in the world. And there will be more stories like yours in the world.

But until that day when you feel called to share from your healing, keep moving forward. Even when you feel like you've taken a few steps back, you are still ahead of where you were in your dark days. A rearview mirror is meant to glance at, not stare into. So occasionally allow yourselves to glance back at where you once were so you can see how far you've come.

Your time will come.

TO HELP YOU **INVEST GENEROUSLY**

1. What are you holding on to that you need to let go of? (A past hurt? A current struggle?)

2. List one thing you can do every day to help you release this thing you continue to hold on to.

3. Is it challenging for you to enjoy the south-wind seasons? Why or why not?

4. Thinking back to some of your north-wind seasons, in what ways did God refine you and make a better version of you?

5. According to the questions asked in this chapter, do you feel it is time for you to begin investing in others' lives with your story?

6. What step(s) does God want you to take toward investing in someone else's life because of what you've endured?

11

God Wastes Nothing

It was a typical summer Saturday morning, and I was going about the regular things I do on the weekend. As much as I love a to-do list, I love a checked-off to-do list even more.

My phone rang around 10:30. I saw a familiar name pop up on the screen. A name that makes me smile. A name I hold close to my heart. A name of someone I always pick up the phone for. This girl's call never goes to voicemail unless I just don't get to the phone in time. I will never screen her call. I will never not want to talk to her. She's that special to me.

"Girl, what is going on?!" I said in a silly voice as I hit the green button on my phone. But her voice was not the voice I heard.

"Cindy, this is Tyler, Megan's brother," he said. He didn't need to tell me who he was. I knew exactly who he was. "She needs to come see you right now. Is that okay?" he asked.

Apparently, the only coherent phrase that Tyler could decipher from Megan was, "I need to see Cindy Beall."

"Of course," was my reply.

"We'll be there in ten minutes," he said.

My heart sank. This was the phone call I never wanted to get.

The phone call from a dear, close friend who needed my service, that service of ably walking with and encouraging someone along the wretched road of infidelity. I knew what this call was about, and I knew what emotional state Megan would be in when she appeared on my doorstep. There is only one reason people call us with that tone in their voice. Because the unthinkable happened. And I was hurting before she even arrived.

I immediately told Chris about the call, and he looked at me rather shell-shocked. Chris was just as close to Megan's husband, Colby, as I was to Megan. We met them when I was pregnant with our youngest son, Seth. They weren't married yet, so we were honored to be able to help them as they inched closer toward marriage. We enjoyed their company and had a lot in common with them.

My eyes burned with tears as I realized now they likely had another thing in common with us: the heartbreak of infidelity.

When Tyler's car pulled into our driveway, I immediately went outside to greet them. I was not completely sure what I was walking into, and thankfully, Tyler met me, because Megan was still on the phone with Colby. Tyler proceeded to tell me that Colby had just called her from out of town and confessed to an affair. He hadn't even been able to confess in person.

I walked to Megan's side of the car and looked at her through the window. Tears were streaming down her face, her emotions unmanageable as she tried to process the worst news of her life. She opened the door, looked at me with grief-stricken eyes, and shook her head. The sides of her mouth that normally formed a beautiful smile now turned down. It was the face of anguished sorrow, and I knew it well.

She proceeded to ask questions of her husband, who clearly didn't have good enough answers, because there are no good answers. There are no answers that make sense. There are no answers that will take away the pain. Even if one answer is found and the pain subsides for 30 seconds, more pain is on its way that insists on being felt.

As she got out of the car, I was close enough to hear Colby talking and crying on the other end of the call. Megan was collapsing into my arms, so I took the phone from her.

"Colby—" I said unable to get out any subsequent words.

"Cindy, what in the &*$@# have I done?" he cried out, not only rhetorically but uncontrollably as well. I tried to speak words to comfort him, but I finally had to hand the phone off to Chris. My bleeding heart was crushed, so I needed my calm-under-stress husband to take over.

The four of us eventually made our way into our house. We were in the bedroom for privacy. Megan sat in the gray occasional chair beneath our wall-mounted plasma TV. Chris sat on our bed. Tyler took a spot on the area rug, while I grabbed a chair from the dining room table. I sat as close to Megan as I could because I knew she needed me to. And honestly, I needed to be close to her too. I felt as if my presence would soothe my dear friend and bring her hope, since I'd already walked down the road she was just starting upon.

She went from a calm, quiet, deep sadness to an onslaught of emotions every couple of minutes. She would look at me as if she were literally hanging on my words and in absolute need of my existence. Like she couldn't live without me. Like seeing me and staring into my eyes expressing compassion would give her the strength to take another breath, when all she really wanted to do was die. I did manage to keep my tears at bay for the time being, even though I was sick over what had transpired.

We all discussed the situation and tried to answer her questions, even if the answer was just "I don't know." We offered hope and encouragement, even though we knew that would not sustain her long, for we knew the next wave of grief was on its way and would crush everything in its path.

She spent the next five hours lying on my bed. I would sit with her for a while, gently moving her wet hair from her face because it was drenched with tears. At times, she needed me close, and other times she needed space. That afternoon I grieved for what she was experiencing in those hours and grieved for what I knew was to come in the days, weeks, and months ahead. I mourned for what she lost. I ached, knowing this would strip away so much of her dignity. Being the spouse of someone who's been unfaithful does that to you. Contrary to what the offending husband or wife says, it still makes you feel like you weren't enough or you didn't look good enough or you weren't loving enough or you weren't a good enough spouse. It makes you sure people are taking pity on you and saying crass things about you like, "She must not have made her man happy in the bedroom," or "If he was a better husband, she wouldn't have cheated." It makes you doubt your entire being and everything about the life and relationship you've had. My heart was breaking for Megan.

And then it hit me. This was the most personal situation of infidelity I'd ever experienced outside of my own story. Yes, I have gotten close to people to help them along their own journeys of infidelity, but Megan is like a sister to me and I carried pain on her behalf.

One of the greatest and most important challenges for Chris and me would be to help this precious couple see there is life after infidelity and to walk them through their restorative process, while making sure we didn't pick sides or get too emotional. Yes, this route was not going to be an easy one.

The Ministry of Empathy

It's likely that, at some point in your own life, you've experienced tremendous loss. It could be marriage related or not. You may be the person who has watched a loved one suffer from an illness for a long period of time with little to no relief. You may be the person who has witnessed family members make poor choice after poor choice, affecting their children whom you love so dearly. You may be the person who has spent hours on your knees praying for a sister to return to the God she professed to love. No matter what you have walked through, what you are currently walking through, or what you will walk through in the future, there is an experience you've been through that God wants to turn around and use to help someone else.

LIE vs. TRUTH

Lie: Nothing good will ever come from this.

Truth: I know that in all things God works for my good because I love Him and have been called according to His purpose. (see Romans 8:28)

Have you ever found yourself feeling sad for someone who is journeying through something you've experienced? Your heart breaks for them. You feel for them so much that you start to cry and want to drive over to their house and just be there. You hate that they are going through that, whether it's the loss of a parent or a child, the loss of a career or a friendship. You feel for them because you've been on that path or one similar to it. This, my friend, is the power of empathy. In simple terms, empathy is putting yourself in someone else's shoes to sense how they may be feeling. And when you've actually walked a similar path it's even easier, because you don't have to imagine what they are feeling. Because you've walked that road, you actually have a pretty good idea. There are definitely differences in each person's circumstance, but the vantage point of empathy gives you a clearer understanding and a greater opportunity to pray for, minister to, and even come alongside that person in need.

This is where the Lord comes in: "Praise be to the God and Father of our Lord Jesus Christ, the Father of compassion and the God of all comfort, who comforts us in all our troubles, so that we can comfort those in any trouble with the comfort we ourselves receive from God" (2 Corinthians 1:3-4). This is where you take the comfort you've received from God and then use that same comfort to comfort another. Because you've been there. You've lived it. You've healed from it and through it. And not only have you lived through it and found divine healing from God, you've come out on the other side of it and actually have a life again. And when someone who has just heard the news that they have breast cancer or they've lost their home to a fire, your empathy connects you to them.

I remember when my friends Andy and Erin Keller lost their home in 2015 to the wildfires here in Oklahoma. I felt it. I ached when I saw pictures of the charred remains of their house. I was uncomfortable at the thought of what was ahead for them: not only replacing a home, but having to purchase things they didn't know they even needed. I was equally overjoyed when they would find subtle messages in the rubble of their home debris, when something should have burned but didn't. I walked that road too. It is as if God literally hides signs of hope for His children to find so we can hear Him whisper, *I see you. I have not forgotten you.*

Someday you will be the one to hold another's hand when they've learned that their life is changed forever by an affair, a trial, an obstacle. You will be the one to offer hope to that person because you are still here, still standing, and still living. And that is the key. People in pain want to know how they will survive it, how they will live again. And while your actions to help them are needed, simply standing by their side is enough. The gift of your presence will do them wonders. More than you know.

Knowing God Through His Word

Without God's Word in my mind, heart, and soul, I'd be a mess. My flesh, like yours, is strong and has a desire to be fulfilled. Mercy, my flesh wants to win against my spirit and often does. So in order to combat that flesh of mine, I choose to feed my spirit instead. Whatever you feed grows. I feed my flesh plenty of things, so I must feed my spirit as well. And there is no better thing to feed it than with God's perfect Word.

Each time I read through all 66 Old and New Testament books, I am truly amazed at what I find. It's easy to locate the amazing stories, including the story of Joseph, who saved millions after being sold into slavery by his own brothers. Or Moses, unsure of his leadership and verbal communication skills, who led the Israelites to freedom across the dry floor of the Red Sea after God's mighty hand parted it. I can quickly find Daniel, who squared off against a lion in a den, and King David, who slung a stone and killed a nine-foot behemoth named Goliath.

But then there are stories that don't usually make the Sunday school lesson plans. They may not keep the attention of young children that some of the more notable stories do because they are more obscure, like the story of Rahab.

If you're familiar with the story of Jericho in the book of Joshua, you know that Rahab's occupation wasn't exactly one you'd tell your little ones about. She was a prostitute, and her home was on the exterior wall of Jericho, which made it easy to find and easy to escape from. I'm sure that location proved helpful to many a man who didn't want his wife to know his whereabouts. It would also come in handy soon for a couple of spies from the Israelite camp.

Joshua sent two men out to spy to see how difficult it would be for them to indeed take over that part of the Promised Land. Jericho was an important city and an even stronger fortress. So for the Israelites to go in and take it over, they would first have to learn more about it to prepare a solid strategy.

When the spies went into Jericho, they "entered the house of a prostitute named Rahab and stayed there" (Joshua 2:1). The original Hebrew language says they went there to "lay down, to sleep" so there didn't seem to be any hanky-panky going on. I mean, most men went to the house of a harlot for one reason alone. But the spies knew of her occupation and decided to stay there for the night because it was the perfect hiding place. They feared the leaders of Jericho would be looking for them, so they chose Rahab's home to limit their exposure and to have an escape route.

The king of Jericho discovered where they were, and he sent a message to Rahab saying: "Bring out the men who came to you and entered your house, because they have come to spy out the whole land" (Joshua 2:3). Rahab not only lied to the king but hid the two men under some stalks of flax on her roof. Before the men left her place, she begged them to spare her life and the lives of her family members because she saved their lives. After making the agreement with her, they left and headed for the hills, just as Rahab suggested.

While there are many mysteries about God, your intimate knowledge of the Bible will give you insight into how God works in our lives. And in this story, we witness how God wastes nothing. He did not waste her occupation, but used her place of business as a place to hide the spies. He did not waste her lie when she wasn't up front with the king. He did not waste her quick thinking when the Israelites needed to be hidden on her roof. She was shrewd, intelligent, resourceful, and an ally.

And she was a prostitute.

God Works in All Things

God wastes nothing. I cannot say those words enough. Those three words are not listed in that order anywhere in the Bible, but you can easily pull this concept out from different stories and situations from within its pages. Probably one of the most-quoted and reassuring verses in the Bible that speaks to this truth is Romans 8:28, which says, "We know that in all things God works for the good of those who love him, who have been called according to his purpose."

This verse doesn't say God sits around and waits for things to happen. It says He works. And He doesn't just work in some things,

He works in all things. Not in some things or most things. Not just in the good things or wise things or beautiful things or powerful things. No, He works in *all* things for the good of His children, those of us who love Him. Those of us called according to His purpose. And if you know Him and have been rescued from the pit of hell, then you are called for His purpose.

He worked in my friend Sarah McLean's life when she was diagnosed with breast cancer at age 26. Now, at 39, she's a two-time breast cancer survivor who runs a nonprofit ministry called Project 31. So many great strides have been made in the medical field to help more people survive breast cancer, yet there are few resources that help aid in the emotional healing of such a tumultuous journey. Because Sarah's own emotional path has been so arduous, she wanted to offer hope and assistance to other victims, survivors, and their family members. The mission of Project 31 is restoring lives and families after breast cancer.

Here are some of the testimonies from women who have been encouraged by Sarah's story and the ministry of Project 31:

> I'm a survivor, almost four years as I write, and this group is a HUGE part of my recovery. They have given me support, courage, love, and the ultimate example of faith and perseverance. Through this sisterhood I have survived! — *Sue*

> I can't put into words how grateful I was to have found Sarah and the ladies in our little "sisterhood"; they were genuinely interested in my journey and what they could do to ease my fears and concerns. I seriously feel they saved my sanity and brought hope to me at a time when I felt none. If someone comes to this place, and I know 1 in 8 will at some point, don't try to face this alone; it's a difficult road to travel without a guide…you will find that the comfort, support, and knowledge offered

> here is all you need to make it through the journey of a lifetime.— *Donna*

> Project 31 came to me at the beginning of my journey when I was so distraught. But having women with the same stories and surviving gave me hope.— *Paula* [9]

Sarah's book, *Pink Is the New Black*, is the account of her journey through two bouts of cancer, a double mastectomy, reconstruction, and various other surgical procedures. You will experience many emotions should you choose to read her book, but feeling sorry for her is one thing you won't do. Sarah is not only a survivor but also a conqueror, a victor, a hero, a winner, a defeater. She has chosen to view life and her path unburdened by a victim mentality that would've left her wallowing in self-pity with a big case of "Why me?" questions. The cancer journey was the path she was given, so she decided she could either grow bitter and doubt her God for the rest of her days, or she could choose to make some tasty lemonade from the tart lemons she was dealt.

God did not waste anything. He did not waste her physical and emotional pain. He did not waste the struggles she and her husband endured. God did not waste a single minute of her suffering and struggle. Not one single bit.

Beyond Your Imagination

When I sit and think about the Bible, I am filled with excitement. Many people think it's outdated and unnecessary for our lives today. People get overwhelmed by the things they don't understand and, in turn, get frustrated with God, because in their minds He doesn't make sense. Here's a news flash for you: He said this would happen. Isaiah 55:8-9 says, "'My thoughts are not your thoughts, neither are your ways my ways,' declares the LORD. 'As the heavens are higher than the earth, so are my ways higher than your ways and my thoughts higher than your thoughts.'"

You see? His thoughts are nothing like ours. His ways are beyond what we can imagine. His thoughts and ways are so far above ours. So why on earth would we expect to understand everything He does or says? If we did, we'd be God, and we wouldn't need Him. We are told in Hebrews 11:6 that if we want to please God, we must have faith. If we understand everything about Him and His ways, then we don't need faith. So I beg of you, quit expecting to understand everything about God and instead rest in the fact that He really does have the whole world in His very capable hands.

> When you minister to someone from a place where great pain once resided, a new level of healing occurs in your own life.

When we help someone through something that we were helped through, we remind ourselves: Hey, what you went through wasn't in vain. What you barely lived through is actually now hope for someone else. What nearly killed you will actually bring hope to someone else one day.

It's a spiritual pay-it-forward concept that not only helps others but also redeems our own pain. Let's revisit what Paul wrote: "Praise be to the God and Father of our Lord Jesus Christ, the Father of compassion and the God of all comfort, who comforts us in all our troubles, so that we can comfort those in any trouble with the comfort we ourselves receive from God" (2 Corinthians 1:3-4).

These two verses were a lifeline for me in the midst of my pain. My mentor, Beth, suggested I read them shortly after my husband's confession in 2002. As soon as my eyes hit those verses, tears began to flow. The truth hit me square in the face and even harder in my heart. It was at that moment that I knew God was going to use our story, our wretched pain, to help others. You can imagine my enthusiasm when I saw Beth the next time. I was ready to get going, ready to get started using our story to help others. The problem was, we were barely a month into our own healing journey. Pain was still a frequent guest in our home. Shame still clouded Chris's eyes and humbled his posture. Tears still streamed down my face on a daily basis. Fear often overwhelmed us when it came to our financial situation and the future that was so unknown. We weren't even near ready to think about helping another couple when we still couldn't tell up from down on most days.

LIE vs. TRUTH

Lie: I want to make a difference, but I don't know if I have what it takes.

Truth: His divine power has given me everything I need for a godly life through my knowledge of Him who called me by his own glory and goodness. (see 2 Peter 1:3)

The reason I saved this chapter for the last section of the book is because it takes the longest to get to this season of helping others with the wisdom we gained through a past pain. When we find ourselves in a rocked state of mind and see our personal world crumbling right in front of us, we feel this urgency to see our lives worthwhile, useful again. So we want to jump right in and help someone, because it does feel good to help others. But when this is done prematurely it can actually hinder your healing process.

Celebrating a New Life

I saw my friends Colby and Megan on their one-year D-Day anniversary. The smile has returned to Megan's beautiful face and Colby no longer looks at me with shame in his eyes. They love each other more deeply right now than they did the first nine years of their marriage. They are more committed to Christ, His church, and studying the Word of God. I said, "You made it! It's been a year. Let today be a day of rejoicing, because one year ago you were in the pit of hell. Today, you are standing tall!"

Even though they are infinitely better, there are still lingering side effects from Colby's choices. They still work on trust and have to deal with triggers. There are still arguments that turn into heated fights, even though neither of them want that. But it just goes with the territory.

Megan has told me that she and Colby wouldn't be where they are without Chris and me. Oh, I so wish they didn't have to know how much they needed us. I wish our friendship didn't get as close as it did this year. Not because we don't adore them. We do. We just wish they hadn't had to start down this road. But they did. And here we are.

They are walking out their redemption story beautifully. They have grown significantly and healed tremendously. I don't doubt for one minute that their time will come. The time when someone they know, their own Colby and Megan, will call them up one Saturday morning and say, "I need to come over now." These two will open their doors. And they will pay it forward.

And you will too. You will take the ashes from your life and allow them to fertilize someone else's. You will offer the shoulder someone needs to lean on during their darkest hour. You will provide godly words of wisdom and comfort because they were once offered to you. But you must heal deeply, build wisely, and live fully before you can invest generously.

TO HELP YOU **INVEST GENEROUSLY**

1. Make a list of some of the good things and bad things you've experienced in your life.

2. Spend some time with the Father and allow Him to show you how He wants to use anything from your past to impact someone else's future.

3. Do you feel that your situation is too fresh? Do you feel it's time to start reaching out? A good indication will be how deep the pain is when you remember that situation. Do you still act out of that pain and make decisions from a place of pain? Then allow yourself to heal.

4. If you feel it's time to begin investing generously, what is your next step? If you feel you need more healing, what do you need to do in order to see your heart healed more deeply?

5. Wherever you are in your healing and wisdom-gathering process, what is a way you can already see God using your season of difficulty? Share some ways that God is not wasting anything He has brought you through.

12

Even If He Does Not

Nicole Knox is the sweetest person I know. Our hearts were instantly knit together in 2002 when we met and she began to care for my oldest son, Noah, who was three years old at the time. Over the years I've watched her blossom from a frightened, insecure young wife and mom who called me many times a day to talk her off the ledge to a bold, confident, and godly one who now encourages others daily. She is not the same person I met all those years ago. It's quite a transformation, I tell you.

But Nicole has had a struggle that few knew about. She battled an illness that often left her confined inside the walls of her home. But the average person who reads her updates on social media would never even have a clue. Those of us who know her, the women she calls her "tribe," do. And to tell you that 10 of us prayed down heaven and earth over this darling girl for years would be like saying Niagara Falls is a nice little waterfall. Like Mount Everest is a nice little hill. Like the wind in Oklahoma is a nice little breeze.

(We don't usually have breezes here in Oklahoma. The wind, oh mercy, the wind; it does indeed come sweeping down the plains.)

This illness that Nicole had was called ulcerative colitis. Without going into much detail, it basically was so bad that she had to be near a bathroom, have a change of clothes on hand, and avoid eating or drinking anything if she wanted to leave her home. Her body basically imprisoned her.

In July 2014 an amazing doctor removed her colon, and she found instant freedom and began a journey of healing. After a couple of months of having a colostomy bag, Nicole had a second surgery to reconstruct a J-Pouch that would allow her the freedom you and I have.

The surgeon said everything went well, and after all the whooping and hollering ended, we whooped and hollered some more. Our girl was fixed, and she would have a life again. She would get to be a great pastor's wife to her husband, Tim, and an incredible mama to her five darling children.

Unfortunately, numerous trips to the ER for dehydration and blood pressure issues over several months took their toll on her body. She has had more testing than a hamster in a chemistry lab. And she and Tim were thrown for another loop with the latest test results and diagnosis: Crohn's disease.

No words.

If this isn't a case for "life is not fair," I don't know what is. I mean, this girl has been through more health-related struggles than you can imagine, including watching her youngest two sons, Judah and Titus, contract bacterial meningitis as infants and get awfully close to death. Through it all, her sweet husband has been by her side as an amazing partner and father, all the while leading the Life.Church campus in Jenks. It's just too much.

Within an hour of learning about the new test results, Nicole told her tribe what God spoke to her while she was praying: "God said, 'Did I not heal Judah and Titus?'"

Bam.

So here we are, standing with her and believing for her healing…again. Although she is a faith-filled woman of God, some days she gets tired and we have to come alongside her and hold her up. That's what a tribe does.

We prayed for her deliverance from this issue. We believed God for her deliverance from this issue. But God did not deliver her from this issue. We are now standing and believing that He will deliver her through this issue. One day soon.

LIE vs. TRUTH

Lie: God leaves us alone in our own messes.

Truth: God is with me, the Mighty Warrior who saves. He takes delight in me; in His love He will no longer rebuke me, but will rejoice over me with singing. (see Zephaniah 3:17)

The Deliverer

Stories like Nicole's don't always make sense to us. You have your own story, I know. We all have a story. Your story could be that you were devoted to your husband and loved him deeply. You supported him and met his needs the best you knew how. But he chose to take another path and leave you and your children for someone else. That's not fair. You did the right things. You loved unconditionally. And yet here you are, experiencing a deep, horrific sadness that you didn't deserve.

You are not alone. I know you may feel that way, but not once has God ever left your side. Even through your doubting, heartbreaking days, He is near to you. His Word says He is.

"The LORD is close to the brokenhearted and saves those who are crushed in spirit" (Psalm 34:18).

God is our Deliverer, even if we can't see proof of that right now. If you don't know Him in this way, there are plenty of opportunities for you to learn more. In Exodus 14 you can read how He delivered the Israelites from the Egyptians by dividing the waters of the Red Sea. In Judges 6–8 you can read how God delivered the Israelites from the Midianites through a guy named Gideon and just a few hundred soldiers. And laced throughout the Gospels of Matthew, Mark, Luke, and John are countless stories showing the miraculous, delivering power of our God: the lame walked, the blind received sight, and the sick were healed.

Oh, our God is a deliverer, all right. *The* Deliverer.

So why doesn't He always do it? Or should I ask, why doesn't He always do it the way I think He should do it? Why doesn't He heal every single time we ask for it?

Because healing Nicole Knox is a no-brainer for me. A total no-brainer. There are so many things I would do if I were God. I would restore every broken marriage, heal every sick child, remove terrorism, and make teenagers listen and obey. (Wait, did I say that out loud?)

> Our job is not to worry about what God will do or what He allows to happen. Our job is to have faith that He is able.

I do ask God why sometimes. And when I start this round of questions with God, He gently reminds me that He sees more than I see, and He knows way more than I will ever know. Even though He has not delivered Nicole yet does not mean He won't deliver her one day.

In order to encourage ourselves, it's wise to stand on the truth that God's Word gives us. It transplants hope into us when our hope tanks are running low.

Into the Fire

Loud, grisly sounds terrified Daniel's family early that morning. Having no idea what the ruckus was, they all eventually got up the nerve and, with trepidation, made their way outside. They were greeted with sights that couldn't be described with mere words, with images that made them bug-eyed and caused their hearts to start pumping blood. Death and destruction were all around them. Blood-curdling screams came from all directions. The sound of horse hooves stomping the life out of people inside their homes, on the streets filled the thick air. Swords were pulled from bodies after the sharp blades took every ounce of life and the corpses were left strewn about this wretched city they once called home. That was what they saw and heard as they tried to make sense of what was happening.

There is no telling how many men came with King Nebuchadnezzar to besiege Jerusalem that day. Enough to take over and destroy an entire city, that's for certain. Once they'd pillaged and captured the City of David and had taken some of the sacred objects from the temple of the Lord to be placed in a house of Nebby's god, they set out for Babylon with their captives.

And God permitted this.

> The Lord delivered Jehoiakim king of Judah into his hand, along with some of the articles from the temple of God. These he carried off to the temple of his god in Babylonia and put in the treasure house of his god. (Daniel 1:2)

See?

Not every life was taken, though. Some were spared only to be used in the king's service in a new city and in a new way of life some 500 miles away. And these captives, these boys were just that—boys, possibly in their early teens. No one really knows. But they weren't men yet, even if they thought they knew more than their parents. (Which I'm sure they did because, clearly, teenagers know more than their parents.)

Daniel, along with his three friends, Hananiah, Mishael, and Azariah, were four of the captives from the tribe of Judah. These four good-looking young men were given new names in hopes it would strip away who they were: Jews to the very core. Newly named

Belteshazzar, Shadrach, Meshach, and Abednego were strong, healthy, well-versed, intelligent, and wise. Had they not been, they wouldn't have been chosen to serve King Nebuchadnezzar. Lucky them.

I wish I understood God. But I just don't. At least not all the time. In fact, on some days I am just winging it based on what my finite mind grasps about the eternal, living, perfect Word of God. And why should I expect to always understand God? I mean, the Bible does say that His ways and thoughts are higher than our ways and thoughts (Isaiah 55:8-9).

But three young Jewish men had no doubts. They knew whom they served, and they did not waver in their belief that their God was absolutely capable and completely willing to step in and show them who was and is and always will be boss. Shadrach, Meshach, and Abednego held true to their beliefs over the years while they were in Babylon. Even though their new leader had a golden image made for the purpose of worship, these boys would not bow down to worship it. Even if it meant death. See for yourself.

> Shadrach, Meshach, and Abednego replied to him, "King Nebuchadnezzar, we do not need to defend ourselves before you in this matter. If we are thrown into the blazing furnace, the God we serve is able to deliver us from it and he will deliver us from Your Majesty's hand. But even if he does not, we want you to know, Your Majesty, that we will not serve your gods or worship the image of gold you have set up." (Daniel 3:16-18)

Bam. Take that, King Nebby. Unfortunately, he didn't take it and instead threw Shadrach, Meshach, and Abednego into a blazing furnace. Not just the furnace with the regular heat, but heat that was seven times hotter. There's no telling what the heat index was in there. Hot enough to make Texans think twice about complaining about their wretched summer temperatures. Once it was hot enough, he had his strongest soldiers come and bind them up and throw them, fully clothed from head to toe, into the furnace.

Trusting His Sovereignty

I long for the kind of faith those three boys had before they were thrown into the fiery furnace. But if I'm being completely honest with you, I don't always have it. But I'm getting there. Maybe 58 percent of the time I have it. The other 42 percent? I'm in a seemingly endless wrestling match with myself and with God, saying, "I believe you *can* do it, God, but *will* you do it?" That's my million-dollar question.

And so I end up fighting this deeply rooted faith within me for fear I might believe too much or too hard or too long for something God is not going to do. Not because He can't. We've established that. He can. He most certainly can. I have not one single, solitary doubt in my mind that my God, our God, is fully capable of doing what He wants to do when He wants to do it and with whom He wants to do it. I do not doubt His ability.

I just wish I understood His sovereignty.

I don't know when God is going to show up and intervene on behalf of someone's financial well-being. But I know He can. I don't know when He is going to heal someone of cancer. But I know He can. I don't know when He is going to step in and break apart a hardened heart for the purpose of marriage restoration. But I know He can. I don't know when He is going to allow the scales to fall from someone's eyes so they will no longer live in deception. But I know He can.

So why doesn't He? Sometimes He does. Sometimes He doesn't.

This is where my wrestling match starts to come full circle. I believe. Then I doubt. Then I remember I don't understand. Then I trust. Then I experience peace.

It goes a little something like this: I believe He can heal my friend's marriage, which actually isn't a marriage anymore because they divorced, but I believe God can shatter through any divorce decree and change things overnight if He so desires. Then I doubt that her husband's heart is going to change because he's so hard-hearted. He has practically turned his back on his faith, and he has decided to gratify his own desires and leave his wife, now ex-wife, and children in the shadows. Then I remember that my ways are so miniscule and God's ways are so gigantic, and what makes sense to me isn't always what is best and part of God's plan because, after all, He did give us freedom of choice. Then I trust that His plan will be accomplished, and He will work out all things for the good of us, but most importantly, for the good of the kingdom of God. And then peace. It rushes into my heart in torrents, like a dam releasing some of its water, like a hurricane coming onto the Atlantic Coast, like a rainstorm pelting the Pacific Northwest.

God's peace. It is indescribable, unexplainable, unfathomable, and incomprehensible. But Friend, you know it when you have it, and you know it when you don't.

God's Deliverance

God didn't deliver Shadrach, Meshach, and Abednego from the fire. They went straight into it.

But wait. When what to Nebby's wondering eyes did appear...four men walking around in the furnace and one of them looked like a god (Daniel 3:25). (Hey, Nebby, it was Jesus. He was protecting them. Just so you know.)

King Nebuchadnezzar was so excited, so overjoyed at this outcome that he got as close to the furnace door as he could and yelled, "Shadrach, Meshach and Abednego, servants of the Most High God, come out! Come here!" (Daniel 3:26). Quite a change in his tune, wouldn't you say?

When they came out of the furnace there wasn't a burn mark on their clothes. There wasn't a single singed hair. And they didn't even smell like smoke. But one thing did burn: the ropes that bound their hands and feet together.

Wait, what?

As Beth Moore says in her Bible study on Daniel, "God didn't deliver them *from* the fire. God delivered them *through* the fire."[10]

That. Will. Preach. Every single day of the week and twice on Sunday.

There are things that hold us imprisoned on this earth. Mindsets, outlooks, ideals, desires, addictions, possessions, expectations, even people. We are imprisoned to what we allow ourselves to be imprisoned by. We have to want freedom. Your counselor can't want it for you. Your spouse can't want it for you. Your mama can't want it for you. You have to want it.

When you finally do want it, get ready to be uncomfortable. The journey to freedom isn't easy. It will be unpleasant for a whole lot of days. You might even feel pathetic. There will be days when your spiritual enemy tries to drench you with shame.

And then one day you will be off of that emotional roller coaster of a journey and you will be walking in wholeness. Instead of being uncomfortable, you will be a person who knows what it's like to choose to rest in the chaos of this world, knowing that while your schedule and to-do list are still incredibly full, just choosing to rest in the presence of Jesus brings peace to your weary soul. Instead of living life burdened by pain, you will be a person who chooses joy over your circumstances, because you will have chosen to use these hard knocks to assist you in stepping up, not letting them keep you down. Instead of feeling pathetic, you will be a person who knows that God shows up in your weaknesses and flexes His spiritual muscles; all you have to do is scoot over and let Him steer. Instead of believing the lie of shame,

> Sometimes we have to go through the fire to be set free from things that hold us in captivity.

you will walk in true humility and brokenness, knowing you don't deserve the generous grace of God that has been lavished upon you. You will choose to deposit that truth into your soul every day, even when you don't feel like it. You will act in faith. And by acting in faith, you will please God.

(I am on a roll, here. Somebody take an offering.)

Through the Fire

Sometimes I'm still in shock that my house actually burned down. The roof was definitely on fire that early morning in June 2013. I've gone through that scenario in my mind dozens of times. What if we'd not done this? What if we'd chosen to do that? What if...? You fill in the blank. Our vision is almost always perfect when looking back at things. It's easy to know what we should have or could have done differently. But you cannot go back and change it. Ever.

I realized through this process of losing a home and all our earthly possessions that God did come through for us. He could have very easily snuffed out the beginning sparks that made our house turn into a blazing inferno. He could have. Without a single thought. He could have spared us from the fire and delivered us from the fire. He did not.

LIE vs. TRUTH

Lie: Our marriage is too wounded and we are too weak to be healed and resurrected.

Truth: Finally, we will be strong in the Lord, and in the strength of his might. (see Ephesians 6:10)

And I don't question Him on that. I did not speak things into existence in six days. I did not create the human body to do what it does so perfectly. I do not know all of the stars by name. I am not Him. So I do not try to be Him. Instead, what I do is try to get to an elevated perspective. Now I can see that while He didn't deliver us from the fire, He did deliver us through the fire. Literally.

I could have been planning a funeral that week. Instead, I was able to have meals with my sons and go on walks with my husband. I could have been begging an insurance company to do what they said they would. Instead, I was finding out about all of the benefits they were offering us that clearly provided for more than we ever dreamed they would. I could have been laden with sadness over lost material possessions. Instead, I rejoiced when our friends Bill and Julie found some of our pictures that weren't completely ruined.

Believing in a Both/And God

Your marriage may be one that God has redeemed. He showed up and both you and your spouse were "all in," willing to do anything and everything to stay together. You now are experiencing more joy than you could have thought possible. It still makes you shake your head that you are even together, considering the rubble that clutters your past.

Or maybe the opposite is true for you. You wanted your marriage to survive from a deep betrayal. You wanted to see God bring back an undying love in your marriage. You wanted to grow old together despite all the junk you've endured. You wanted to allow God to use your experiences to help someone else. But your spouse didn't want that and chose a different path.

So many people think we serve an either/or God. Listen, God is way bigger than our choices and consequences. We shouldn't think that just because our lives don't turn out as we expected or as other people think they should have that there is no future for us. Hello, what about repentance? Doesn't that play a role? Doesn't His grace cover everything?

I prefer to think we serve a both/and God. Yes, God will restore and bless many marriages after betrayal, *and* He will restore your life even if things don't turn out as you hoped. Yes, He works by delivering us from the fire, and He also works in delivering us through the fire. He is a both/and God. Because He is a life-saving, grace-giving, forgiveness-offering, working-it-all-out-for-the-good kind of God.

Resurrected Hope

Never in my wildest dreams did I imagine that Chris and I would be where we are today. The day my husband sat me down on our sofa over 14 years ago, he devastated my heart and killed my hope with his words. During that season, there were days when I could barely lift my head from the pillow, but thankfully God gave me strength to get out of bed. At times, images of my husband's infidelity came flooding into my mind, and then God gave me peace as I took my thoughts captive. For hours at a time, pain bombarded me and suffocated me like a blanket in 100-degree weather, but my God comforted me with the promise of eternity.

He will provide the same for you. *Strength. Peace. Comfort. Hope.*

Now I can't promise He will remove the storms from your life. I can't promise you'll have a comfortable, pain-free existence on this earth. I can't promise you'll get everything you want and dream of.

What I can promise is, when you are weak, He'll be strong. When you think you can't take another step, He'll carry you. When you are in despair, He'll be your hope. We find these truths:

> Even youths grow tired and weary, and young men stumble and fall; but those who hope in the LORD will renew their strength. They will soar on wings like eagles; they will run and not grow weary, they will walk and not be faint. (Isaiah 40:30-31)

Hope in the Lord.
Hope in the Lord.
Hope in the Lord.

TO HELP YOU **INVEST GENEROUSLY**

1. When have you, in the past, felt that God had abandoned you? How did hindsight help you to see the presence of the Deliverer later?

2. If you are currently walking into the fire and feeling the fear of uncertainty, how does the story of Shadrach, Meshach, and Abednego give you courage for your situation?

3. How has your biggest "fire" experience freed you from a belief, behavior, or situation that held you captive in your life or faith?

4. If you are in the middle of the uncomfortable journey to freedom, how can you choose joy in your circumstances right now? What step of faith is God calling you to take?

5. Do you trust your Deliverer? Write down how you need or are experiencing the following from your mighty Deliverer:

   Strength:

   Peace:

   Comfort:

   Hope:

Where Are They Now?:
The Beauty of Rebuilt Marriages

I would love to be able to tell you that every marriage can handle the betrayal that infidelity brings. Not all can. But I have seen couples who have stayed together and now experience a marriage they would never have imagined. They are living the dream! Many have stated that they are thankful for their painful journey because it gave them the marriage they dreamed of.

I've seen other couples walk away and not attempt to walk the road of reconstruction. They felt there was just too much damage to repair. Many others have found happiness with someone else, and others have stayed in a pit of despair. Still other couples have not divorced but are not making any progress due to hard-heartedness or an inability to move on despite their shattered vows.

For a couple to somehow find the strength to rebuild a marriage relationship that has been utterly destroyed is a tall order. The task ahead will seem daunting if the focus is on the difficult weeks, months, and years ahead. But choosing to take steps each day, rejoicing in the small victories, and finding new ways to truly love one another will help you find your way to having a marriage that is beyond your wildest dreams.

In my first book, *Healing Your Marriage When Trust Is Broken*, I shared the stories of several couples. I wrote about those various couples because one story does not fit all. Chris and I have been in their lives and have seen such tremendous growth. If you have not read about their stories, I would encourage you to do so. That way, you will be able to see the progress each couple has made and continues to make.

Brian and Jenni

I've known this couple for about seven years. Jenni and I have the privilege of serving together through Leading and Loving It, a ministry to pastors' wives and to women in ministry. While we don't get to see each other nearly enough, our friendship is deep. We get each other and totally enjoy being together.

I was one of the people Jenni reached out to after her confession to her husband. You see, Jenni was unfaithful and broke her husband's heart. Their marriage obviously hit rock bottom, but through prayer, counseling, and the power of the Holy Spirit, they have emerged stronger. In years past, they were bold enough to share their story on Jenni's personal blog and have been featured on a television show. They have coached many other couples through infidelity recovery by sharing their own story. If you ever get the opportunity to hear from them, you will be blessed.

I asked Jenni about their D-Day and how often they still think about the past. Here's what she said:

> D-Day for us was in February 2009. In the first couple of years after D-Day, we thought about the past quite a bit. It was important. It was a big part of changing our future, and as painful as it was, it was worth every minute of pain to get to healing. We rarely think about

it now. At least not the same way. It's a normal part of our lives now. We don't pretend it didn't happen; it just doesn't own or define who we are today.

Brian and Jenni are also no strangers to triggers and emotions that come on when they remember their past. Jenni said that she still feels regret and sometimes shame, but it just reminds her of how far they've come and how she never wants to be that person again. Thankfully, they always talk when those things come up to remind them of the past. They even said, "Triggers will always be a part of our lives, and it would be silly to think we can move forward without them. It's what keeps us in the tension of health and unhealth."

If you spent any time with Jenni, you'd know she's a total crackup. The girl is silly and loves to have fun and laugh. When I asked her what role humor plays in their marriage, she said that humor was huge! Brian loves to laugh as well. She said, "Life is just too short to just not find the funny." I like that. We have to find the funny because sometimes it's hidden. Brian and Jenni served their time in the darkness and occasionally still have moments there, but they do not have real estate in their past.

It's not easy to share your story publicly, especially if the TV show you aired it on was the Oprah Winfrey Network. But their choice to share their story on television was intentional. They had a go-first attitude because they believe it spurs others on to be real and honest with their own junk.

Hope from Brian and Jenni

I've asked Brian and Jenni many questions over the years. But my final question to them was this: If you could say anything to the person who just found out about his or her spouse being unfaithful, what would you say? They said this:

> Don't do this alone. Reach out…but be selective. Reach out to the people that have your best interest in mind

that *won't* take sides. Talk to people who will love you both. In the end, the one who was unfaithful is still fiercely loved by God. We are all flawed, and though you have every right to be angry and hurt, the end goal is always restoration in our whole being. Do not sin in your anger…and don't sweep it under the rug. Get down on your knees and pray. And ask the people you trust most to pray with you. Once you've done this, schedule a counseling session. None of us has extra money to spend on this…but we spend money on the things that are important to us. This is where it counts. Get a good counselor *right away*. You are not alone. There are so many resources now.

Wade and Christi

Oh, the story of Wade and Christi is an amazing one. What God did to get Christi's attention is one of the most miraculous stories I've ever witnessed. Talk about someone who ran from God. Boy, did she ever. And rightly so. Her wounds were deep and hard to overcome. But God let her know that He had good plans for her and that restoration was possible if she would trust in Him.

Wade and Christi's D-Day happened during the summer of 2008. They told me that there are definitely still triggers that remind them of the past, but they have experienced so much healing that they don't dwell on it. Wade said, "I do feel embarrassed sometimes. It still feels a little bit like an out-of-body experience. As more time goes by, it seems even crazier to me that I allowed it to get as far as it did. I do find it healthy at times to remember the hurt and the pain that I caused as it serves as a deterrent."

Wade and Christi enjoy life together in a rich way and humor plays a huge role. Christi said that one of the first things that attracted her to Wade was his sense of humor. Even after all they have been through, he still keeps them laughing and enjoying life.

Christi often gets asked how she can ever trust Wade again. She often says, "I trust God in Wade." Wade said her response is good accountability for his walk with Christ, and they are very open with one another. Christi said, "Sometimes I feel a sense of panic when I am reminded of the past. The biggest difference for me is that I feel more confident in talking to Wade about how I am feeling. At first if something was bothering me I would hold it in as long as I could. I was nervous that he would just think I'm paranoid or that I don't trust him. Now I know he understands my need to talk things through." They said they know trust will be a work in progress for the rest of their lives, but they do trust each other as they press on together.

Hope from Wade and Christi

Wade and Christi are still on a healing journey. They are fully confident that God will continue to work in their lives as they truly follow Him. When I asked them if they would like to say anything to you, here's what they said:

> We heard a pastor speak about accountability when we lived back in Kansas. He said when his accountability partner would confess to him, he'd say, "I forgive you, God forgives you. Now stop being an idiot and don't do it again." We are going to mess up. We need to confess, and we need to understand we are forgiven. And we need to stop messing up. We strongly encourage everyone to make sure they are seeking the right counsel. Everyone is quick to offer opinions and advice. And there are a lot of non-Christian counselors out there who will give ungodly guidance. It's so important to make sure you are listening to the right voices, to make sure you are in the Word, to make sure you are praying to Jesus regularly.

Kevin and Nicole

This couple is dear to my heart, but they are the only couple I haven't met yet. All of our communication has been mostly through e-mail over the years. But it's amazing how connected you can feel to someone without meeting them. I chalk this up to a kindred spirit between us. And I'm pretty sure you will think they are pretty awesome as well.

Kevin and Nicole's world fell apart on September 29, 2008. They said they don't really think about the past much anymore, even though it took a long time to get to this place. Nicole said, "There are times that it feels so long ago and distant that it doesn't even seem real (but believe me it was!) Perhaps, I've just gone everywhere mentally that a wife can go after receiving such a shock, but I like to think it's because God has taught me the discipline of taking my thoughts captive and allowing Him to heal the broken places."

And heal those places He has. Kevin and Nicole have shared their story many times in the past with other couples, at conferences, at churches and retreats, over the phone, in writing, and at just about any time or place God provides them with the opportunity to tell what He did in their marriage.

Hope from Kevin and Nicole

I know many people have been inspired and given hope by Kevin and Nicole's life. Once they were pit-dwellers, and now they are standing on God's mountain shouting what He did in their lives. And here's what they want to say to you:

> From day one, we were determined that God was going to get the glory in our story and that our new ministry (that clearly no one would ever choose on purpose!) was going to be for couples whose lives have been decimated by pornography and infidelity. Though for quite some time we had to crawl, scratch, and claw our way forward,

we can confidently say that He has restored what the
locusts have eaten, and, beautifully, He has allowed us
to use our story to minister to and breathe hope and life
into other couples who believe that this darkness cannot
be overcome. It can! He has made a way!

Not only can you survive this, but you can thrive in spite of it.
There is hope for you. Real, unending hope. Press in to Jesus, deeper
than you ever have. You can trust God. He is still good. Read that
again: He. Is. Still. Good. Be attentive to His voice, even when it
seems He's far away and isn't listening. (He isn't far away, and He
is listening.) Be tenacious. Pursue healing with a relentless tenacity
that would make grown men shudder (and it will). *Trust the Holy
Spirit to tell you when to fight and push through a tough time and when
to rest and let Him just hold you.* Don't walk this alone. There are people you can trust who will walk alongside you, and there are people
who won't. Be discerning. This is the bottom line: God will make
you more beautiful on the other side of this if you let Him. I promise. More importantly, He promises.

Matt and Andrea

I adore this sweet couple. Of all the couples I've told you about,
this is the only one who lives in our city and attends one of our
Life.Church campuses. While we don't see them often, we still have
the ability to visit with them from time to time. There is such a
sweetness in where they are today. They've been blessed with many
children and are truly enjoying married life together.

February 7, 2009, was their D-Day. At first, they thought about
it daily, as most couples do. And still there are times when Andrea
thinks about it more often than she would like. She tries not to dwell
on it, but sometimes those all-too-familiar feelings emerge and she
has to talk herself through it. Matt said, "When triggers come, it's
a combination of guilt and shame. Not really current guilt, but

remembering the guilt I felt in those days." Andrea said she experiences fear when memories come flooding back. She said:

> Whether it is the sudden triggers that cause it to flood back beyond my control or the triggers that quietly cause me to doubt for a longer period of time, it's always fear that takes root. The brief heart-catching triggers I don't talk about with him. They're too brief, and it's such a blatant attack I don't address it. But it's the ones that lock in for a few days that I always bring up and talk through. Several years ago Matt made it mandatory that I bring it up because it had torn me up significantly trying to handle it alone. So that's what I do.

Chris and I have spent time with many, many couples over the years. Some have experienced infidelity, and some have not. And out of all of them, Matt and Andrea are one of the healthiest couples we know.

Hope from Matt and Andrea

Matt and Andrea have been through the fire, and there is not a smell of smoke on them. I know their final words will bless you:

> We want to tell couples we know how they are feeling and we understand. We also want to tell them that God can, will, and wants to do something amazing in your lives through this situation. God can bring a closeness you never knew existed out of the pain you are feeling right now. It's a hard road to walk down. But as the road is traveled, the life it leads you to is more than you can ever imagine. God can and will work all things together for good for those that love Him and are called according to His purpose (Romans 8:28). He can take that pain, guilt, shame, and feelings of betrayal and turn those feelings into a love and closeness that only He can bring.

Where Are You Now?

I'm not sure what part of the healing journey you are on in your marriage. Maybe your wound is recent, and just remembering or mentioning anything about it still cuts you deeply. Or perhaps you've been walking this road for months or even years. Regardless of your location on this path, you are on this path. Good job, my friend.

Marriage is difficult even when we don't break our marriage vows. It takes a daily dying to self on both parts to see a marriage succeed. But not everyone is willing to do that. If I've said it once, I've truly said it a thousand times: I can't want it for someone. Nor can you.

But you're here, and if you are still reading this far into the book, bravo. That says something about where you are, where you want to go, and where you'll end up. People don't typically read marriage books until they have to. So maybe you're one of the have-tos. What would really be awesome is if people would make investments into their marriage before tragedy strikes. Wouldn't that be better?

So where are *you* now? Are you doing well and finding great joy in your marriage? Have you hit a bump in the road and feel stuck? Do you even wonder if you can attempt to come back from such betrayal?

Well, I'd like to offer you some hope. Hope from a girl who spent her fair share of time in the pit of despair. Hope from a girl who begged God to take her life, even though she would be orphaning her son. Hope from a girl who had no idea who she was after her whole life and ministry was abruptly taken away from her. It's that kind of hope that you think doesn't exist, but it really does. The hope that is Jesus.

I guess what I'm trying to say is, coming back from the proverbial grave, which is where I felt like I was for a season, is possible. With Christ, all things are. He will be your comfort when your heart is fractured. He will be your counselor when you need guidance. He will be your joy when yours is depleted. He will be your guide when you can't see the path. He will be your defense when the arrows are flying. He will be your foundation when things are shaky.

Basically, He will be your everything. And that's exactly what He should always be.

Acknowledgments

Harvest House Publishers and LaRae Weikert, you have been so good to me from the moment my first book, *Healing Your Marriage When Trust Is Broken*, was pitched. I always call myself a no-namer in the author world, but you treat me like I'm a *New York Times* best seller. Thank you for believing in me.

Jana Burson, you took a risk representing me. Had you not, I don't know if this book would have happened. You tirelessly edited my proposal, more than once, and went to bat for me. I appreciate you more than you know. #bestagentever

Hope Lyda, what can I even say to the best editor on earth? When you suggest ideas and edit my work, I heed it. Your brilliance with the written word astounds me. You are equally encouraging and motivating, especially when I'm on the home stretch. I want to be like you when I grow up.

Craig and Amy Groeschel, it has been and continues to be the greatest honor of our lives to serve under your leadership. Life.Church will forever be special to us because we experienced our darkest hour here as well as the highest heights. Thank you for making it easy to follow you. I love you both!

Ali Bergin, you prayed me through these 60,000 words, week in and week out. Receiving a text message from you each and every Monday asking "What can I pray for this week?" was without fail so good for my soul. Thank you for believing in me and being my friend for 14 years. I love you!

To my friends who helped me navigate God's Word more thoroughly: Natalie Witcher, Kim Heinecke, Jennifer Edmunson, Amy Newberry, Markey Motsinger, and Ryan Motsinger…you all know your stuff, and I'm truly grateful.

My three sons, you bring me never-ending laughter and unexplainable joy. There was no book to explain the love I would feel as a mother.

You each have a distinct personality that so uniquely fits our family. You boys have outdone yourselves! I would not trade anything. Well, maybe the incessant messy rooms and frequent passing of gas. Other than that, I'll take all of it. I love you so much!

Chris, I am absolutely smitten with you. You are the love of my life, my co-laborer in the ministry, and my best friend. It feels like just yesterday we got married, and yet here we are 23 years later still going strong with hardly a hiccup in the road (#please). Thank you for believing in me, for your opinion matters most. I love this life we live together.

My Jesus. My answer is always *yes*. Regardless of the pain. Thank You for choosing me.

About the Author

Cindy Beall is a writer, speaker, and mentor to leaders. She has been married to her husband, Chris, since 1993, and they have spent most of their marriage in full-time ministry. Chris and Cindy spend obscene amounts of time on their back porch and also love working out together. They have three sons between them, which means there is very little pink in their home, but there is a plethora of airsoft guns and camouflage.

Cindy's husband, Chris, serves as the Oklahoma City campus pastor at Life.Church and also oversees half of the Oklahoma City metro Life.Church campuses. In addition to serving with her husband, Cindy is the director of Equip on the Leading and Loving It team that ministers to pastors' wives and to women in ministry. Her first book, *Healing Your Marriage When Trust Is Broken*, released in 2011 with Harvest House Publishers.

For booking information, please visit Cindy's website at www.cindybeall.com.

Notes

Chapter 5

1. Gary Chapman, *The 5 Love Languages* (Chicago: Northfield, 2004).

Chapter 6

2. Dr. Phil McGraw, "Dr. Phil's Ten Life Laws," Dr. Phil, http://drphil.com/articles/article/44.

3. Judith Orloff, MD, "Strategies to Deal with a Victim Mentality," *Psychology Today*, https://www.psychologytoday.com/blog/emotional-freedom/201210/strategies-deal-victim-mentality.

Chapter 7

4. Neil T. Anderson, *The Bondage Breaker®* (Eugene, Oregon: Harvest House, 2000), 43-44. Used by permission.

5. Anderson, *The Bondage Breaker*, 43-45. Used by permission.

Chapter 8

6. Luke Gilkerson, "Get the Latest Pornography Statistics." Covenant Eyes, http://www.covenanteyes.com/2013/02/19/pornography-statistics.

Chapter 9

7. Craig Groeschel, "From This Day Forward" (Life.Church, August 2012).

Chapter 10

8. The Source of Abundant Joy," March 7, 2015, http://utmost.org/the-source-of-abundant-joy/.

Chapter 11

9. http://www.project31.us/.

Chapter 12

10. Beth Moore, *Daniel: Lives of Integrity, Words of Prophecy* (Nashville: LifeWay Press, 2006), 46–66.

How to Believe in Restoration

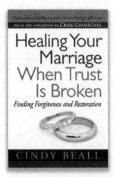

A few days after an ordinary Valentine's Day, Cindy Beall's life changed forever. She listened with disbelief to her husband, Chris, a respected pastor, as he confessed to pornography addiction, numerous affairs, and to the startling news that a woman was pregnant with his child.

With raw honesty and intimate knowledge of pain and of God's power to resurrect something new out of the debris of betrayal, Cindy reveals how to:

- seek guidance, counseling, and prayer support when deceptions surface
- help your family heal from the grief and humiliation
- rebuild trust after porn, sex, and other addictions undermine a relationship
- protect your marriage from lies and unfaithfulness
- rely on God to pursue forgiveness and move forward in new promises

Cindy's compassion, grasp of God's Word, and the Bealls' remarkable story will help you trust God with your broken heart and follow His leading, hope, and redemption.

Foreword by Craig Groeschel, best-selling author and senior pastor of Life.Church.

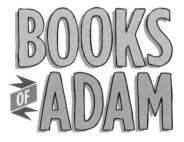

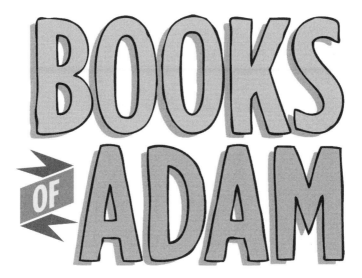

THE BLUNDER YEARS

ADAM ELLIS

GRAND CENTRAL
PUBLISHING

NEW YORK   BOSTON

Grand Central Publishing
Hachette Book Group
237 Park Avenue
New York, NY 10017

HachetteBookGroup.com

Printed in the United States of America

RRD-C

First Edition: July 2013
10 9 8 7 6 5 4 3 2 1

Grand Central Publishing is a division of Hachette Book Group, Inc. The Grand Central Publishing name and logo is a trademark of Hachette Book Group, Inc.

The Hachette Speakers Bureau provides a wide range of authors for speaking events. To find out more, go to www.hachettespeakersbureau.com or call (866) 376-6591.

The publisher is not responsible for websites (or their content) that are not owned by the publisher.

LCCN: 2013938335
ISBN: 978-1-455-51698-8

For Kristin and Trevor:
I couldn't choose just one, and I hope this inspires you both
to fight for my approval.

CONTENTS

THE ART OF MOVING ON

I wasn't paying attention when Zoe started explaining her project to the class. It was mid-April and the weather was strangely warm for Boston. School was the last thing on my mind, especially since I was set to graduate in a few weeks. The students were gathered in one of the stuffy ground-floor art rooms, fidgety and restless as each person presented their final undertakings. Over the past hour the quality of the work had been steadily declining, since the kids with the most impressive projects had all volunteered to go first. Prior to Zoe, a moody guy with floppy hair covering half his face had discussed his "work": several pieces of dirty cardboard that he'd pinned to the wall.

The signs and his subsequent explanation received a warm enough response from the professor and the class, but by the time he was finished I'd mostly checked out, content instead to stare out the window and watch a bag lady with a single giant dreadlock rummage through a trash can. *She's probably looking for her cardboard sign*, I thought.

When I'd arrived at college, I couldn't wait to join a community bursting at the seams with artists like myself. But four years in art school had inspired a degree of apathy in me, at least regarding certain facets of the art world. Perhaps I'd simply grown tired of my professors responding so positively to what I deemed to be total bullshit. Several weeks before, a student had spilled paint on a white sheet, then ridden his skateboard back and forth through the mess, and the response from the school's faculty had been alarmingly favorable. I'd overheard one teacher in the hall saying, "This is going to be huge. They'll be knocking down his door after this piece goes public." I didn't know who "they" were, but by that point I'd accepted the possibility that maybe I just didn't have my finger on the pulse of the art world. While I'd always received positive feedback on my own work, my stuff was more illustrative and usually humorous, and even if my professors never said so outright, the general attitude toward illustration and cartooning at my school seemed to be that it was a lesser art. This was disheartening, if not outright insulting, as I'd always taken my work seriously, even when it was silly or absurd.

The kid with the signs unpinned them from the wall, crammed them into his messenger bag, and Zoe was called on to present her final piece for critique. Out of the corner of my eye I noticed her set something on a rickety metal stool. Her explanation was brief and matter-of-fact, and at first I wasn't sure I'd heard her right.

"I put a condom on the Virgin Mary," she said flatly.

Her words took a moment to sink in. I turned my attention toward the front of the room. Sitting on the stool next to Zoe was, in fact, a cheap plastic figurine of the Virgin Mary—the kind you'd find at a dollar store—and it was sheathed in a latex condom. I wasn't sure if she was serious or if it was just a prank. It seemed she'd spent all of forty seconds slapping it together. I glanced at her face for a sign that she was joking, but found none.

Nobody spoke. I assumed it was because everyone was as baffled as I, but I couldn't be sure, as everyone's face held a similarly blank expression. The professor kindly asked Zoe to explain the piece.

3

"Well, like, it's meant to be a criticism of the Virgin myth and a commentary on the absurdity of divine impregnation." Zoe shifted her weight a bit and cocked her head, as if she didn't quite believe herself. I sort of got the idea, and might've even put some stock in the concept, but what it boiled down to was that Zoe had crammed a tacky figurine into a condom and called it a day. I'd seen this kind of thing a hundred times before. Freshman year, the kid across the hall from me had made a mural out of Cheerios and Froot Loops, and we were all pretty sure he'd forgotten about the project entirely and scrambled to make something from materials in his dorm room in the hour before class. That sort of behavior was understandable for a new student, but this was supposed to be the culmination of a semester's worth of work by a senior. It was supposed to have taken a week to complete at the very least. I expected the professor to tear Zoe a new one for wasting everyone's time, but instead she clutched her chunky stone necklace and gushed about it.

THIS IS BRILLIANT! SO DEEP!! SO BRAVE!

"Tampon in a teacup..." I whispered to myself, though apparently louder than I'd realized, because it caught the attention of the professor.

"Adam, do you have anything you want to add about Zoe's piece?"

"Oh, uh, no," I stammered, "I was just saying, uh…there's this movie, and a girl puts a tampon in a teacup as a commentary about the expectations society places on women, or something. This just, uh, reminded me of that. I guess." The movie I was referring to was *Ghost World*, and the tampon-in-a-teacup sculpture is meant to be ridiculous and pretentious. I was sure I was about to be outed as the class jerk, but nobody seemed to get the reference.

"It's almost, like, defiant in a way," said one girl, her head tilted thoughtfully at the figurine. Other students murmured in agreement, someone else adding, "Yeah, it's kind of daring." I rolled my eyes. The professor added a few marks in her grade book, and then it was my turn to share. For a moment I considered leaving class and taking a failing grade on the project. My work was far less conceptual, and I feared a backlash. I pinned several paintings to the wall and turned to face the class.

Since Netflix had recently been inexplicably suggesting shows from my childhood, I'd been on a '90s cartoon kick for a few weeks. I had started painting characters from the shows as a sort of warm-up, but then a larger idea had developed. For my final project I'd decided to paint characters from *Captain Planet*, but in an art nouveau style, in an attempt to juxtapose art in the 1890s with animated media in the 1990s. "Well, I feel that art nouveau has become homogenized and mundane to the point of every dorm room having a reproduction of *Tournée du Chat Noir avec Rodolphe Salis*, or some reprinted vintage perfume ad," I explained. "So I've taken that notion and drawn parallels with how kids' cartoons in the nineties degraded into little more than half-hour commercials designed to sell toys." I had worked hard and thought my final project was rad, but my professor wasn't so sure. She grilled me about my paintings.

"I wonder about the relevance these works have in the grand scheme of things," she told me. "I think you need time to let your talents gestate. Cartoons might not be the best subject matter for you." She turned back to the class.

She had missed the point of my project. Behind her, through the window, I noticed that the bag lady with the giant dreadlock had taken her boob out and was holding it in one hand while she yelled at a bicycle. I wondered if I was living in a less crazy world than she was. I imagined that if the homeless lady had been standing indoors instead of out, she would have been considered a creative genius by my professor.

As I stood on the subway platform waiting for the Green Line train after class, I tried my best to feel anger about my professor's comments on my artwork, but the truth was I couldn't muster anything. I'd grown jaded, and the complacency I felt scared me. For the first time in years, I was worried about my future, and it wasn't because my professor hadn't responded positively to my paintings. I'd learned years ago to not take critiques personally, and I had no real desire to make a living displaying my work in galleries anyway. But the fact that the skateboard/paint piece and the prophylactic Virgin Mary were considered successes made me question my chosen field. I'd always been hopeful that I could incorporate my creativity into a more standard job–like scenario—Cake decorating! Painting children's faces at the county fair!—but now that I was thinking about it seriously I realized my options as an artist might not be as plentiful as I'd fantasized. For a split second, I toyed with the idea of grad school, but I was weary of being in school and felt eager to embark on a new chapter of my life. I was sick of Boston too, with its subzero winters and Red Sox fans charging the streets with their faces made up in red and white. Up until this point, I hadn't given a lot of thought to what I'd do after college. Most of my friends were staying in Boston or migrating south to New York, and I had planned to do the same, hoping to find a job in one place or the other. But on that platform, I suddenly knew I needed a drastic change of scenery.

That night in my room, I started plotting my escape. I turned to the back of an old geography textbook and scanned over a map of the United States: I wanted to go far away. The West Coast seemed like the logical leap, but where to? Southern California was out (earthquakes!), as was Seattle (I refuse to live in the same city as Sir Mix-a-Lot). I briefly considered Hawaii, but that fantasy faded when I remembered that they have giant cockroaches and none of their Taco Bells are open twenty-four hours, which I personally believe should be classified as a crime against humanity. San Francisco was too expensive, British Columbia was too cold. I wanted to be in a larger city, so the only remaining option was Portland, Oregon—a city that I had never, up until that moment, given a passing thought to. I grabbed my computer and powered it up. When I Googled "Portland, Oregon" pictures of food carts, lush green parks, and crystal blue skies popped up on my screen. *They got pretty trees*, I mused. I imagined Portland shining like a beacon, beckoning to me from a distant horizon. I pictured myself growing a giant beard and trading in all my existing clothes for soft, comfy flannel. And just like that, I was Portland-bound.

THE CHOCOLATE MILK
INCIDENT

About a week before graduation, I found myself riding the college's shuttle bus, which chartered students to and from the different campuses located in Cambridge and Boston. Usually I refrained from riding the shuttle because it was primarily used by rambunctious freshmen, and riding around with them made me feel like a field trip chaperone. Worse, the shuttle was decrepit and seemed to lack any sort of shock absorbers. It wasn't unusual to see students bouncing a few feet into the air when the vehicle crossed especially rough terrain. On this particular day, I'd just wrapped up a meeting with my adviser and was forced to utilize the shuttle since it was free. Earlier that morning, I'd crammed my backpack into my locker in a hurry, forgetting to grab my wallet before I left for my meeting. I had a habit of procrastinating and scrambling to be on time, and being flustered made me forgetful. Likewise, I'd been so busy trying to tie up loose ends before the close of the school year that I'd forgotten to eat anything all day, and sitting on the shuttle, I realized I was ravenous. I'd gone from being merely hungry to feeling shaky and light-headed in a matter of minutes, and I felt that if I didn't get food in me soon my stomach might start consuming itself. *This must have been how Karen Carpenter felt*, I thought as I gazed out the window.

I sank into the scratchy, faded fabric of my seat and closed my eyes, imagining crispy, golden chicken nuggets falling from the sky like big deep-fried raindrops. I could almost taste them. I was devising a mental list of food I'd devour when I got to the cafeteria when I heard a loud *bang* that sounded like a gunshot and felt the shuttle lurch to the right. The driver cursed and quickly parked. He pulled out his cell phone.

"*Mi llanta se explotó!*" he barked into his phone. I don't speak Spanish, but I didn't need a translator to tell me what *explotó* meant. We'd obviously blown a tire. A few moments later, the driver hung up and notified the passengers of what we already knew. "Everybody off!" he instructed, motioning for us to exit the vehicle and wait on the sidewalk. We did so, grumbling. "New shuttle soon. Half hour," the driver shouted.

I immediately began to panic. Perhaps my blood sugar was dropping too low and clouding my judgment, but I felt like I didn't have time to wait around for a new shuttle. I needed food. I broke away from the group and made my way down the street, keeping an eye out for a deli or a food cart, or even some discarded takeout in a trash can. In my soft suburban upbringing, I'd never experienced real hunger, and it made me nervous to feel so jittery and dizzy. Fortunately I found a supermarket only a couple of blocks away. In my heightened awareness, the blue-and-yellow neon sign seemed to pulsate with vibrancy, more colorful than I remembered. Once inside and overwhelmed at my food prospects, I wandered through the aisles, searching for something cheap and easily edible— anything that might hold me over until I could get a proper meal. I started taking inventory: Hot Pockets would have to be microwaved, and everything at the deli's hot bar had crusted over under the heat lamps. But there was so much else to choose from. I was starting to feel relief at the plethora of food I saw when it dawned on me: I didn't have my wallet.

Even if I chose something to eat, I wouldn't be able to pay for it.

Well, that's it, I thought. *This supermarket shall be my final resting place. I found Rome built of brick ... I leave her clothed in marble.*

Certain death was close at hand, so I considered my options. I thought about my friend Agnes, whose favorite pastime was shoplifting, and how she'd never been caught. In fact I'd watched her blatantly leave clothing stores, her coat bulging with pilfered goods, and nobody had ever lifted a finger to stop her.

I decided that if Agnes had always been so flippant about it and had never suffered any repercussions, I could get away with it too. Something small, I thought, would surely go unnoticed. Who would I be hurting? The giant chain grocery store? They wouldn't miss anything. They probably wouldn't even notice. Besides, it was a life-and-death situation. I walked the aisles a bit longer, searching for the right item.

It didn't take me long to find something suitable.

Chocolate milk! Protein and sugar. *Perfect*. I lifted a bottle off the shelf and hesitated, unsure of what I was about to do. The only other thing I'd stolen in my life was a couch from the Harvard student lounge, and that was in the middle of the night and under the influence of *at least* nine beers. This, I figured, would be easier.

The intense hunger I felt acted as its own sort of drug.

Almost involuntarily, I reached for the bottle with trembling fingers that hardly seemed like my own. Quietly and discreetly, I sheathed the bottle of chocolate milk in my jacket's front inside pocket. It fit perfectly, as if the jacket were designed for this sole purpose.

As I walked toward the giant exit sign at the front of the store, I felt like there was a spotlight on me. I maneuvered as casually as I could, swinging my arms, hyper-aware of my movements, like a robot learning to walk for the first time.

I made it to the door without detection and was just reaching to push it open when I felt a firm hand on my shoulder.
Alarmed, I spun around, and my heart sank. A scruffy-looking
guy, short and somewhat disheveled, stood behind me holding
a tiny, silver badge.

His badge was smaller than any I'd seen a policeman carry,
so I assumed he was just a security guard. For a brief moment

I considered making a break for it, but in my weakened state I wouldn't have made it far. I knew I had no alternative but to face the music. My best friend in high school had once gotten out of a trespassing fine by crying, but that wasn't an option for me. (I've only cried twice in my life, and both times occurred while watching *Homeward Bound*.)

The security guard instructed me to follow him and led me into a tiny back room with a little metal table and a wall of television monitors. Already my mind was racing with thoughts of exorbitant fines and possible jail time. *They'll make an example out of me*, I thought. *I'm headed for the big house. I'll*

never survive, I'm too soft! Oh God, my eyebrows will grow back together! I envisioned my future incarceration, complete with orange jumpsuit and prison tattoos, my heart sinking lower and lower.

"ID please," the guard instructed, but since I didn't have my wallet I had to give him my information verbally and it didn't even occur to me to lie. He copied my answers onto a cream-colored form attached to a clipboard. When he asked me where I lived I gave him my local address in Cambridge, but told him I was graduating soon and wouldn't be living there much longer. He made a note of it. "So young man, why were you stealing chocolate milk?"

19

"I was starving, and I don't have any money," I said. I paused and added, "Just like Aladdin." He gave me a look of absolute pity and wrote down a few more scribbly lines. He then set his clipboard on the table, and I braced myself for punishment. Instead he told me I could leave, but added a final warning for good measure.

YOU CAN COME BACK INTO THE STORE...

BUT NOT FOR THE REST OF THE DAY!

Trembling slightly, I rose from the table and left the store, shamed but relieved. I felt like I'd dodged a bullet, though in reality I was probably just one of many shoplifters the security guard had caught that day. I'd missed the shuttle back to campus and had to walk, but somehow I no longer felt as hungry as before.

I graduated a few weeks later, moved out of my house in Cambridge, and returned home to Montana for the summer before making my move to Portland. I only had a few weeks there, but the days passed like any other vacation spent at home. I lounged around in the basement and zoned out on junky television. I'd put the shoplifting episode behind me, eager to start the adventure that would be my life in Oregon.

I was sleeping late one afternoon when I awoke with a start to my mother shrieking my name in the furious tone of voice I'd heard only once before as a teenager when I'd accidentally left the stove on for an entire weekend. I shot out of bed with a start, and emerged from my room half-asleep and very confused. My mother stood in the kitchen holding a piece of paper and a newly opened envelope. She was clearly livid.

The grocery store I'd stolen from hadn't quite forgotten the incident as I'd hoped. They had sent a damages bill to my apartment in Massachusetts to the tune of two hundred dollars. It had arrived after I'd moved out, and since they'd received

21

no payment, they'd escalated the bill to *five* hundred dollars. My school had finally forwarded it to the only other address they had on file: my mother's home in Montana. She, unfortunately, had been the first to receive the mail that day. She frequently opened my school mail since it was usually about tuition and my loans were under her name. This was obviously not the kind of letter she was expecting to open.

"What the hell did you steal that cost five hundred dollars?" she roared, outraged that she had raised a thief.

"Nothing!" I croaked, "I mean, I tried to steal chocolate milk, but only because I was about to *die*! I was just hungry, I swear!" For a moment it seemed like she didn't believe me, but when my embarrassed, guilty expression made it clear that I was in fact telling the truth, her face rendered the same look of pity I'd received from the security guard.

"This is ridiculous, Adam. What is wrong with you?" She set the bill down on the counter and picked up the telephone, then dialed the number of the grocery store. "Yeah, hi," she said into the receiver a few moments later. "We just received a bill for five hundred dollars, for *chocolate milk* ... Adam Ellis ... Yes ... Yes, I understand it's for shoplifting, but five hundred bucks is bullshit ... I don't care, it's *bullshit* ... Yeah, we're not paying that. How much does chocolate milk cost in your store? ... Mmhmm ... Okay, then we'll send a check for $1.49 ... Okay, great. Goodbye." She set the receiver down and glowered at me. I felt like a child, not like a newly graduated twenty-two-year-old ready to start a grown-up life.

"I would've paid it ..." I said meekly. I would have too, and I'm sure my mother knew that, but I think she was secretly thrilled at the opportunity to argue with someone in retail. After all, this was the woman who once convinced Target to accept a return on boots she'd purchased at Payless. Still, I could tell she was disappointed in me, and I was embarrassed for myself. Not a month into my post-college life and I'd already done something idiotic. Worse, my mother had bailed me out of the situation. What a wonderful start to my adult existence.

CITY LIVIN'

When I was a teenager, I had a list. It was a loose, ever-changing inventory of features my future home had to have, and since I was young, it was rightfully insane. My prospective living space (a Dubai high-rise, or maybe a Tokyo loft) had to feature hardwood floors supplied from endangered Peruvian forests, modern enameled lava countertops, floor-to-ceiling windows overlooking panoramic views of whatever gleaming cityscape I'd decided to call home, plus a service elevator that opened into my cavernous living room. I figured by the time I was twenty-five I'd somehow be a millionaire and able to afford every expensive thing I saw on television or read about in a magazine.

When I graduated college, I had naught to my name but a thousand dollars in the bank and a 1994 Nissan Altima. I'd had enough of the East Coast for a while, and besides, I'd never be able to afford rent in New York or Boston's nicer areas. As for Tokyo, I'd seen enough bizarre Japanese commercials on the

Internet to nullify any desire to become an expatriate, though that was most likely an excuse to avoid learning a foreign language. Still, a small part of me clung desperately to the hope that someday, somehow, I'd magically come to live in the kind of apartment that only existed in '90s sitcoms. I moved to Portland in part because it was so much cheaper than other cities, and I felt it wasn't such a wild notion to expect at least *some* of my fantasy features to come to fruition, despite barely having the funds for an IKEA desk, let alone a gold-plated Jacuzzi or one of those giant room-dividing aquariums that I could fill with piranhas. I kept my chin up, dreams of extravagance burning brightly in my heart.

I had little time to orient myself in Portland at first. I slept on a friend's floor for a couple of days while I called around and checked out apartments. Because time was short, I had to choose the first livable place I could find. I didn't really care, though. Portland was shiny and new. The air smelled cleaner, the streets miraculously clear of Dunkin' Donuts wrappers, and everyone seemed almost too friendly not to be on some sort of upper. Maybe they were all intoxicated on the fresh summer breeze. It was easy to see why. Portland was beautiful.

My first apartment was far from impressive, but I viewed it as a sort of starter home. It was entirely basic: a square living room connected to a similarly shaped bedroom. It was bland, but over the next few weeks I filled it with furniture and covered the walls with posters and photographs until it felt more like a home. I forgave most of its faults because it felt so thrilling to be on my own. It was located just off Hawthorne in Southeast Portland, a hip neighborhood full of vintage houses and coffee shops. It was close to a multitude of bars and restaurants, so I overlooked the fact that half of its outlets didn't work and there was a large mysterious stain on the living room carpet. I forgave the fact that the water was sometimes brown, and I tolerated the management, who seemed indifferent to the safety of the tenants.

On my first afternoon in the apartment, I was startled by the unit's former tenants unlocking my front door from the outside and stepping partway into my living room before realizing the place was occupied. I had barely unpacked all my stuff, and I was already experiencing my first break-in of sorts.

Apparently the building's owners hadn't bothered to demand the keys back from the past occupants. Since I was hidden behind the door and out of the couple's view, they didn't see me and quickly closed the door. The whole encounter, if you could even call it that, lasted no more than a few seconds, but I stood there for what seemed like an hour feeling baffled and unsafe. I have no idea what they'd come for, and I never saw them again. As I listened to them hurry away, I wondered how many other people in the city might have keys to my apartment. I made a mental note to buy a Taser and get the locks changed, and continued suckling my Popsicle. The incident left me feeling a bit violated, but I rationalized it to be an honest mistake on the part of the former tenants.

Over the next several months I heard talk of a few robberies in the building and became increasingly suspicious that my downstairs neighbor might be a drug dealer. And yet none of this bothered me as much as it probably should have. This was my first home that wasn't subsidized by my college or ruled by my mother, who had a tendency to paint everything in the house taupe. I was thrilled to feel independent. It was comforting to know that if I was robbed or murdered in my apartment, the newspaper article would read, "Local Man Dies at the Hands of Coked-Up Thieves," and not "Student Dies."

It wasn't until the complex became infested with cockroaches that I decided my time in the building had to end. I may be perfectly willing to live in constant fear of robberies and meth lab explosions, but I won't put up with bugs. Bugs are icky. I noticed a single cockroach one night while doing dishes, and had it been a viable option, I would've packed up everything on the spot.

Adult Apartment Number Two was a step in the right direction, allowing me to hold on to the delusion of someday living large. Though it was nothing like the spacious fantasy apartments I dreamed of as a teenager, it was surprisingly equipped given what I could afford. I'd stumbled upon it by chance while wandering through a Northwest neighborhood I'd never been to before. It was a corner unit on the top floor and had those desirable hardwood floors, plus exposed brick in the living room *and* the bedroom. Brick walls always felt romantic and bohemian to me (though I'd later learn that brick just means "lots of places for spiders to live"). It seemed that this apartment was worth a lot more than what the management was renting it for, which should have made me suspicious.

During my tour of the place, the landlady explained that in the spring she'd lost a dozen or so college-aged tenants who had graduated, and since she was having trouble filling the vacancies, she'd dropped the price. This made sense to me. She described the building as a hotel from the 1920s that had been shut down in the '30s, reopened as apartments in the '60s, and renovated in the '80s. My brain translated this to "former brothel, probably haunted by ghost hookers." I was sold. When I was growing up, a girl down the street had claimed her attic was haunted by an Indian chief, and I had always been jealous of her. I couldn't wait to have a haunted house of my own.

I only had enough cash to rent a U-Haul for one day, so the move was marred by stress, sweat, and ugly frustration. I had a friend help me, and frankly I'm surprised the move didn't ruin our friendship forever; hauling a couch up six flights of stairs is enough to break even the strongest bond. I told myself

I'd stay in that apartment for years and wouldn't have to lug furniture up narrow staircases again until I was thirty. Plus the giddy anticipation of ghost hookers kept me strong and focused.

I expected at least one slutty poltergeist to show up in the apartment, but I had no such luck. No mysteriously disappearing valuables, no faint whiffs of stagnant rosewater, no soft wailings traveling up and down the hallways. (Still, I never truly gave up on the possibility of my apartment being haunted, and I like to believe the ghosts and I just never got the scheduling right for a proper haunting.)

Before signing the lease on my new place, I'd had to do a fair amount of internal convincing since the apartment was slightly out of my price range, but once I made up my mind to splurge on rent, I settled into the apartment like cake batter being poured into a pan. I loved it instantly and completely. It felt like home in a way my childhood house never did, because I'd found it on my own and I was in charge of it. If I wanted to decorate it with animal skulls I bought off eBay, I could—and I did. I rationalized the pricey rent by telling myself it would even out in the long run if I bought smaller Americanos every morning and didn't eat out as much. I'd opted for cable television in my old apartment, but I forwent the luxury in my new place because I was already overspending. It didn't matter to me. As with any first love, I made excuses to be happy. And I *was* happy. I was deliriously happy in that apartment, and even when things started to spiral downhill, I continued to convince myself that this building was the place I'd live forever.

Winter came, and with it arrived the first little annoyances. The building was old and poorly insulated, and though Portland winters are not fierce, the winds can be biting and the chill finds its way through windowsills and cracks in the walls. One brisk night it snowed (as it does once or twice a year in Portland), and the next morning I awoke shivering. My fingers and toes felt numb and my eyeballs ached dully in my skull, barely shielded behind my eyelids. I recalled chilly January nights walking home from the pubs in Boston, and curled up into a ball. My bedroom felt as arctic as it looked outside my window. Disgruntled, I wrapped myself up in my blanket, trudged out of bed, and made my way into the living room to inspect the radiator. I twisted the icy black nozzle, but nothing happened. I kicked it and still nothing. I thought, *Maybe it takes a while to initiate after the weather gets colder. Maybe the heat hasn't been activated yet.* I waited patiently for a week, but still my radiator lay dormant. Eventually, I was able to see my breath in my own living room.

I notified my landlady of the issue, and she assured me it would be fixed. She seemed unfazed by my complaint. "Sometimes it takes a while for the heat to get going. I'm sure it'll kick in later tonight. You'll know when the heat's starting up, since the pipes rattle a bit."

My landlady saying the pipes "rattle" was like calling North Korea "bashful." I awoke that night at 3 a.m. to such a ruckus,

I thought an airplane jet engine had crashed through my roof like that early scene in *Donnie Darko*.

A quick scan of my darkened room revealed no sign of demon rabbits or other horror-movie characters, and in my half-awake confusion I briefly hoped the racket might be all those ghost hookers finally making their presence known. When I realized it was just the building's pipes coming alive, I was understandably disappointed.

Despite the heating issues, I still felt like I'd lucked out in finding that apartment. From that point forward, I decided to keep the heat turned off—the noise just wasn't worth it. I spent the winter months wrapped up in blankets, and I wore extra socks and fingerless gloves, bundled up like a survivor of some post-apocalyptic nuclear ice age. I took lots of hot baths to thaw my frozen limbs and brewed tea several times a day to warm my insides. It didn't matter that I was becoming a one-man rendition of *Grey Gardens*. The apartment was a freezing hovel, but it was *my* freezing hovel. Sometimes I'd forgo heat for weeks at a time, but I stayed put, steadfast and defiant to my apartment's faults. I swore I'd never leave.

Winter passed and the heating concern became a memory, though new problems arose in its place. The building was just off Burnside, a busy street that acts as a main artery through the body of the city. Not far away was a homeless shelter, and at night the homeless folks would disperse and wander up and down Burnside, often congregating on the sidewalk outside my building. This had never bothered me, but one morning I noticed a flyer in the lobby window that made me uneasy.

DON'T LET THIS WOMAN INSIDE. SHE DOESN'T LIVE HERE. DON'T LET HER IN.

DON'T.

I soon learned from another tenant that whoever this woman was, she'd been idling about in the lobby waiting for someone with a key to open the door; then she'd slip in behind them and just sort of hang out. She'd amble about the halls and mumble to herself until someone kicked her out, only to return a few days later for a repeat performance. She'd never go into any apartments, and nothing had gone missing, save for the flowers in the lobby once or twice. For some reason she insisted on returning time after time, and it had become enough of a problem that management had put up flyers in an effort to keep her out. It caused a shroud of uneasiness to fall upon the tenants.

The intruder woman eventually ceased her visits, but less than a week later a haggard-looking man was discovered in the basement rummaging through someone's freshly dried laundry. He refused to leave and became vocally aggressive, so the police were called. A couple of tenants demanded a doorman be hired to combat intruders, but management refused, citing the cost. I shrugged off the intruder scare, figuring I'd rather put up with trespassers than pay higher rent to cover the cost of a doorman. Not everyone in the building was so forgiving, and both my upstairs and downstairs neighbors fled, prompting a shift in the type of tenants inhabiting the building.

The upstairs unit was the first to be reoccupied. A pair of elderly Russian immigrants moved in, and though I saw the man only twice and never his wife, I garnered enough information about them simply by listening to their arguments through my paper-thin ceiling. They screamed at each other from morning to night, with no real anger, but with the weary frustration I assume results from eating nothing but cabbage soup for sixty years. They had no television that I could tell, but listened instead to an old tinny radio at maximum volume throughout the day while they argued. Because I am a product of the American schooling system, my knowledge of other countries and cultures hovers somewhere between *zero* and *Britain's Got Talent*, and as such I crafted a crude depiction of my upstairs neighbors that resembled something akin to Boris and Natasha from *The Rocky and Bullwinkle Show*.

When the apartment below me was filled, the result was far less tolerable than my upstairs neighbors' constant Slavic shrieking (which was actually somewhat therapeutic to listen to—almost like an angrier, atonal Enya). My new downstairs neighbor was a girl about my age who, I learned, worked as a florist. From what I could tell from first appearances, I liked her. She wore a lot of long flowy dresses, and her hair was always the perfect amount of tousled. She had a penchant for bulky jewelry. She was quiet and seemed like a nice neighbor to have until a couple of weeks after she moved in, when her boyfriend joined her. I found myself trapped in the elevator with him on a few occasions, and each time was galling. He wore the same hoodie *every day*. He described things as "faggy." He had a tribal tattoo that looked like his buddy did it for free in a garage, all jagged edges and jerky linework. One morning he didn't say anything, just farted in the elevator and laughed to himself. He'd complain to me (or rather *at* me, as I did my best not to engage him) about the homeless people milling about our block, grumbling about how they were always in the way and "smelled like garbage." He was insufferable, but I would've dealt with it fine if it weren't for the music he blasted from his girlfriend's apartment all day long while she was at work. He blared an endless stream of Black Eyed Peas, David Guetta, and LMFAO, like a playlist created by Satan himself. I was working from home during this time doing freelance design work, a reluctant subject to his musical predilections, and I knew if I ever asked him to keep his music down he'd probably only crank it louder. I prayed regularly for his girlfriend to dump him or for him to find a job, but months passed and I eventually learned the lyrics to every Black Eyed Peas song in existence.

After several months of this, I'd had it. Eager to avoid confrontation and bordering on a manic, Peas-induced hysteria, I did the only thing I could think of: I drafted an anonymous, threatening note with cut-out magazine letters. I've always been nonconfrontational, but I was desperate. I feared speaking to the guy face-to-face might lead to my corpse being zipped up in a body bag, so I took the passive-aggressive route instead. I sliced tiny letters out of my back issues of *Portland Monthly* and methodically glued them to a piece of paper.

Ignoring the fact that such a letter could easily be construed as criminal harassment, I folded it up in an envelope and prepared to drop it in my neighbor's mailbox the next day. It was the perfect crime, I thought, since the letter could've come from anyone in the building. I felt calm wash over me, knowing the ordeal would soon be resolved. But that night the girl downstairs had an explosive fight with her boyfriend, which rendered any future action on my part moot. I'd just come home from dinner with a friend and the fight was already in progress, but what I heard was more than enough to make sense of what was going down.

"...in our bed!" the girl was screaming. "Not even our bed, *my* bed. My bed! It's brand-new! That bed was from CRATE. AND. BARREL. And now it's ruined!"

"Baby, come on, you're overreacting!" I heard the guy say.

"Shut up, Jared! I can *never* sleep in that bed again! It's covered in slut germs now!"

"Come on, let's talk about this! I'm not even gonna see her again."

"You're not gonna see me again either, that's for sure! Get out!" This was followed by the sounds of objects being thrown, ceramic pieces shattering against walls, maybe a mirror breaking, then a door slamming, followed by silence. Several days later the apartment was vacated entirely, assumedly because the "slut germs" had made the air unbreathable and the apartment unlivable.

I felt like I'd weathered a storm, having survived breakins, arguments, and unbearably loud music. I thought that I'd come out victorious, and was still entertaining the idea that I'd stay in the building until I died when my landlady raised the rent. It was a standard hike and entirely reasonable, but suddenly the apartment was just too expensive for me. The extra hundred dollars a month made my new rent firmly outside my price range, and just like that I fell out of love with the place.

I packed up and moved.

CREEPY FRIENDS

Making friends in a new city is tough. It only takes a few clicks on the Internet to find a new apartment or a new job, but if you troll through the classified ads looking for new friends, you're likely to end up murdered or cannibalized. Or worse, trapped in a knitting circle with a lonely girl who collects kitty stickers.

They say it gets more and more difficult to make friends as you get older, and I was determined to prove this notion wrong in Portland. At the very least I hoped to be the exception to the rule. That said, I was at a loss for how exactly to make new friends, short of standing on a street corner with a big sign that read FRIENDS PLEASE. So, for a brief time when I first arrived in Oregon, I routinely forced myself to attend every social gathering I could find. I went to a couple of art openings before realizing I wasn't ready to analyze and discuss art so soon after graduating. I went to a vodka launch and decided professional boozers might not make the most reliable friends. I felt ready to give up on the prospect of friendship altogether, but after some prodding from a friend back in Boston, I decided to give it a final shot and enrolled in a pottery class. I figured at worst I'd come out of the endeavor with a new ceramic vase to store my ashes in when I inevitably died a lonely loser.

I don't remember what led me to think a pottery class was a smart idea, since my knowledge of ceramics was limited to high school textbooks featuring illustrations of natives making ceremonial bowls, and perhaps that one scene in *Ghost* where Demi Moore gets molested by a spectral Patrick Swayze. Perhaps it was this last idea that led me to the class, considering my fondness for ghosts. Of course with my luck, I'd probably encounter a decidedly less seductive ghost-predator. Muammar Gaddafi, maybe. Or Bea Arthur.

Unsurprisingly, pottery wasn't my forte and I struggled through the first lesson, creating lopsided pots, lopsided vases, and my specialty: lopsided mounds of nothing. The class was supposed to be four sessions long, but I decided this would be my first and last pottery lesson, since my lack of talent would surely not win anybody over. I decided to politely withdraw from the class. Oprah says you should turn your wounds into wisdom, and I came out of that class with the wisdom that pottery is stupid and I hate it.

After my surrender, as I stood waiting at the bus stop, two kids around my age walked up to me. I recognized them from the class.

"Pottery's kinda dumb, huh?" one of them said offhandedly. He was a tall redheaded guy with freckles and a sort of floppy Mohawk. A girl stood next to him, similarly freckled but with a darker shade of auburn hair. I figured they might be siblings, but they very well could have been dating, or married, or members of a ginger cult.

"Yeah," I agreed. "I'm not very good at it. I just wanted to make a nicer vessel to store my drugs, but I guess I'll keep using a hollowed-out box set of *Alf.*"

They laughed at my joke and introduced themselves as Harrison and April. *This is it!* I thought. *You're making friends, Adam. Don't blow it, kid. Keep your cool!* We made small talk for a while longer. My bus appeared in the distance and I began to panic. It seemed to approach at a snail's pace, crawling toward me ominously. I could feel time slipping away and, with it, the potential of newfound friendship. I was considering intentionally missing my bus so I could stay and talk more when Harrison said, "April and I are going hiking. You should come with us if you're not doing anything."

"Yes." I said automatically and robotically. "Let's go. *Yes.*" Like a puppy, I followed them away from the bus stop to where their hatchback was parked and climbed into the backseat. The car was clean and organized, but it smelled a little odd. There was a faint but familiar odor that I couldn't quite put my finger on. I tried not to dwell on it because really, whose car is perfectly clean? The ensuing ride might've lasted twenty minutes or ten hours; I was too entrenched in the *awesome friendship* that was blossoming in front of me to notice where we were headed or how long it took to get there. When we arrived at their house, we were in a part of Portland I'd never seen before: some grungy suburb that wouldn't be out of place in a Harmony Korine movie. Their house was a shabby hovel decorated lov-

ingly with uncollected garbage and discarded bits of furniture. I noticed a few broken appliances leaning against the side of the house, which seemed to be sinking slightly on one side. I passed by a homemade wind chime dangling from their hovel-porch that should've sent my spider-sense into-overdrive.

Sun-bleached skulls hanging from the roof should be a fairly obvious red flag, but since I have minimal common sense as it is and a penchant for decorating my own digs with morbid items, I ignored the first in a series of glaring warning signs that day. April offered me a drink and I obliged. I took a seat on their front steps, Harrison following suit. April stepped inside and emerged a few minutes later with a mason jar full of amber liquid. I assumed it was iced tea, but I wasn't sure. I was raised on a steady influx of SunnyD and purple Kool-Aid, so I'm not sure I'd recognize iced tea if I drank it. It could've been anything, really, but I was so excited at the prospect of my new friends that I didn't think twice about it.

I sat there for a time chatting with the possibly incestuous ginger cult siblings. It was a sunny, cloudless day, and in the cooling breeze I found them accessible and genial. I learned that April had heart palpitations and had a spent a number of years in a back brace. I discovered Harrison once got stung in the butthole by a jellyfish. And yet I somehow neglected to glean whether or not they were related. When I mentioned I'd recently graduated from art school, April chimed in.

"I did a semester at Pacific Northwest College of Art," she said. "I was gonna major in video but, y'know, shit's expensive."

"Yeah, shit's so expensive," I agreed, happy to have some common ground with my new friends.

Harrison kicked a golf ball-size rock loose from the dirt with his foot and suggested we get a move on. I'd almost forgotten there was a hike planned. April momentarily disappeared around the side of the house and returned with a backpack and something zipped up in a large, semicircular nylon case. I didn't know what it was, but I didn't think much of it. We set off behind their house, following a bike path that led into some trees, and soon we were surrounded by foliage. Before long we deviated from the path and the trees grew thicker. Sunlight weaved through the branches and I was struck by how lovely it was, realizing how long it'd been since I'd experienced nature. The concrete grayness of Boston had never offered much in the way of natural wonder. After a while we came upon a clearing and I glimpsed a rabbit in the distance grazing on clover. The only thing that passes for wildlife in Boston is the rats that feast on discarded pizza crusts, so I was struck by the novelty of seeing an actual rabbit. It looked impossibly soft. Its little nose twitched as it chewed. I pointed it out to Harrison and April, but they'd already taken notice. Without a word April handed the nylon case she was carrying to Harrison, and he quietly unzipped it. When I saw what was inside, my heart skipped a beat. It was a bow. An expensive bow. The kind with which one *kills adorable bunnies*.

My mouth agape, I watched silently as Harrison readied an arrow in the bow, aiming ahead into the clearing.

He let the arrow fly. It was clear he had done this before. The arrow hit its mark, and there was a sudden spray of crimson as the rabbit was taken down.

"Nice shot," I muttered, bewildered, eyes wide, unsure of what else to say. Immediately I realized why their car had smelled funny. I'd smelled that same odor only a couple of times in my life, once as a kid when my neighbor had butchered a deer

in his driveway, and once when my friend's mother had worked in a butcher shop for a summer. The car had smelled faintly of death. Harrison lowered his bow. He and April headed in the direction of the rabbit. I observed them, alarmed, racking my mind for some prior mention of this being a hunting trip. I couldn't recall either of my new friends mentioning *murder* being on the agenda. I suddenly felt unsafe.

"That's a nice one," April said to Harrison with a sly smile. "He'll be tasty."

Of course you're going to eat it, I thought. *And afterward I bet you'll make jewelry from its feet and eyeballs, you creeps.* My faith in these new friends was shifting. And yet there was another side of me that was curious to see what they'd cook, because *actually* rabbit *is* pretty tasty . . . and all I had to eat at my apartment was a moldy lime and an expired Lean Cuisine pizza. *Maybe I'm judging them too soon*, I thought. *Maybe it's admirable that they hunt their own food. Back to the land, and whatnot.* On the trek back to the car I tried to hide my unease.

What I thought would be a quaint hiking excursion had taken a dark turn, but I couldn't decide if I was overreacting. I'd grown up in Montana, where hunting is common, but I'd never experienced it outright, save for that one instance of seeing a deer carcass hanging in my neighbor's garage, blood draining from it and trickling down the driveway. I remained as chipper as possible on the ride back to the house, the limp bunny carcass still warm, resting on the seat next to me.

Back at their house, April and Harrison immediately set to work planning dinner. Their kitchen was small and cluttered with pots and pans, cooking utensils, and more spice jars than I thought possible. It had the permanent savory smell of a kitchen that sees regular activity. April nonchalantly rattled off ingredients she planned to include in a rabbit stew and asked if there was anything I was averse to eating. *Besides Thumper?* I thought. I mumbled that whatever she cooked was fine, paying minimal attention to her. I had my eye on Harrison. He'd taken a small knife from the backpack and was turning the rabbit over in his hands. The bunny flopped about limply. It barely resembled the animal I had seen grazing serenely before. I flinched as he made a few cuts into it. He motioned to April, and she joined him. They fumbled a bit with the rabbit, each grabbing a different end, and with a skilled, practiced motion ripped the fur clean off the animal.

RIIIIIP

I was immediately light-headed. My mouth felt dry. I'm not sure I would've been able to speak if I'd wanted to, and yet I still couldn't determine if this was normal behavior or not. Surely this rabbit met a more humane end than the chickens used to make my Boneless Barbecue Chicken Blaster Bites, so who was I to object? I concluded I was being overly sensitive.

Dazed, I continued to watch Harrison work. With the knife he made another calculated cut into the rabbit, and its guts suddenly spilled forth, seemingly in slow motion, glistening like diamonds in the afternoon sun.

I was thoroughly grossed out. *Stop being a wimp*, I told myself. *The Native Americans used every part of the buffalo. I bet buffalo guts are way bigger than rabbit guts.* I tried to picture how large buffalo guts might actually be, and that notion led my brain on a tangent about that scene in *Star Wars* where Luke sleeps inside a tauntaun to keep warm. I would've digressed completely into a pop-culture spiral of nonsense were it not for April's voice snapping me back to reality.

"All right, let's get dinner ready!" she announced, nonchalantly wiping a bit of blood on her pants. Harrison and I sat at the kitchen table while April hacked away at things

53

on the countertop, throwing chunks of vegetables and bits of herbs into a pot. I palavered with Harrison, not knowing what else to do; all the while in my peripheral vision I could see April breaking down the rabbit into pieces until it no longer resembled an animal at all. I could hear the crunching of rabbit parts, and somehow, I still clung to the hope that these people might just turn out to be the best friends I'd ever known.

Dinner was served on faded plates that could have been hand-me-downs or purchased from Goodwill. We drank out of mismatched glasses; mine was a Weight Watchers mug.

The stew was delicious—rich, hearty, and with a depth of flavor I'd never be able to match on my own, though I couldn't get over the fact that the food I was eating had been hopping through a meadow earlier that day.

This might have been a turning point for future vegetarianism, had I dwelled on it. I made a loose connection between the animal on my plate and the pets I'd cared for in the past, but April's cooking was so good that by the time I'd finished eating, I'd decided that if she cooked the Taco Bell dog in a casserole, I'd gladly devour it.

I helped clear the table, my faith in Harrison and April somewhat recovered, but I looked forward to getting home. I still had little bits of dried clay under my nails and I needed to unwind. I wanted to scrub the ceramic dust from my fingertips and wash the image of glistening bunny innards from my brain. I was about to thank Harrison and April for dinner and make my exit when Harrison cut me off.

"April, you should show Adam your video before he leaves!" he exclaimed, displaying a level of enthusiasm I hadn't yet seen in him.

I was momentarily confused, but then I recalled April mentioning her art school film. I blanked on viable excuses to leave, so I shrugged and agreed to watch it with them. I situated myself on their slouching, faded green couch, and April selected a nondescript DVD from a nearby shelf. My distress over the day's events had given way to general ennui at this point, but truth be told, graceful exits were never my strong suit. In high school I worked in a toy store and sprained my ankle one day on the job, but limped around for three hours until my shift was over because I couldn't think of an eloquent way to tell my boss I needed to go to the hospital.

April poked the power button on the television and it came to life. She popped the disc, labeled "Final Project," into the DVD tray. She clicked a few buttons on the TV, then took a seat on the couch with Harrison and me. The film opened with a close-up shot of a pair of freckly breasts, and to be perfectly honest I expected nothing less. Tits are de rigueur for art school students. What happened next, however, was somewhat unexpected.

Off screen, someone began tossing baby carrots at the exposed breasts. They bounced off the girl's chest, making her boobs jiggle ever so slightly.

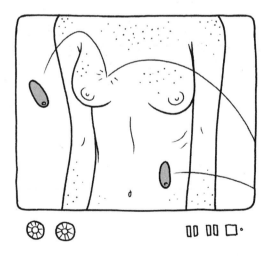

The camera panned back, and April was revealed to be the owner of said breasts. She was seated in a wheelchair. She wore a diaper. The word vegetable was scrawled across her forehead.

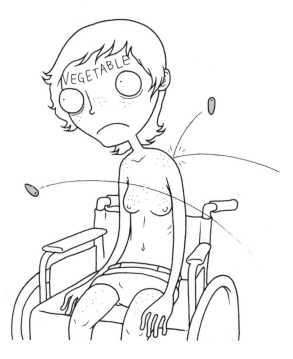

Okay, I thought. *Carrots are a vegetable. And she's supposed to be, like, a human vegetable or something? It's sort of conceptual. I get it. It's stupid, but whatever, I get it.* The film continued for six or so minutes in this fashion, with various other small foods being tossed from somewhere out of frame. Wedged between April and Harrison, I wondered how long this nonsense was to continue, but I feigned interest in the video to be polite.

On screen, the camera rotated slowly and aimlessly around April. I desperately hoped the film would end soon. I was trying to formulate an excuse to leave when April did something unexpected. Quietly and discreetly, she put her hand on my knee.

April's hand rested there for a moment, gentle and motionless. Neither of us said anything. I couldn't fathom why April felt this was a suitable time to put the moves on me, but I wasn't sure how to delicately avoid the situation. I have a tendency to freeze up in awkward situations. One time in middle school I accidentally walked in on the deaf janitor pooping, and I stood there in the doorway of the stall for *way too long*. He hadn't seen me, so I stayed there frozen until I could snap back to reality and quietly exit the scene. I sat on the couch now, inert, willing April to move her hand away. I felt dizzy. Beneath me the couch seemed to sway slightly, like a canoe on the water. I opened my mouth to speak, and that's when Harrison put *his* hand on my other knee.

"I HAVE TO GO," I blurted suddenly. The notion of a tactful exit was a lost cause. I leapt up from the couch and scrambled to find my jacket before realizing I'd never had a jacket. I halted briefly at the door and artlessly added, "Dinner was ... great, thanks." I left before they had time to formulate a response.

Outside, I glided past the creepy wind chime and across their cluttered lawn. On the sidewalk, I brought up bus schedules on my phone and calculated a route home using the GPS application. I took no heed of the neighborhood I was in, focused only on getting away. I stared at my phone like a treasure map, following the little blue line on my screen to safety.

As I walked to the bus stop, thoughts cluttered my mind. *Friends are overrated*, I told myself. *I don't even need friends! I'll just get a chinchilla, and it'll be my best friend, and I'll never eat it.*

WORLD'S BEST BOSS

In high school my friend Dylan said something to me that changed my life. We'd gone to a smoothie place on our lunch break, and when I attempted to order a medium smoothie, Dylan said, "Just get a large. It's only a dollar more. If you're gonna spend four dollars on a smoothie, you might as well spend five and get a large." When Dylan said that, I felt like I'd been blessed with wise counsel from Confucius himself. His words rang so true to me. Since I was already spending too much money on pulverized fruit, why not go for broke? For the rest of the afternoon during calculus I suckled contently at my oversize peach smoothie, peaceful and serene, oblivious to the world's problems. I believe I came away with something greater than tiresome math facts that day, and that was a newly adopted adage for life. That simple concept of indulgence would stick with me, and I would go on to apply it to every aspect of my adult life. Whenever possible, I upgrade.

I treat myself. I find a way to convince myself that I deserve it, even when I don't. As a result, I always live beyond my means.

In Boston, it was easy to live large. Housing and food were paid for, so I was able to spend my funds on whatever I wanted. Eight-disc-at-a-time Netflix membership? Why not? Top-shelf vodka every Saturday night? Certainly! When I moved to Portland I figured I'd be able to keep up my extravagant ways. I assumed I'd immediately land a killer job as something vague and creative, like "image consultant" or "emotional architect," unaware that Portland was already bursting at the seams with unemployed, entitled youths. I believed I'd send out a few cleverly designed resumes, be hired immediately, and proceed to live a baller lifestyle, like a skinny, white Soulja Boy.

Such was not the case. At first, I applied for jobs with an unwavering can-do attitude, tailoring resumes for job specificity and carefully crafting cover letters to email prospective employers. Sadly, it soon became clear that I was essentially sending resumes into the void. Not one of my applications was replied to. Somewhere around month four of my job search, I began to suspect that my expectations had been flawed, and I started to worry. Why wasn't my phone abuzz with messages from employers looking to hire a fine arts graduate with no adult work experience? In twelve weeks I'd only received one callback, and it turned out to be a mix-up. They'd meant to call a German girl named Ada Ellis. Disheartened, I sank into a mild depression.

My joblessness wasn't for a lack of trying. In addition to the countless resumes I emailed, I estimate I printed a metric ton of hardcopy resumes and hoofed them around town to anyone who I thought might take one. I gave up the notion of job-related pride. I begged restaurants and coffee shops to keep one on file, even though they weren't hiring. I handed out copies to video store managers six years younger than me. I wouldn't be surprised if my job hunt alone caused the annihilation of every forest in the Pacific Northwest.

Weeks passed and my checking account declined steadily. I put my student loans on hold. I sold my car because I couldn't keep up with the payments. I started using coupons at the grocery store, donning huge sunglasses and a fake mustache so nobody would recognize me. Every night on my way home from an unsuccessful job search, I'd pass the Taco Bell on my block, more and more aware that my future might involve a career in fast food.

My mom would call me on the phone and ask how I was doing, and I'd always tell her "fine," though I was anything but. At night I'd lie awake, terrified of what would happen if I couldn't find a job and all my money ran out. I had no other option, no fallback plan. Moving home to Montana wasn't an alternative I was willing to consider. I'd rather sleep on the streets and eat garbage. I'd made the decision to move to Portland and I had to make it work. It just *had* to work. I had too much pride to admit failure and move home, and even then I don't think my mother would have allowed it. I felt a similar disillusionment with adulthood to the one I'd felt after my years in art school. *I bet that Zoe chick is making millions off her condom-covered Virgin Mary figurines*, I thought. But I couldn't give up. There was no alternative battle plan. There was no tactical withdrawal.

When I finally landed an interview at a bookstore, it only proved I had more to worry about than simply getting callbacks from employers. Apparently my interview skills had atrophied and died. I arrived to the interview on time wearing my most professional outfit. But I was so nervous that when the interviewer asked what the last great book I read was, I froze up. Suddenly I couldn't remember a single book I'd ever read. I sputtered a nonsense answer about "reading so much it's hard to decide," and then stared at the interviewer awkwardly until he moved onto the next question. The saddest part is that I really do read constantly. I could've talked about being swept up in the haunting tragedy of *The Brief Wondrous Life of Oscar Wao*, or how *Kavalier & Clay* was so achingly beautiful I didn't know what to do with myself after finishing it—as if nothing else really seemed important anymore—but instead I gave some Palin-esque response about liking everything. I might as well have responded with, "What's a book?" and flicked a booger at the interviewer's face. Needless to say, I didn't land that job.

I was down to ninety-seven dollars in my checking account when I finally found work, and ironically it wasn't a job I'd even applied for. It was an overcast Tuesday afternoon when my phone rang with a number I didn't recognize. A woman named Patricia introduced herself and asked me if I'd be interested in a paid internship at her interior design and staging company. She told me that she'd stumbled upon my website and figured I might be a good fit.

"I need someone to design promotional materials and stuff," she explained casually. "Brochures and the like. Maybe someone to do social media crap. Can you use Twitter? I'm terrible with the computer."

I wondered if she could hear through the phone the giant tears of relief splashing onto my unwashed hoodie.

The next day I met Patricia for an interview. She was a well-dressed woman of about forty, prim and poised, though to call her attire dated would be putting it softly. She looked like she should be bossing around copywriters at a 1980s fashion magazine with a name like *Belles Ordures* or *Quite!* Her hair was large and unmoving, probably hair-sprayed within inches of its life. She wore a mauve pantsuit with shoulder pads and gaudy gold jewelry. Scanning the resume I'd brought, she asked which computer programs I was familiar with and if I could use Adobe InDesign. I lied and said yes, figuring I could learn it later if

I needed to. She set my resume aside and gave me a brief run-down of what I could expect from the job. Then she sipped on her latte for twenty minutes and talked about her cat, Evita. I listened contently, happy to even be considered for what was in all honesty a lifesaving opportunity. I had no idea what made me stand out in her mind, but by the time her coffee was empty, she'd offered me the position. I couldn't help but be thrilled. She told me her business was small and that I'd be doing mostly menial tasks, but I didn't mind. I'd be working in my field, more or less.

Patricia ran her business out of her home, and I started work the next week. My first morning, Patricia sat me down to dis-cuss my salary. It wasn't much, but it was enough for me to live on for a while. In the months that followed I figured out that Patricia was completely forgetful and disorganized as a rule. Oftentimes I'd benefit from her absentmindedness, but just as frequently it created problems, and I quickly became the company's Swiss Army Knife, solving dilemmas left and right. One day I'd spend three hours on the phone with the printers over a mix-up with a typo on a flyer, and the next I'd have to sync Patricia's email on her cell because she'd some-how reset the device back to factory specs for the fifth time. Besides Patricia, there were only a couple of other people at the company, and they mostly dealt with deliveries, so the bulk of the problems fell to me. I made sure never to complain about the mountain of odd jobs dumped on my lap, as I still felt the position was a godsend. For the most part I stayed on top of things, but Patricia was constantly flustered, all the time. I'd walk into her office with some paperwork or a design issue, and she'd almost always be screaming at someone on the phone. She never sounded angry, just batty and stressed, like a tornado of polyester blazers and tarnished costume jewelry. Still, I found her amusing and was happy to help her. For all her yelling, she never screamed at me, and the fact that she'd employed me at such a difficult time endeared her to me, nutty as she was.

Although Patricia had been in business for a decade, I frequently wondered how the company stayed afloat. She seemed to be eternally out of touch. I once accepted a delivery for fifteen rolls of sea-foam-colored wallpaper accented with big pink flowers. It was hideous, and I couldn't imagine anyone using it. Patricia told me she was staging a beach house in Depoe Bay, and I thought, *Is it a beach house for Scott Baio?*

Are you traveling back in time to 1986? I figured her aesthetic catered to a specific clientele, so I kept my mouth shut. In the end the wallpaper must have been rejected by whichever client it was intended for because it sat slumped in the corner of Patricia's office for the rest of my time there.

Patricia seemed to be trapped in a bit of a time warp herself. I wondered how she kept her hair so eternally motionless and if she had to get blazers with shoulder pads specially made. I pictured her hunched in front of *Designing Women* reruns, brow furrowed, jotting down fashion tips onto a ledger. Whatever the case may have been, Patricia's idiosyncrasies seemed to work for her so I went about my business and she went

about hers. Eventually we fell into a routine where I could come into work and field various problems on my own. Some days Patricia and I never even crossed paths. When we did it was usually because Patricia had a task for me to do that she considered urgent but that didn't make much sense.

I'd been working for Patricia for about three months when I came into her office one morning and found that she had turned off all the lights in the room and was peering out the window cautiously. As I ventured toward her, she flapped her hand at me and made a shushing noise. "Uh, why's it so dark in here, Patty?" I asked.

Without turning toward me, she said, "I may or may not have a home business license. The homeowners association is trying to oust me." I stood in the doorway for a moment longer, then gingerly set some forms on Patricia's desk.

"Okay, well, I'm going to go work on the Rosier account," I said and turned to leave.

"Wait!" Patricia whispered, smoothing one side of her concrete hairdo. "If anyone comes up to you outside and tries to talk to you, just say you're visiting a family member. No! Say you don't speak English. Can you speak German? Aren't you German?"

"Um, I think my great-grandmother was?" I replied. "I mean, I don't *speak* German..." I started inching toward the door slowly. "I'm gonna get to work..." Patricia didn't turn around.

As the months rolled on, Patricia's expectations of me seemed to change. She became less and less concerned with the quality of my work and instead seemed to view me as a friend she paid to hang around her house. She'd routinely call me into her office to discuss what had happened on *Desperate Housewives* the night before, seemingly unconcerned that I had no idea who the Housewives were or why they were so Desperate. When she started demanding I take care of her cat while she made phone calls, I began to question my future at the company.

It dawned on me that working in someone else's home office might be a slippery slope. I pictured myself years down the road, sitting on the couch next to Patricia, both of us in matching terry-cloth robes, our hair in similar pink curlers, with

Evita stretching out on the cushions between us. Despite this alarming prospect, I stayed on.

One afternoon a few weeks later, there was a knock at the front door. We weren't expecting any deliveries that day, so I was immediately cautious, expecting to see the homeowners association with torches and pitchforks. I opened the door with trepidation and was instead bombarded by a couple of chipper, rosy-cheeked missionaries. Dressed in identical black slacks and crisp, pressed white shirts, they greeted me with such cloying earnestness I almost felt assaulted.

The missionaries began their standard speech, asking kindly if they could tell me about The Jesus. Though it would've been perfectly acceptable for me to decline, I told them I'd be happy to listen. For the most part, I find it impossible to say no, usually out of fear of offending someone. In college, while roaming a satellite building looking for a seminar on printmaking, I accidentally stumbled upon an Alcoholics Anonymous meeting and unknowingly joined it, and didn't leave until the session was over. I was afraid if I got up and left, someone would call me out on it, so I stayed and listened for the entire hour, occasionally nodding to let them know that *yes, I got it.*

While I half listened to the missionaries inform me about angels and stuff, Patricia appeared behind me in the hallway.

Seeing that I was in need of saving, she devised what I'm sure she thought was a clever way of getting rid of the visitors.

The missionaries had seemed very pleased at being heard, so when I saw their expressions falter at Patricia's words, I felt a mild pang of guilt. The missionary who'd been speaking trailed off midsentence, his eyes shifting to the grinning woman behind me. His smile remained steadfast, if a little more strained than before. A few moments of silence passed, and then the other one said, "Have a blessed day," and as quickly as they had appeared they were gone. Behind me, Patricia chuckled. I knew she was joking, but I'd already become a willing ear for television gossip and the caretaker of her cat. I wondered if it was such a leap to suspect one day she might walk into my work space wearing nothing but oversize brass earrings and gold pumps. I tried to push it out of my mind, but at that moment I began to wonder about other job opportunities.

Four or five weeks after the missionary incident, I learned through a series of misguided emails that Patricia was being sued by two clients, and was in trouble with the government for withholding taxes. Before realizing I wasn't meant to be on that particular email thread, I'd gleaned that Patricia was clearly at fault regarding at least one of the lawsuits, and that she was in hot water with the tax issue.

She was a total flake of a boss, and she'd possibly sexually harassed me on a couple of occasions—albeit a gentle sort of harassment (I'm sure it would never have reached *Nine to Five* levels of inappropriateness)—but still, I liked Patricia, and was grateful that she had rescued me from unemployment. It pained me to know that I'd have to start formulating my departure. The troubles at the company were nothing I could help with, and probably nothing Patricia herself could circumvent in the long run. I knew I had to get off the ship before it went down. I couldn't ride that one out. I had to bounce.

When I crept into Patricia's office a few days later with a quitting speech memorized in my head, I expected her to be angry or hurt. I told her I'd need to put in my two weeks' notice, telling her that my time had come to "explore alternate paths in my career," whatever that meant. I figured it was best to keep things vague and polite. Patricia appeared to understand what I was getting at.

"You've been a huge help," she said sweetly. "I'll miss you, and if you ever need anything, let me know." Her response surprised me. I suppose people quit jobs all the time under perfectly friendly circumstances, but this was my first experience in voluntary termination. Every time somebody quits a job in the movies, there's yelling and fighting and possibly a gun involved. I didn't know how this sort of thing went down in real life. My only other real job was in high school working the phones for a company that installed and maintained pools. I was supposed to field simple questions like, "How much chlorine do I add to my pool?" I regularly screwed up my math while answering questions and might've caused a few schoolchildren to get chlorine poisoning. I was fired from that job after a couple of months.

My final weeks passed by quickly. I cataloged and filed with all my heart, trying to prepare Patricia as best I could for my exit.

One day during my last week I came into work to find the house oddly quiet. Patricia, who would normally be jabbering on her phone already, was silent, and the living room TV, usually fixed on the *Today* show, was cold and dark. It felt sort of lonely, but I shrugged it off and unpacked my laptop and got to work on the last bit of lingering paperwork I had left.

I heard Patricia come up the stairs around ten. She bypassed the room I was working in and walked down the hall to the bathroom, where I heard the shower turn on. Something wasn't right. The water ran for about fifteen minutes, then stopped, and a few minutes later I heard a blow dryer. Finally I heard Patricia emerge and make her way back down the hall. This time, she noticed me working in the spare room. She gaped at me, hair blown out and messy, a toothbrush dangling from her mouth.

"It's Saturday," she told me plainly. "Do you not know your days of the week, Adam? I wish you'd told me sooner, there are a ton of tax credits for hiring people with special needs."

"I guess I got mixed up," I said, embarrassed. I usually calculate what day it is by referencing whatever TV show was on the night before, but somehow the days had started blurring together for me.

"I'll clear out," I said and began stuffing papers into my backpack.

"Well, you're already here," Patricia said. She paused for a second and returned to the bathroom to spit out her toothpaste and gargle some mouthwash before returning and continuing her thought. "I just bought a Wii and I can't figure it out. Wanna set it up for me? I'll pay you for the time you're here."

I zipped up my backpack. "Yeah, that won't take long. Welcome to this century, by the way."

She smiled. I removed the Wii from the box and had it hooked up to the television in a matter of minutes. I directed her through the on-screen menus and loaded up a game for us to play. She learned the mechanics of it quickly and promptly kicked my butt. Granted, I was impaired by Evita trying to chomp my ankles. I would have called interference, but after a year of creating spreadsheets that amounted to nothing, color-correcting nonsensical brochures, and endlessly filing things I knew would never be retrieved, it felt good to be accomplishing something worthwhile, even if it was just as simple as helping Patricia indulge herself in Wii Boxing.

NIGHT PEOPLE

One of my most vivid early memories might not actually be my own. It feels like mine and I'm mostly certain it is, but I wouldn't bet my life on it. It might be a false memory, and were that proven to be the case, I wouldn't be surprised. After all, I've always found the line between fantasy and reality to be fuzzy at best. For a number of years I believed Geena Davis and my mother were the same person, due to their similar appearances, and that our VHS copy of *Beetlejuice* was unique to our household. Likewise, I distinctly remember loving peanut-butter-and-onion sandwiches as a kid, but then I caught the beginning of the movie *Little Monsters* on cable one night in college and realized I'd adopted that particular memory from Fred Savage's character. In the grand scheme of things it probably doesn't matter. Man's memory is his own private literature, and so what if mine happens to have a healthy dose of fiction?

In this probably-real-but-possibly-fake early memory, I'm standing on a beach in California late at night. The weather is warm and somewhere nearby there's an arcade where I can hear the ambient sounds of people yelling and laughing while music echoes out toward the ocean. The beach is mostly empty except for me and a few other idle stragglers. It's peaceful, yet the night seems electric and alive. The details surrounding how I ended up on a beach in the middle of the night as a child aren't apparent to me. I know that at some point during my childhood I went on vacation to California, but I don't know why my mother would allow me to stay up so late or wander the beach alone. The other, more likely scenario is that I assumed the memory from someone or something else, most likely a forgotten, decades-old teen movie with a name like *Valley Girl Robot Surfers*. Real or not, this memory stands out in my mind as a critical factor in shaping my eventual personality. It's when I realized I was fonder of the nighttime than the daytime, and it's how I began my problematic life as a night owl.

Since then, I have frequently found myself at odds with the rest of the world, as society does not cater to those who creep in the shadows and slumber away the daylight hours. I try to blame some imaginary internal clock for my vampiric ways, but in actuality I simply choose to be awake at night whenever the situation allows. I feel more productive after the sun has set. There are fewer distractions at night, and it's easier for me to clear my head. I jog at night, and I've only once been mistaken for a rapist—but then again, if you saw a tall bearded figure hurtling toward you at 2 a.m., you'd probably fear for your life too.

I prefer nighttime because a new society emerges after dark and it's always unique and unpredictable. It's one I've grown more and more familiar with in recent years, but it's a strange group. Once, during my nightly walk home from the 24 Hour Fitness in the Pearl District, I stumbled across a couple of homeless ladies engaged in the most fervent grind session I've ever witnessed (granted, it was my first time seeing homeless women scissor each other and I haven't observed it since, but the enthusiasm they displayed was astounding nonetheless). I halted in my tracks, dumbstruck, and when they noticed me standing there a moment later, the awkward silence that blanketed us seemed to last for an eternity.

Briefly, I wondered how uncontrollably aroused one would have to be to deem the 405 underpass suitable for sex, but then I gathered myself and apologized for intruding.

In retrospect, I suppose it's uplifting to know that even exhibitionist lady-bums with no shame can find love. It was almost heartwarming in a way, but not three days later when I stumbled upon a similar sight beneath the exact same underpass. This time, a young woman stood on a waist-high concrete wall, holding a lit cigarette in one hand and lifting her skirt with the other. A man stood in front of her, his face buried in her crotch. He, too, had a lit cigarette. It struck me as odd for them to both have lit cigarettes, given the nature of their intimacy. The girl noticed me walking and made no effort to halt the act; in fact she seemed entirely uninterested in what was happening to her lower half.

I kept my head down and hurried past them, making a mental note to find a new route home in the future.

Creepy late-night sex acts aside, I find the nighttime pleasant and peaceful. Were it easier for me to get the things I want at night, namely food, I fear I'd never see the light of day again. When I lived in Northwest Portland, the only things near me that were open all night were a small sandwich deli and a tiny convenience store that mostly sold cat food and pints of ice cream, oftentimes past their expiration dates. There was also a Taco Bell a block from the sandwich place, but my frequency at that establishment was becoming problematic. I like to pretend Taco Bell is for special occasions, like weddings and bar mitzvahs and Saturday nights when you've had nineteen shots of Jose Cuervo, but in recent weeks any occasion was special enough for a Taco Bell run. Because I find it impossible to think ahead and keep my fridge stocked with food, most nights I'd find myself starving with the only viable options for nourishment being cat food and bland subs. After a while I grew tired of eating Fancy Feast and reluctantly became a regular at the sandwich place.

It was a small, narrow deli with harsh fluorescent lighting— a place whose clientele seemed to consist solely of late-night drunks and insomnia-stricken weirdos. I suppose I fell into the latter category. Not once in over a year did I get a sandwich as I had ordered it, but I suppose beggars can't be choosers. Usually my meal was simply missing a key ingredient or two, or maybe the cucumbers had frozen in the storage fridge and crunched when I bit into them. One time, I almost received the perfect sandwich, but at the last moment the guy behind the counter squirted so much sauce that my sandwich became almost inedible.

One night while I was paying for my sandwich at the register, a scruffy-looking homeless man appeared at the door and
shuffled up to the ordering counter. In his hand he clutched
three wadded-up bills. "What can I get for this?" he mumbled to the sandwich maker and presented his three wrinkled
singles.

"Nothing," said the kid behind the counter. "The cheapest
thing we got's the veggie sub. That's five." The man with the
bills looked frustrated. He let out a sigh. I felt bad for him.

I figured I might be able to help, but I didn't want to

embarrass the guy, so as I paid for my own sandwich I quietly slid the cashier a couple of extra dollars and nodded toward the homeless guy, hoping the cashier would understand I meant to help pay for his sandwich. I hoped my gesture would go unnoticed and I'd be able to slip out the door undetected, but the homeless man apparently picked up on the exchange that had just occurred. He looked at me, cocking his head a little. I opened my mouth, intending to tell him it was no problem, that I was going to leave a couple of bucks as a tip anyway, but before I could say anything, the homeless man made his feelings on the matter clearly known.

"It's fine, really," I said, gathering my sandwich and drink. I averted my eyes and turned to leave, desperate to avoid confrontation, but the homeless man closed in on me.

"I don't need nobody to take care of me!" he loudly informed me. "I'm a goddamn veteran, you hear? You owe me your life!"

Still trying to inch away, I feebly tried to make conversation and alleviate the situation. I asked what war he served in, expecting the answer to be Vietnam, or maybe Iraq. The only other wars I could think of off the top of my head were either before his time or fictional battles from movies. His answer surprised me.

In all fairness, I might have misheard. His speech was somewhat slurred, and he could have said something else entirely. He might have said *Great War*, which would have made him a very young-looking 102-year-old. He also might have said *race war*, which would've taken the situation to an entirely more alarming level. Given the pace of modern technology and my relaxed understanding of science in general, *Space War* wasn't entirely outside the realm of possibility, and it's what I heard.

"Well, thank you for your service," I said awkwardly, edging a little more intently toward the door. The homeless man had embarked on a tangent by this point, and my desire to avoid a tense situation was a lost cause. The man began yelling—at me, at the deli employees, at the world. Unsure of how to deal with his outburst, I simply turned and left, praying he wouldn't follow me, but luck was not on my side this night. He clamored after me, screaming about nothing in particular, causing a ruckus behind me as I made my way down the sidewalk. He stomped and jabbered so rapidly I couldn't make out much of what he was saying. I caught bits about wormholes in space and evil beings hiding behind planets, but I was too focused on trying to lose him to make sense of his speech. I walked briskly, but I didn't want to give the impression I was trying to escape, which was exactly what I was doing. I figured running would make me seem vulnerable, so I tried to keep my cool.

When I reached my apartment building, I purposefully kept walking, keen on keeping my address a secret from my pursuer. I had no real plan of action, but I hoped that he'd lose interest shortly. My brain was preoccupied listing hypothetical

places I might find sanctuary. The twenty-four-hour sex store was just a couple of blocks away, and that seemed like as good an option as any . . . Perhaps I could lose him among the sticky DVD cases and oversize vibrators. But as I turned the corner with my head partly twisted behind me to monitor my follower, I unknowingly began to veer off the sidewalk. Had I been paying attention, I would have noticed the large cardboard box I was heading toward. Instead I collided with it and tripped, losing control of my sandwich and drink. My dinner flew out of my hands as I toppled. The box barely moved and as I fell, I realized with horror that it wasn't empty. Someone had been sleeping inside it, and the impact woke him with a start.

I landed on the ground next to the box. It wasn't a violent fall, and besides the momentary shock of tripping, I wasn't hurt save for the stinging palms I'd used to land. But then I noticed a rustling. The man inside roused angrily. Cursing, he

scrambled out of the box and rose to his feet. *Great*, I thought. *Now I'll have two of them after me. There's no way I can lose both of them. I'm done for!* But I was wrong; on the contrary, the man who'd been asleep didn't so much as look at me, instead turning his sole attention to the man who'd been following me, believing him to be the cause of the disturbance. The two men scowled at each other. Suddenly I was no longer of importance, simply a spectator at the unfolding battle between Box Guy and Sandwich Guy. As quietly as possible, I stood and watched the scene unfold. The men hollered at each other for a few minutes, but with an odd sort of intimacy that led me to believe they'd argued like this before. This would explain why I'd so abruptly become insignificant to them. At first, no punches were thrown, just wild insults followed by a lot of posturing. Sandwich Guy said something; I couldn't hear it clearly, but it incensed Box Guy. His eyes widened, as if he couldn't believe the nerve of his opponent. He scowled and kicked his foot forward angrily, sending up a flurry of dead leaves toward Sandwich Guy.

I found the action to be almost comical, but Sandwich Guy reacted as if the leaves were made of fire and he was in real danger.

Sandwich Guy shot his opponent a look of pure contempt and clenched his hands into tight fists. Noticing this, Box Guy did the same, and they both shifted into defensive stances. They snarled at each other angrily, and I felt my body tense up in preparation for what would surely be a brutal fight. For a moment neither of them moved, both seemingly waiting for the other to attack. Then, as if on cue, they simultaneously launched at each other, arms waving fanatically. The ensuing skirmish was a chaotic frenzy of growls and tangled limbs, though surprisingly nonviolent for such a passionate dispute. Though they fought with enthusiasm, both displayed a remarkable lack of skill. They flailed about, slapping each other like two drunk, boneless children having seizures.

I watched, speechless, from the sidelines; my jaw slack. I was just about to slip away unnoticed when a new presence made itself known. From across the street I heard a booming voice. I turned my attention toward it and was surprised to see a colossal woman marching toward us. She wore a stretchy gold tube top and a tight white pleather miniskirt. Her gold belt and hoop earrings matched her long, shimmery press-on nails. Her hair was so large I could've climbed inside it to hide from the homeless guys, had that been an option. Clearly she was a prostitute, and strangely, I recognized her.

I'd met her a couple of weeks prior while struggling to parallel-park my car in a tight space. It had been late at night and I'd just returned from a party across the river. Noticing my plight, this working girl had kindly offered her services in the form of standing next to my car and informing me of how much space I had left between my car and the one behind me. I doubt I would have been able to park without her help, and afterward she didn't even solicit me for sex. *Because she was classy.* Now, in the midst of witnessing a bum fight unfold, I was stunned to see the exact same hooker advancing toward us, shouting at the top of her lungs.

Upon seeing her, the two men immediately ceased their scuffling. Their hands dropped to their sides and they took a step back from each other, like bickering children on the playground who just got caught by a teacher. The lady of the night, who towered over the three of us, strode up and forcibly separated Box Guy and Sandwich Guy, wasting no time in chastising them like toddlers. I was amazed to discover she knew them both by name.

93

"Roger! Jeremy! How many times we gotta go through this?" she bellowed. The two men looked at their feet shamefully. She reprimanded them and I watched, astonished that for the second time in as many weeks, I was being rescued by a streetwalker who dwarfed me in size. After a few minutes of thunderous scolding, she sent the two men in opposite directions. Sandwich Guy (I wasn't sure who was Roger and who was Jeremy) sulked away in the direction of the deli, and Box Guy snatched his box and dragged it off the other way. As quickly as it had started, the bum fight had dissolved into

a memory, and suddenly I was standing alone with a gigantic hooker on the side of the road in the middle of the night.
Somehow I wasn't surprised.

FOUR DAYS PRETENDING
TO BE A RABBIT

I wish I could justify the decisions I make. I'd like to think of myself as a spontaneous, carefree vagrant, but at this point in my life I think it's safe to assume the truth is that I'm simply an impressionable ne'er-do-well who lacks impulse control. It's becoming harder and harder to convince myself otherwise. One look at my bank account and you'd think, *This dude clearly has no foresight.* That and *Did he* really *eat at Taco Bell four times this week?*

One day I was talking to my friend Jeanie on the phone and she started telling me about this all-juice diet she was on. Jeanie is the kind of hippie-dippy gal who makes her own clothes, keeps her own kombucha cultures, and can spend an entire afternoon Dumpster diving. I maintain a sort of polite bewilderment toward Jeanie's lifestyle, and usually don't put much stock in her whims, but on this particular day I indulged her.

> YOU GOTTA TRY THIS CLEANSE, MAN. IT'S JUST APPLES AND KALE AND CELERY AND GINGER ROOT AND CARROTS AND SHRIMP AND CRUDE OIL AND CLOWN FARTS AND...

CELL PHONE CARVED OUT OF DRIFT WOOD

POTATOES 15 LBS

"That sounds like it would make you shit *constantly*," I said.

"Oh yeah," she replied. "I'm shitting right now."

She explained to me how juicing would clear out all my toxins. It was clear that neither of us actually knew what toxins were, but that was beside the point. If asked, I'd probably describe toxins thusly: angry cartoon blobs who go around munching on your white blood cells.

BWAH!

Of course, the moment Jeanie mentioned toxins, I could practically feel my body swarming with tiny parasites making me lethargic and cranky. *I have so many toxins*, I thought. *I gotta get rid of all these toxins!*

At first, juicing sounded like a lot of work—more work than I was willing to do. There are certain microwave dinners I won't buy simply because they involve too many steps ("I have to stir it halfway through the cook time? Are they *serious?*"). The more I thought about it, however, the more appealing it sounded to drink nothing but fresh juice for a whole week. *Besides*, I thought, *taking responsibility for my own health and well-being would be a very mature thing to do.* In the closet I had a big hulking juicer I'd received for Christmas and hadn't put to use yet, so I figured this might be an interesting little experiment.

The next morning I woke bright and early and hoofed it down to the farmer's market in search of fresh fruit and vegetables. Ladies in sundresses and floppy hats milled about as bearded men struggled to load up their bicycle baskets with produce. I felt entirely accomplished just being there.

It didn't take me long to locate and purchase the items on my list, which I'd constructed in my head haphazardly (apples, green stuff, maybe a tomato just for show, et cetera), but as I wandered around the vendors' tables, it dawned on me what odd places farmer's markets can be. Apparently anyone can rent a table and sell whatever they want.

I may or may not have purchased a gourd with googly eyes, and it may or may not be sitting on my bedroom dresser next to a full cat skeleton I purchased at a taxidermy shop in San

Francisco. I've always been an impulse shopper, and for some reason the more macabre the item is, the more I like it. I blame my grandmother, who let me watch *Cannibal Holocaust* when I was eight, bless her heart.

Back at home, I unpacked my juicer, skimmed the directions, then plugged it in and started feeding big chunks of apples into the spout. I was immediately alarmed at how loud the juicer was. It sounded like it was in excruciating pain.

Despite the juicer's robotic shrieks of death, it pulverized the apples efficiently. I added kale, some lemons, then ginger and celery, and after a few minutes I had a large cup of what easily could've passed as pond scum. Excited, I opened my mouth and took a huge gulp. Sure enough, it tasted like pond scum. Pond scum with lemon and ginger, but pond scum all the same. "This is horrifying," I said aloud. Still, I decided I was committed to ridding myself of those insidious toxins, so I slurped it down and made some more for later (spoiler alert: It tasted even worse chilled).

Truth be told, I felt pretty good for the rest of the day. I went about my work with a bounce in my step and a smile on my face. I even thought about cleaning my apartment. I didn't *actually* clean it, but the fact that I considered it felt like a winning event. The next day I felt even better. I remember one summer when my mom had our cat shaved because it was getting matted hair, and afterward it pranced around the house feeling nimble and liberated. I felt just like that. Despite the wretched taste of the juice sludge, I discovered it gave me more energy throughout the day, and I no longer saw flaming, cackling skulls when I closed my eyes at night. The first few days, I felt mildly euphoric.

The honeymoon phase didn't last long, though. By the third day of my juice fast, I was craving meat. Juicy, unadulterated *meat*. In fact, that night I actually dreamed about cheeseburgers. Sweet, sexy cheeseburgers.

Throughout the day the cravings only got worse. I wondered how I would do this for a whole week, and I started to get ornery with people. I stumbled around like some malnourished zombie, muttering about mozzarella sticks and Oreo McFlurries.

That evening, I passed a food cart serving Mexican food to hungry passersby. A smiling couple in matching polo shirts stood on the sidewalk, feasting on bulging, succulent burritos, struggling to keep all the fresh toppings from falling onto the ground. I stopped in my tracks and stared at them with a mixture of pure jealousy and unbridled disdain. They noticed me glaring and, clearly frightened, walked hastily away. At that moment I realized what a creepy curmudgeon I'd become. I knew this had to stop.

So on the fourth day, I caved. I found myself at a grocery store, where my feet had unexpectedly taken me. Mouth watering, eyes wide, I stopped to stare longingly at the frozen pizzas. Thankfully, like an angel sent from on high, a spirited employee was serving samples a few aisles over, dishing out mouthwatering Bagel Bites. Their oil glistened under the fluorescent lights.

Following The Great Bagel Bite Debacle of 1994 (which involved me spilling a plate of piping hot pizza bagels all over my bare chest and giving myself second-degree burns), I'd sworn them off for good. But standing in front of a tray of those cheesy, freshly microwaved little morsels, I couldn't

imagine a more divine treat. I plucked one off the table with my bony, corpse-like fingers, struggling to lift it in my weakened state. I raised it to my lips. It felt like taking communion.

I've found that something peculiar happens when you deprive your body of real food. (I'm not saying Bagel Bites are "real food," but bear with me for the sake of argument.) I don't know what it is exactly, but it's like your taste buds begin to hibernate after a few days of choking down repellent green slime, and when you present them with something tasty and savory, they *flip the hell out*. When I put that first Bagel Bite in my mouth, the insides of my cheeks actually ached, like I was biting a lemon. I salivated like a dog. It tasted glorious.

NOM
NOM

Is there a moral to this story? Probably not. I learned I shouldn't structure my diet around buzzwords like *juice fast* and *toxin*, and that walking around like a zombie for a week, snapping at those who are letting themselves eat, is not very productive. And I learned that kale tastes like dirt, no matter what you pair it with. If anything good came out of it all, I suppose being reunited with Bagel Bites is a plus.

Or maybe that's a negative. It's up for debate.

CALL OF THE WILD

One afternoon while I was doodling at my desk, my phone vibrated. It was a text from Annie, a girl from college I hadn't spoken to in nearly a year.

hey dude! i'll b in portland next month w/ my sister. we're gonna go camping, u should come! it'll b fun!

I grimaced. I hadn't gone camping since I was a child and had no burning desire to do so as an adult. I flicked off my phone without texting Annie back and tossed it on the couch cushion next to me. I made a mental note to politely decline her offer later. I wasn't going camping. No thank you.

As I cycled through the four local channels my TV received, I thought about the camping trips I took as a kid in Montana. For some reason I had no clear memories of the hiking and swimming that we did, but I did remember one recurring theme—something I've spent years attempting to quietly suppress. My typical behavior on those outings was more than a little sinister, and it's not something I make a habit of sharing with friends. Every time my family would go camping, my mother would send me off into the woods to play while she set up the tents. Before scampering off, I'd secretly grab a box of matches from the car. I generally keep this nugget of personal history a secret because what I'd do with those matches was just plain weird.

I liked to build things as a child. School recesses were spent creating little villages out of sticks and leaves, tiny hamlets consisting of a few huts or tepees. On camping trips I had the whole forest at my disposal, which meant I could build cities instead of villages, castles instead of huts. I'd disappear into the woods for hours, constructing whole metropolises out of twigs and rocks and mud, laboring over every detail. Then, since my cities needed citizens, I'd search for dead bugs or empty snail shells to populate my towns. Every now and then I'd get lucky and find a partly decomposed mouse. Once I found a frog with its guts hanging out on a rock near a lake. He became the king of my city.

The forest always had plenty to offer. On one occasion, I found a shoe box in the back of the car filled with plastic cutlery and napkins. I emptied it and I refilled it with whatever I could find in the woods, returning to my makeshift kingdom with a box full of new citizens to inhabit the city.

My cities were strictly populated with already-dead creatures. In my imagination, they were plenty alive, and that was good enough.

"None of this sounds all that creepy," you might remark. "In fact it's sort of quaint." Aside from playing with dead

things, I suppose it's a somewhat charming anecdote, were it not for the gruesome fate my cities would succumb to. Inevitably, my creations would be met with ruin, and always by my hand. I'd imagine meteors falling from the sky, or perhaps a rebel in the castle would immolate himself, and the flames would spread, causing the city to fall. This is what I needed matches for: destruction. To be clear, I was always careful to keep the blaze contained to my city, mindfully building in dirt clearings or on sandy patches near water, though looking back I'm lucky I never burned down the Gallatin National Forest. Still, it doesn't detract from the fact that I was a nine-year-old with a spiteful god complex.

They say setting fires is one of the early warning signs of a future serial killer, but only when coupled with other warning signs, notably cruelty to animals and wetting the bed into adolescence. I don't think I ever wet the bed, and the fact that I colonized my cities exclusively with already-deceased animals leads me to think I'm probably in the clear serial-killer-wise. I haven't killed anyone yet, so I believe I'm off the hook. Plus I only set fire to my own creations, which is almost noble when you think about it. There's sort of a Zen quiescence to accepting that your own handiwork must be met with obliteration.

Still, the whole thing paints me as a relatively disturbed kid, so I tend to keep that one under my hat. I told my friend Chloe about it once, and she didn't even bat an eyelash. "Eh, kids are fucked up," she quipped. "One time I found a dead cat on the side of the road, and I roller-skated around my neighborhood with the thing on a shovel, going door to door and asking anyone if they were missing a pet."

After that I didn't feel so bad about my own behavior. Still, I had soured to the idea of camping.

After a couple of days I forgot about Annie's text completely, but the following week she contacted me again—this time on Facebook, urging me to join her. I stared at the picture of Annie on my computer screen. I hadn't seen her in a while and realized it might be really nice to catch up. Suddenly I found myself considering her invitation. I didn't want to go, but the more I thought about it, the more I felt like I *should* go. Besides, I didn't want to be the only adult without a grown-up camping story. Everybody needs at least one outdoorsy tale they can reference in mixed company. I texted Annie back telling her I'd go.

With my fate sealed, I made a mental list of things I'd need, since I had no camping gear to speak of. I figured Annie and her sister would have the necessities, whatever those might be. (Flares? Snakebite anti-venom? Machetes?) Most of the gear I found online was superfluous and unnecessary, like solar-powered alarm clocks and hammock/tent hybrids you can hang between trees. I found a little tent on Amazon for cheap, and figured I could forgo a sleeping bag in favor of lots and lots of blankets. As for food, I can barely cook meals in my apartment, and I figured attempting to do so via campfire would be an unmitigated disaster. I went to the grocery store and picked up whatever looked filling while requiring zero preparation.

A week before the camping trip, I was all equipped. I felt like Survivorman. I congratulated myself on being a wilderness guru and rewarded myself by eating an entire box of Girl Scout cookies, which gave me a stomachache and caused me to have nightmares about a lipless Adele.

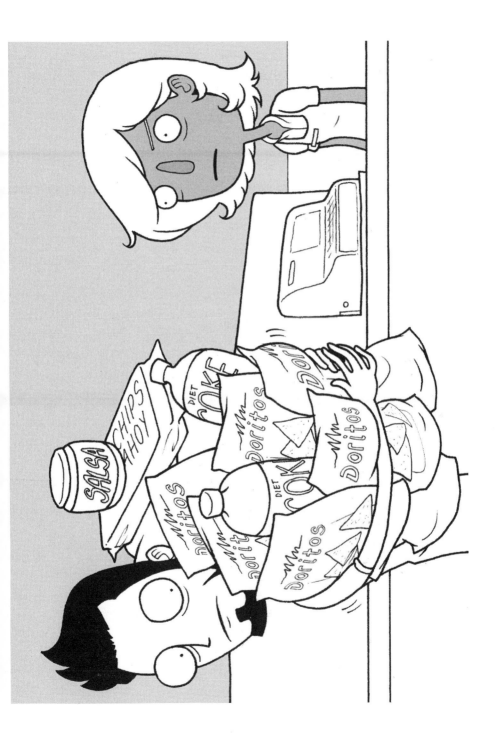

Two days before Annie was scheduled to arrive in Portland, I received another text from her.

so i got a dui and they took away my licence so i'm just gonna stay home this wknd and watch sex n the city on my laptop. i'm such a samantha lol

"What the hell, Annie," I said out loud. I'd invested time and money into preparing for the trip, and despite my own expectations I had been getting excited for it.

I stood in my living room, sipping a cup of coffee, staring at the little pile of supplies I'd amassed for a camping excursion that would no longer happen. Briefly, I thought about float-ing the idea past my other friends in town, but I knew none of them would be up for a camping trip. Most of my friends are soft-handed, gentle souls who would wilt in the woods like dying lilies. In my newfound identity as a mountain man, I was on my own.

Then a thought occurred to me: *So what if I'm on my own? I can still go camping by myself, right?* I pondered this notion. It's not like the campground Annie had chosen was in the middle of nowhere. It probably even had cell reception should I find myself being torn apart by wolverines. What was stopping me from going camping solo? The more I mulled it over, the more viable this option seemed. It might even be peaceful to go alone. It would be refreshing. I would exercise my indepen-dence and self-reliance. I made up my mind to soldier on with the plans by myself.

I made another journey to the supermarket to round out my cache of provisions. I bought some Dora the Explorer Band-Aids since they were on sale and picked up a bottle of bug spray. I pur-chased matches, making a mental note not to set fire to any dead animals. Since it was summer, there was a display next to the register stocked full of s'mores ingredients. I grabbed a box of graham crackers, some candy bars, and a bag of marshmallows.

A few days later I packed everything into the backseat of the car I'd borrowed from a friend and set out toward the Hood River. The area Annie had selected was small and relatively secluded, and when I arrived I managed to find a place to set up camp that appeared quiet and private. It was a secluded little clearing surrounded by tall oaks, big enough for a single tent and a campfire. I picked a spot under some low-hanging branches to assemble my tent, which only took me an hour and a half to set up. It didn't come with directions. I had no clue what I was doing and in the end my tent had an odd lean to it, but the results were more or less satisfying. I was thankful I was alone in that moment, as there was nobody to be embarrassed in front of. There was plenty of daylight left, but I knew if I didn't get a leg up on attempting a campfire, night might fall before I'd succeed, leaving me in darkness. I gathered sticks and some dry brush, and it was another hour before I managed to create a lasting fire. My meager flame kept going out before I could add more wood, but eventually I got lucky and it grew larger. The sun was setting by that time, and I was hungry. I snacked on chips and salsa for dinner, feeling accomplished, then dutifully tore open the bag of marshmallows and unwrapped the chocolate bars. I paused then, an idea forming in my mind. I decided it would be a good idea to make the whole s'more beforehand and then roast the entire thing over the fire, causing the graham crackers to toast and the chocolate to become warm and gooey. Using two long sticks, I awkwardly extended my s'more over the fire.

The result was a burned, goopy mess. I imagined if I were a contestant on *Top Chef*, I'd be the first one voted out. It would be a cookout challenge, and Padma Lakshmi wouldn't even try my dish before sending me home.

I held the s'more in my hand and stared at it. It did not look appetizing. I ate it anyway because I had created it, which meant I must destroy it as well. It was only camping tradition.

After that I sat around for a while, wondering what people do in the woods. I peered around my campsite, not sure what I was looking for. I could hear crickets and branches rustling softly in the breeze. I started to feel a little bored, but refused to accept the notion that camping solo was a dumb idea, because I'd committed to it and wouldn't accept defeat.

Tomorrow I'll go hiking or something, I thought. I got up and went about putting my fire out. *Or maybe I'll sharpen a stick and try to spear a fish.* My confidence was growing, and I was beginning to think maybe I liked camping after all. With my campfire out, I noticed how dark it was, much darker than it ever got in the city. I looked up and could see the stars clearly. They were pretty. It reminded me of Montana. I crawled into my tent, curled up in my blanket nest, and fell asleep.

When I woke up, I thought I was in my apartment at first. From my bedroom, I can sometimes hear people's footsteps scraping the ground and causing the floorboards of the hallway to creak, and I mistook the rustling sound outside my tent as just that. When I realized where I was, and that the sound I was hearing was something different, I sat bolt upright, eyes wide with sudden alarm. *There is something outside my tent making noise*, I thought. I froze, listening as it meandered around the side of my tent toward the front, where it then stopped. It sounded bigger than a fox or coyote, but thankfully not large enough to be a bear. Still, that left plenty of dangerous animals as likely possibilities.

Because my tent had a camo pattern and since I'd set it up under some branches, I figured that whatever the thing was, it didn't know I was there. I remained motionless and listened, waiting for the intruder to continue on and leave my campsite, but it didn't. Curious, I reached for my tent flap and, as silently as possible, unzipped it. I stared out into the darkness, waiting for my eyes to adjust.

At first I only saw the last smoldering embers of my campfire. I fixed my vision into the abyss and faintly saw something crouching in front of my tent about twenty feet away. I couldn't quite make it out. I squinted. The thing shifted slightly, and I suddenly realized what it was. My eyes grew wide and my jaw slackened in surprise. It was a girl. Her pants were down around her ankles and she was squatting. I heard a small strained grunt emerge from her. I couldn't believe what I was seeing.

I could only stare. I was paralyzed. From my few short years in Cub Scouts, I knew how to escape a moose attack and how to make a splint, but nothing in the handbook had prepared me for this. Had I been able to form words, I don't know what I would have said. "Excuse me, miss, would you mind defecating elsewhere?" I was too terrified to move in case she noticed me, so I just watched, horrified.

I sat there, praying it would end soon. I didn't want to be witnessing this, but I couldn't make any movement without giving my position away. I knew if she saw me, I would be caught looking like a Peeping Tom. *What is taking her so long?* I thought. *This girl needs to eat more vegetables.* She inadvertently turned her head in my direction but didn't notice my camouflaged tent right away, nor did she make

out my baffled face peering back at her from the void. For
a moment she stared right at me. Then her eyes bulged in
realization.

"Eep!" she chirped as she scrambled to pull up her pants. She clambered away into the woods.

For a long time I didn't move. I just gazed straight ahead to the spot where the girl had been. Then, as slowly and gingerly as before, I zipped my tent flap closed and lay back down. I stared up at the low roof of my tent. I could see the stars through a mesh opening on the side. They seemed dimmer than before.

I couldn't sleep. I felt violated, as if the offender had pooped in my own living room. I couldn't say for certain, as I didn't have a clear view, but I suspected that there was a turd lying in wait outside my tent. In the dark, I listened to myself breathing. The silence seemed oppressive and thick. The phrase *girl turd* swam through my thoughts as I drifted back into slumber, and in my dreams manifested into a single mantra: *gurd*. The terrible gurd, lingering ominously outside my tent.

In the morning, I stayed wrapped in my blankets for a long time. I didn't want to venture outside. I knew what was out there. Eventually my back started to hurt on the hard ground, so I rose with trepidation. I emerged from my tent with all the solemnity of an escort leading a funeral procession. I saw the thing immediately, lying on the ground a stone's throw from where I stood. I walked over to it. It was small, almost dainty, and covered in glistening morning dew.

It was clear from its shape that it had been pinched off in a hurry. I hated that this turd told a story. I stood there for a minute or a day, I couldn't be sure. Time seemed meaningless.

I sighed and looked up at the sky. It was blue and cloudless. *I've had enough of camping*, I thought. I collapsed my tent,

gathered my supplies, and left. The turd remained. For all I know, it's still there, collecting crystalline dew every morning.

On my way home, I stopped at my favorite Thai restaurant. I sank into a window seat and stared out onto the street, pondering my brief camping excursion. I wondered if I'd been out there long enough for it to be considered camping at all. *Maybe camping just isn't my thing*, I mused. *I still like the woods and stuff. Just not, like, for days on end.* I'd hoped camping would be a revelatory exercise in independence, but it turned into just another experience dealing with other people's shit.

WHAT COULD GO WRONG?

It snows maybe once a year in Portland, and even then it's usually a light dusting of powder that melts upon impact. Portlanders are accustomed to their temperate climes, coddled by the cool northwest breeze, spoiled by the lush views of endless green. When that fantasy threatens to fade, Portlanders lose their shit. Such was the case in the winter of 2008, my first year in Portland, when it actually snowed a great deal. About a foot of snow fell that December, but having spent the previous four years in Boston, I was unfazed by the abundant precipitation. My attitude was not shared by the rest of the city. People flipped out. The media dubbed it "Snowpocalypse." The city *shut down.*

Walking around outside that winter, it felt like the world had ended. Nobody ventured out, save for a few brave souls on their way to the grocery store to stock up on Tyson Any'tizers Buffalo Style Boneless Chicken Bites (such as

myself). In Boston one year there was a blizzard that caused three feet of snow in some places; it piled up to eye level around trees and up against the doors of my dorm. *That* was a Snowpocalypse. I couldn't understand why everyone in Portland was losing it over a mere foot of snow. It was almost eerie how desolate the city felt, as if something terrible was about to happen. I feared I'd turn a corner and come face-to-face with marauding bandits or a yeti looking to feast on human flesh.

If there's a point to be made here, it's this: Freaky weather makes people *act a fool*, and it's an important factor in the account of how I ended up in handcuffs that year. I hope it will aid in understanding the events that led up to me sitting alone in jail, watching the same nighttime news cycle play over and over on a tiny television affixed to a concrete wall. It began, as most things do, with a girl.

That summer Portland had similarly extreme weather, though at the opposite end of the spectrum. It was late August and my childhood friend Paige was in town for a couple of days, passing through on her way back to San Francisco, where she lived. I hadn't seen her in a long time. Several years prior we'd had a falling-out, but neither of us could remember the exact details of the fight, so we took her visit as an opportunity to reconnect. We met up for drinks that evening at a bar in the Buckman neighborhood and had a lovely go of it, easing back into our friendship and finding it remarkably simple to pick up where we'd left off. The awkwardness of not speaking for so long lasted mere minutes, and before long all was forgiven.

The bartender announced last call just before 2 a.m., and we walked out into the steamy night air. We milled about on the sidewalk for a moment, debating the next plan of action. It was unbearably hot during our walk home from the bar— strangely hot for Portland, in fact, and combined with the extreme humidity, it felt like we were trudging through guacamole. After a few blocks we were dripping with sweat, and felt disgusting.

"It would be really nice to go swimming, huh?" Paige remarked offhandedly. "Yeah," I agreed, and for a moment we both remained silent as the notion sank in.

I make no excuses for the events that followed. As kids, Paige and I made a number of stupid decisions as a team, so I suppose that night was par for the course.

There was nobody around to be the voice of reason—no Velma to convince the rest of the Scooby Gang that what they're about to do might not be wise—and Paige and I have always fed off each other's reckless spontaneity. I brought up Google Maps on my phone and located a high school a couple of blocks away. We figured there might be a pool inside where we could take a quick dip, so we set off down the street.

We found the school in question, dark and still as an abandoned factory, and we set about looking for a door that had been left unlocked or a window left ajar. The building spanned a whole city block, so we had to creep around the premises looking for an entrance. All the while, the school loomed over us, silent and mysterious. It was hard to imagine such a foreboding thing housing children during the day. I spotted a window that wasn't quite closed all the way. It was on the second floor but easily accessible by a flight of cement stairs leading up to the main entrance. It seemed almost too easy, like the window had been left open specifically for us. The window beckoned.

Paige hoisted me up, and I lifted her in after me.

We found ourselves in a small bathroom, only big enough to house one stall and a sink. I closed the window behind us and we ventured forth into the darkness of the empty school. The bathroom opened into a long hallway, with bulletin boards and classroom doors appearing on either side of us as we crept down the hall looking for the elusive pool. I hadn't set foot in a secondary school since my teenage years, and it felt strange to be back in one. I looked over at Paige as we walked down the hallway and realized that the last time I'd been inside a middle school, Paige had been my classmate. We'd been the only two good drawers in school, and it had set the groundwork for a friendly rivalry. I smiled in the dark. It seemed pointless to have ever fought with her in the first place. I realized I'd missed her terribly.

The halls of the school were dim and cool, and as we explored the building, finding a pool became less of a priority. Our footsteps echoed and we tried to tread lightly, even though nobody was around to hear us. Our search led us not into the cool embrace of water, but into the dank depths of the school's basement, where we meandered around the boiler room. But there was little to see.

We decided to leave the grounds and declare the adventure a bust. We walked back downstairs, past the lockers and water fountains, sweaty and ready to go home. On our way out, we passed a console against the wall and noticed a flurry of activity happening on the dashboard. Dozens of little red lights were flashing on and off.

Suddenly it dawned on us that we had tripped a silent alarm somewhere, and with no way of telling how long ago it had gone off, one thing was achingly obvious: We needed to escape. *Fast.*

"We should..." I started.

Paige nodded, adding, "Yeah, let's bail."

We didn't need to say anything else; we shot each other the same uneasy look. If they didn't already, someone would soon know the school wasn't empty. We tore out of the building.

Paige and I had made it halfway across the front lawn when we were intercepted by a cop. I saw a flashlight turn on me and knew we were caught. It happened so quickly, I barely had time to make sense of the situation. A clean escape had been a futile idea from the start.

"Hold it!" I heard the cop say. This all felt a little too famil-iar. I wondered whether the chocolate milk debacle had made it onto my record. If so, I would surely be considered a hardened criminal. I was looking at a year in prison, at least. "What're you doing here?" the policeman barked.

My head dropped, and I knew it was pointless to fabri-cate a story. Paige and I were both cuffed within minutes, cold metal bracelets placed on our wrists as we feebly attempted to explain that we had just been looking for a pool to cool off in.

"We were just hot! That's it!" I exclaimed.

We were met with a look of disbelief, which gave way to a sort of awkward bewilderment once the cop realized we were probably telling the truth. Another cop showed up, lights on but no sirens blazing, and then the superintendent of the school, who decided to make an example of us and press charges. Paige and I were split up into separate squad cars to have our information taken. I couldn't see or hear her, but I assumed she was getting the same rundown that I was.

I find that in stressful situations I'm unable to take things seriously and tend to make jokes as a defense mechanism. Even in the worst situations I find myself at the very least giggling inappropriately. I didn't have a driver's license at the time, having lost it on a beach in Connecticut, and had been using my passport as identification. Since it lacked many of the required details the cop needed, I had to dictate my information to the officer orally.

From the front seat of the squad car, he asked me what my hair color was. "Dark brown, with some gray. More gray than I'd like, but what can I do, right?" (Later I would learn the cop had listed my hair color as simply "gray.")

He asked me my weight and I told him I weighed 143 pounds. He replied, "Really? Usually people tell me an even number—142 or 144. I almost never get odd numbers." I got the feeling that he felt the situation was as ridiculous as I did, which would explain his amicable attitude toward me.

"Well, I'm 143," I told him. "You can put down 144 if you want."

"I'm gonna write down 146 just to mess with you," he said, chuckling. On the way to the police station we discussed our favorite episodes of *COPS*. He told me that if it had been his call, he wouldn't have arrested me. I liked him.

I'm not sure what I expected lockup to look like. Ironically, it sort of looked like a public pool, all harsh lighting and concrete walls painted sea-foam green. The cops on duty took all my possessions, fingerprinted me, and told me to settle in. I sat down in the open seating area with the other detainees, situating myself on one of the nailed-down plastic chairs and feeling out of place in my polo shirt and Montauk Red chinos, looking like I'd been arrested for hosting a clambake without the proper permits. I surveyed the folks around me. Each of them had a similar weary, disheveled look. Most were drunk or asleep. Paige was across the room in a separate area for women, with only one other occupant. I waved at her, and was reprimanded by a guard. Paige looked the way I felt: exhausted and uncomfortable. We had a tacit understanding over the absurdity of the situation. *We're idiots*, I thought, and I'm sure Paige thought the same.

I knew we'd be in jail until morning and I hoped things would stay quiet and uneventful. I turned my attention toward the little television. The news was reporting on Sarah Palin's book tour. I watched for a bit, then folded my arms, put my head down, and closed my eyes, thinking I could maybe sleep for a few minutes. I was drifting off slightly when a new detainee appeared in lockup, screaming his head off about his arrest, to nobody in particular. He wore an ill-fitting wifebeater, and his hair was greasy and disheveled. None of the officers even seemed to notice him. From his rant, I gathered he'd been booked on domestic assault charges, but according to him, *he* was the one who'd been abused, not his girlfriend.

I considered mentioning to the guy that he meant "judicial," not "judicious," but thought better of it. He marched around the holding area for a while but eventually settled down and began mumbling profanities under his breath. Respite from his disturbance was fleeting, unfortunately. I'd just turned my gaze back to the television to watch a second cycle of the previous news story when an even louder man showed up. He was worse for wear than the last dude. His long, matted hair hung about his bony face, and his clothes looked like they hadn't been washed in months. He was clearly high, *covered* in meth scabs, and it was obvious from his scrapes and bruises that he'd resisted arrest. During the next fifteen minutes I watched as he made collect calls to no fewer than eight people, trying, to no avail, to find someone to bail him out. With each subsequent phone call his story changed drastically, yet he always painted himself as the victim. All the while, he scratched at his lanky arms and sunken face, spinning tales about how he was simply minding his own business and had been arrested for no reason. Every person he dialed hung up on him before he could get his full fabricated story out.

In my head, I knew the guy was probably harmless, but his appearance unnerved me. I do my best to stay neat and tidy; if I don't get a shower every morning, my whole day feels like a failure. Seeing someone so completely out of the hygienic loop made me instantly feel dirty. As I watched him dial number after number, I could feel my heart rate increasing. I prayed that when the guy finally gave up on calling someone to get him out of jail, he wouldn't sit next to me. I am not a religious man, but I prayed for it, desperate to be heard by whatever deity might be listening. "Oh please, Baby Jesus, righteous Vishnu, merciful Kabbalah Monster, someone hear my prayer..."

I'm afraid of very few things in this world. Zombies scare me, sure, and I'm not too fond of bees because they'll kill themselves just to make you uncomfortable for a few hours. Bugs in general don't thrill me, but the only thing that makes me *truly* squeamish is meth scabs, and I shouldn't even have to explain why. I'm uncomfortable with scabs of any sort, but meth scabs in particular are horrifying. They conjure thoughts of dirty needles and rotting teeth. I listened to the meth guy blather on the phone and scratch his arms absentmindedly, and I suddenly felt rather itchy myself. My teeth ached. I pushed on them with my tongue to make sure none of them were loose. All the while, I thought about this man sitting next to me—his methy, scabby skin flakes rubbing off on me. This in itself was enough of a deterrent against ever breaking the law again. I swore up and down that I'd learned my lesson.

Someone must have heard my prayer because amazingly

meth-man retired to the bathroom after he'd run out of contacts to dial. He treated us to an off-key rendition of Hot Chocolate's "You Sexy Thing" from behind the closed door, and I didn't see him again after that.

Morning came; both Paige and I were notified that we had court dates the following day, and then we were released into the crisp, early air. Paige looked sleepy, and I shuddered to think how I must've looked. Though we'd only spent the night in lockup, it felt exhilarating to be free once again, like getting out of school on a Friday afternoon. For two mostly well-behaved kids from suburbia, the night had seemed endless. Exhausted, we had one thing on our minds: coffee. Paige took out a cigarette and lit it as we walked. After a few blocks we spotted a Starbucks, shining like a symbol of freedom. We ordered drinks and took them outside.

"So, uh, that was ... interesting, huh?" I said. Paige chuckled and nodded as she took a sip of her coffee. We sat there in the comfortable silence of old friends as we finished our drinks.

Paige was the first to stand. "Well, see you tomorrow in court," she said, smiling. I grinned back and Paige turned and walked toward the train station.

When I got home I fell asleep almost instantly, and it was a deep slumber. I awoke hours later, briefly wondering if the whole ordeal had been a dream before remembering I had a court date.

For my hearing the next day, I arrived an hour early, terrified I might not be able to find the building and would miss my appointment. In a bid to look presentable, I wore a new sweater I'd bought recently. It had been sitting on my floor for a few weeks, though, and my attempt to get the wrinkles out of it had been only marginally successful. I waited for Paige to arrive, anxious about what penalty the judge might dole out. When Paige finally appeared in a yellow dress, her hair pulled back into a ponytail, it struck me how out of place she looked in the courtroom. Tall and pretty, she looked like she should be heading to a garden party, not awaiting punishment for a crime.

The hearing was short and sweet. Our crime was downgraded merely to a violation, meaning it wouldn't appear on our records once we'd completed the allotted hours of community service. After the ruling, a clerk gave us a list of places we could choose to do our service. Paige and I perused the same bright green sheet of paper.

"I wonder if there's a way to do community service online," Paige half joked.

"Right?" I agreed. "Like maybe I can be the moderator of a video game message board for a couple days or something." In the end I chose to work in a meal center for a weekend.

A few days later, I opened the mail to find a jury duty summons. *What a strange twist of fate*, I thought. The timing could not have been more surprising, but I reported back to court the following week prepared to do my civic duty. It felt strange to be returning to the exact same building, but for an entirely different purpose. I felt like an imposter, sneaking into a party I hadn't been invited to. As a sort of disguise, I wore my glasses, which I rarely do, thinking someone might recognize me as a hardened criminal. During the preliminary interview process, I was asked a few questions by the defense lawyer.

"Have you ever been to court before?" she said, and I couldn't help but smile.

Marching out of the courtroom, I reflected on the turn of events. *Would I rather spend a few hours in the clink, or days and possibly weeks on a jury for some girl who shoplifted a tube of mascara?* In an odd way, the circumstances had turned out in my favor. A few hours in lockup had saved me from a God-knows-how-long session of jury duty.

I felt a little guilty over how my stupid mistake had ironically worked out in my favor. It was like someone behind the scenes had mixed up my life's paperwork and I was reaping the benefits. I just hoped the mistake would stay unnoticed.

TO SERVE AND ANNOY

I had a fight once with my friend David about altruism. He claimed it didn't exist and that people only do good out of inherently selfish desires. I think he'd just read *Atlas Shrugged* and was on an Objectivism kick. I tried to no avail to convince him that at the very least it was a gray area, but he wouldn't budge, and the more we argued, the more I worried he might be right. Stubbornly, I refused to concede, so the argument went nowhere.

I choose to believe in the goodness of people. I make it a point to notice when people do unwarranted good things, and try to live life by that example. At the grocery store recently the cashier forgot to scan a bar code on my to-go box of lobster meat and raw shrimp. The guy at the seafood counter had put my lobster and shrimp into the same container and affixed two separate barcode stickers, one on the top and one on the side. When I took the box to the cashier, she scanned the top bar code, missed the second one, and placed the box in a bag with the rest of my items. Without missing a beat, I pointed out her error.

"There's a second bar code there, on the side," I said. "There's lobster in the box too, not just shrimp."

"Oh, thanks," she replied, lifting the box out of the bag and scanning the bar code she'd missed. I paid her and left the store, and it didn't dawn on me until a few minutes later that I'd done something honest without even thinking about it. At the time, it hadn't even occurred to me that I might get free lobster and nobody would be the wiser. *I'm such a good person*, I thought. *No, I'm a fucking saint.* I was so proud of myself that I had to text my friend Kristin and tell her the good news. Despite the fact that my abundant self-praise probably negated the good deed altogether, I tucked it away as proof of mankind's innate virtue and deemed myself a model citizen. Humanity was good, and I was a shining example.

Of course, even saints stumble now and then. After my arrest for trespassing, I was assigned three days of community service in a cafeteria-style meal center for homeless and disadvantaged seniors. It was a small, shabby place with faded yellow linoleum floors and aging wood paneling on the walls. My job was to clear plates and trays of leftover food, sort dirty dishes, then wash those dishes at the end of the day. I didn't love it, but I did my job without complaint because it was my punishment, and in the end I was probably getting off easy. Likewise, I knew in the back of my head that there were people in the world doing far more grueling work voluntarily, and I had no right to whine about giving a weekend up to do community service.

During that weekend, I worked with a number of people who were also clocking service hours involuntarily. On the first morning, I learned that most of them had been assigned hours for DUIs or MIPs, and were quite put off to be working on a weekend. I reminded myself that a bunch of people who had recently been arrested might not be the greatest sample group from which to judge society, and I found myself clinging feebly to the notion of humankind's inherent goodness.

The first day I was paired up with a girl named Heather. I took one look at her perfectly coiffed hair and lavender cashmere sweater and knew she'd be trouble (I mean, who wears cashmere to work at a soup kitchen?). The first thing she said to the center director was that she'd like to work in back in case somebody she knew walked by the building and saw her through the windows by the street. "None of my friends know I'm here, and I'd like to keep it that way." Her request was honored, which meant she was paired up with me at the cleaning station. The two of us were in charge of taking messy plates from patrons, clearing away leftovers, and sorting dishes and utensils.

As we worked through lunch, I learned she'd been assigned twenty-four hours for a second DUI, an infraction she felt was of little consequence.

"I swear, it's like cops have nothing better to do in this town," she prattled as we cleared trays of food. "I wasn't even that drunk, and I'm a good driver anyway. They should be catching murderers or whatever. It's so annoying having to be here." I tried to engage Heather as little as possible and busied myself clearing trays as they were handed to me. The bulk of the work fell to me, as Heather seemed more concerned with keeping her clothes clean. She'd scrape food from plates slowly and methodically, then dispose of the trash gingerly and carefully, as if everything around her were covered in Ebola.

Near the end of the lunch rush, she disappeared into the kitchen somewhere and didn't return. I didn't mind, since I actually worked faster without her. After the cafeteria had mostly cleared out, I took a stack of dishes into the back to wash and found Heather reapplying her makeup in a mirror over the sink I needed. I stood behind her, my arms straining from the weight of the dinnerware. When she noticed me, she exclaimed, "I'll just be a minute!"

On the second day, right before dinner service, a woman arrived with her two preteen daughters and was assigned to the cleaning station with me. The woman was dressed conservatively, her hair pulled back into a simple ponytail. Her daughters had similar ponytails and wore subdued collared blouses. They looked like they came from the type of family that shuns R-rated movies. The mother cheerfully explained to me that she and her daughters had been assigned a few hours of community service by their pastor, and made some inspirational quip about feeding the hungry "just like Jesus did." Since I was a dish-clearing expert by this time, I gave them a quick rundown of the process. "It can get sort of hectic, so it's easiest to just form a line and pass dishes down as you clean."

The mother nodded. Then she asked, "Do you know when dinnertime is over? We're parked outside and we have to leave before the meter runs out." I shrugged and told her that dinner ended at different times every day, whenever the dining hall cleared out. Secretly I thought, *I wonder how often Jesus was concerned about parking tickets.*

During the dinner period, the mother stood motionless with her arms folded, seemingly content to monitor her daughters' work. They were helpful enough and did the job dutifully, although more leisurely than was necessary. At the very least neither of them complained when they got splashed with murky dishwater, which was often. Many of the patrons seemed to have Tourette's of the limbs, sending their trays and dishes flying toward me at mach speed.

Near the end of dinner, an elderly man with a yellowing beard and drugstore eyeglasses approached me, jabbed his empty tray at my chest, and griped, "There were no fucking cucumbers today. I asked for cucumbers. Why didn't I get any goddamn fucking cucumbers?"

"I'm sorry about that," I replied. "I'm not sure. I haven't been back in the kitchen today."

"Make sure they got cucumbers tomorrow," he stammered and wandered off. There was a lull, so I took the opportunity to check on things in the kitchen. Since the man had brought it up, I was curious as to why no cucumbers had been included in the meal when they were apparently supposed to be available. I snapped off my latex gloves, asked the mom and her daughters to staff the station for a moment, and walked toward the back of the building.

I glanced around the kitchen and spotted a girl at one of

the counters. She couldn't have been older than seventeen and wore heavy raccoon eye makeup behind choppy, stringy bangs. She held a long knife in her left hand and was chopping absently at a cucumber. In her other hand she held a BeDazzled iPhone and was speedily texting someone with her thumb. She seemed to be giving the bulk of her attention to the text instead of the food. On the counter, to one side of her, a large pile of cucumbers rested, waiting to be chopped up. On her other side was a neat little pile of cucumber slices, perhaps ten or twenty little green discs in total. *That explains the shortage of cucumbers*, I thought.

I couldn't see what she was texting, but I imagined how her message read.

I watched as she halfheartedly chopped at the vegetable. The knife slipped a little, causing an entire cucumber to roll off the counter and onto the floor. She glanced at it, resting on the dirty wet ground, then finished her text, pocketed the phone, and picked the cucumber up off the floor and placed it back on the counter. She continued slicing it into discs.

I would have been disgusted by her total disregard for cleanliness, but I was too horrified by the lower-back tattoo I'd caught a glimpse of when she bent over. It was a poorly drawn rendition of a stripper adorned with massive butterfly wings, the sort of tattoo you might see on a fifty-year-old Hell's Angel with a nicotine-stained beard.

I furrowed my brow and sent judgy vibes at the back of her head, then grabbed a new pair of gloves and went back to my station.

On the third day, Heather was back at the cleaning station with me and I could tell she was eager to be finished with her hours. She folded her arms and leaned against a door frame.

"These people all have such terrible attitudes. We're feeding them for *free*, they could at least show a little gratitude."

"I mean, I guess so," I replied, careful to avoid conflict. "But we don't really know their stories, y'know? And this food isn't exactly tasty, right? Would you eat it?"

"Of course not." Heather rolled her eyes. "I pack my own vegetarian bento box every day."

Most of the patrons who came to get meals were a little rough around the edges, though understandably so. Many of them were veterans who had been dealt shitty hands. They'd all fallen through society's cracks one way or another. Some of them had mental illnesses, some were victims of poor investments and apathetic family members, and some were simply alone in the world.

The center had a few regulars. There was one woman, Luann, who came in each day for both lunch and dinner. I couldn't tell her age; she could have been forty-five or eighty-five. She always had a messy look about her: unkempt hair, wrinkled clothes, fingernails all different lengths. Something wasn't right with her, but I could've only guessed as to what it was. Upon arrival she'd make the rounds, greeting everyone loudly, mealgoers and staff alike, chattering incessantly about anything and everything. Her friendliness was the opposite of the other patrons' demeanors. She chattered unwaveringly. I imagined she could've carried on a pleasant conversation with the cash register. After bringing me her tray, she'd linger at the cleaning station to talk. On my first day, she told me all about her daughter in Michigan (I'd later learn from the center director that she had no children). On my second day she bragged about the house she owned down the street that she painted a new color every year (I didn't need to be told that there was no truth to this). The lady was nuts, but she was friendly and entirely harmless. Heather, however, was terrified of her.

"Did you see how much hair she has on her chin?" Heather whispered to me that afternoon as Luann walked away from us. "It's disgusting. I feel like vomiting." She stuck her tongue out in a mock gagging gesture. We both watched as Luann shuffled around, babbling at people. She seemed a bit more animated and excited than normal. Then she did something odd. She loudly announced that she was going to take off her shirt.

Before we knew it, Luann was peeling her shirt off, revealing a faded, flesh-colored bra that might have been white at some point. As she did so, I looked around at the other people in the room. Only one or two lifted their heads.

IIIIT'S TITTY TIME!

Nobody else in the cafeteria seemed to care about what had just gone down. I could only assume this sort of thing had happened before. Perhaps it was a regular occurrence. After a few minutes of parading around, Luann sat back down at a table—still shirtless—and began eating, as if all was well.

"Huh," I said to myself. I noticed Heather's mouth was agape. She was clearly appalled. She made a sharp *huff* sound, looked up at the ceiling like she was trying to gather her senses, and gasped, "I do *not* feel *safe* here." She shook her head slightly, like she was trying to shake off the memory, and marched back into the kitchen, where the center director was filling out an order form. I followed her, curious as to how she would handle this.

"Something just *happened*," Heather proclaimed indignantly, "and I don't think I can stay here!"

The director, a portly man with thinning hair, looked up, bemused. He didn't even ask her to explain. "Go get your community service sheet," he said calmly. "I'll sign off on your hours."

Heather left, and I shuffled across the squeaky yellow linoleum and got back to work, cleaning plates until the crowd dwindled and eventually cleared out. By the time I was finished with work that day, I wondered if my friend David had been right about the state of humanity after all. The patrons I'd encountered over the weekend had been unfriendly, albeit understandably so, but worse, the staff had been completely indifferent. I finished my duties, took my sheet to the director for his signature, removed my apron and gloves, and left.

Outside the center, I took a deep breath. It was nice to have some fresh air, but I still felt bothered. I feared none of the people I'd worked with had really learned anything. I wondered if I had, either. Were any of us better people for having spent a weekend serving the community? Heather was probably getting drunk and whining to her friends about how awful her service was. The mom and her daughters were probably saying grace over a piping-hot pan of Tater Tot casserole, feeling smug about the 2.5 hours of good deeds they'd performed for Jesus. I'm not sure what I'd expected, really. I wasn't exactly one to talk. It's not like I'd been feeding the needy out of goodwill. It was court-ordered. I had no real right to judge anyone. I couldn't shake the feeling that perhaps I'd held on to a false belief about human kindness my whole life. I pondered the consequences of such a morose revelation.

The sun was beginning to set, so I started on my way home, slinking along with my hands in my pockets, frowning slightly.

I'd walked several blocks when I noticed a little girl with loose pigtails and knee-high striped socks staring at something on the sidewalk. I could see her mother about fifteen feet away at an ATM, poking at the screen. My eyes followed the little girl's gaze. In the middle of the sidewalk was a dead sparrow. A pigeon was pecking at it, and the girl looked incensed.

"Hey!" she shouted at the pigeon. "Stop that!" I could tell she was gravely concerned for the sparrow. She must not have realized it was dead. Her little hands made fists when the pigeon didn't follow her orders. "I said *stop that!* Leave him alone! He's hurt!" The pigeon took no heed of her.

Then the little girl did something surprising. She marched forward and kicked the pigeon. Since the girl was small, there wasn't much force behind the kick, but the pigeon was startled and it tumbled a few feet away.

My jaw dropped in a mixture of surprise and sudden admiration for the girl. The pigeon, its feathers ruffled, flapped about in the street for a moment, then flew away. I stared at the girl. She stared down at the dead sparrow. She bent down and gingerly stroked its wing with a few tiny fingers. When she realized it was a dead, she ran back toward her mother.

I stood there, dumbfounded by what I'd just seen, but more than anything I felt complete and utter respect for the girl. Despite her seemingly violent action, I knew in her head the pigeon was a bully and she'd done the only thing she could think of to protect the smaller bird. She had cared enough about that poor sparrow to try to help it. Suddenly I felt a little better about humanity as a whole. *The world needs more pigeon-kickers*, I decided as I walked the rest of the way home.

I thought back to the argument I'd had with David so many years ago, about how people only really care about themselves and just want to feel good, others be damned.

Maybe he was right. But maybe he wasn't. The fact that it was still up for debate made me hopeful.

THE BREAKUP BREAKDOWN

In February 2010, I entered into a relationship. The following January, I exited. I dated Riley for less than a year, and the details of what occurred during that time are of little importance. It was not a remarkable romance. What is important is that I fell in love despite all my efforts not to. That's the sneaky thing about love; you don't know it's there until it's *there*, and by then it's too late to do anything about it. I'd figured I had time to kill before love grabbed me, so I just went along with it, telling myself I'd cut the relationship off if things got too serious. I wasn't even especially happy, but I didn't particularly want to be alone. Plus it was nice to have someone to sleep next to (although the fact that I was most content when Riley was unconscious should have raised some flags).

In hindsight, I should have aborted the mission after the first date, the moment I set foot in Riley's apartment. Warning signs that we had nothing in common were conveniently parked in plain view, stacked on bookshelves and hanging on walls.

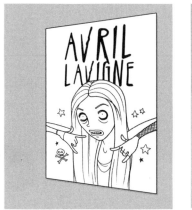

. . .

In an effort to rationalize our glaring differences, I told myself that what someone chooses to read or watch or listen to doesn't determine their character. I was sure we could transcend these differences. So, I accepted a second date and then a third, and then seemingly out of nowhere I was six months into a dysfunctional relationship, torn between the stubborn love that had taken root in my heart and a nagging desire to escape something I knew was unhealthy. We argued, we belittled each other, we tested the boundaries of acceptable behavior, waiting for the other to break. Riley would intentionally show up late for movies and I'd purposefully wait too long responding to texts. "Oh, sorry. My phone was charging in the other room." Honestly I'm not sure we ever even liked each other, but strangely that's not always a factor in love. We grew accustomed to one another, and the hurt became routine.

To this day I'm still baffled as to why I let the relationship play out for months after realizing it was doomed. I wasn't waiting to find someone new so that I could bridge my way into another relationship, and I wasn't scared to be alone, at least not in theory. I'm an only child; I excel at being alone. I told myself I wanted to avoid the confrontation of a breakup, despite knowing our relationship was built around confrontation. I somehow convinced myself that everything would work out if I simply waited. Not surprisingly, things only got worse, and shortly after Christmas 2010 I found myself on Riley's blue IKEA couch in the midst of being dumped. Somehow, astoundingly, I was surprised it was happening. I will not recount the conversation that took place. I cried. I wept. *I sniveled.* And then it was over and I was alone, walking back to my apartment, newly single and thoroughly stunned.

When I was a kid, I figured everyone in their twenties had it all figured out. I was nine when my babysitter got married, and I remember how my mother and my stepfather had both warned her against the union. I never understood their wariness; I idolized the guy she was engaged to. I thought he was the coolest person I'd ever met. He played video games with me. He was a line cook in the college's cafeteria, which I thought sounded so adult. I was too young to realize a grown man spending all his free time playing Super Nintendo with a child was pathetic at best and downright creepy at worst, and that his job made him little more than a glorified lunch lady. All I knew at the time was that he was twenty-four and *awesome.* A couple of years later he and my babysitter divorced, and over time I would learn that he'd been frequently unfaithful to her.

In the hazy moments after my breakup with Riley, it dawned on me that I was now roughly the same age my babysitter's husband had been when she was first married to him. Though I had never been unfaithful like him, it was impossible to ignore my numerous faults in the relationship, and I drew parallels in my mind. I'd been passive-aggressive, manipulative, sometimes downright cruel. Frankly I'd been a shitty boyfriend, not unlike the way the man I'd so fiercely admired had been a terrible husband. In that moment, I felt the slow collapse of my childhood hero come full circle with the realization that I was now an adult, and not the sort of one I'd hoped to be. I thought, *Nothing really changes. Nobody actually grows up.* It was certainly a melodramatic thought to have, but breakups have that effect on people.

I walked home from Riley's apartment in a dream state. I felt broken, confused, and ashamed. More than that, I felt scared, because I knew what was coming: the Breakup Breakdown. This is what I call the aftermath of a relationship's demise. It's a bastardization of the Kübler-Ross model with some tweaks and added stages, and it's a bad enough process without the realization that your childhood hero was actually a flawed, fragile human being, and you just might be one too.

In the past, the Breakup Breakdown had been fairly cut-and-dried, a few weeks of moping followed by a gradual turnaround wherein I start dating again like new. This time, because it had been such a harsh and complicated affair, I dreaded the coming days and weeks. For once, I recognized my role in the dissolution of the relationship, and it was sobering. And yet I knew the process was inevitable, so I hunkered down and prepared for the worst. After all, I was already in the thick of it.

PHASE ONE: FLAT-OUT DENIAL

Floored as I initially was over my breakup, I wasn't altogether surprised. I hate to do the dumping, so I avoid it at all costs. I tend to cling to failing relationships like a coyote gnawing on a rotting squirrel carcass, mostly because I can never find the right time to broach the subject of ending it all. There's no polite way to dump someone, so I carry on with the crumbling affair, dying a little bit inside with each passing day. On occasion I'll falsely convince myself that things are actually getting better, or that living a life of quiet misery is somehow noble, and just when I've resigned myself to a lifetime unfulfilled, I'll get eighty-sixed by the other party.

Sometimes it doesn't hit me at first. Since I've spent so much time in my own head analyzing the relationship, I forget there's another person involved, and on more than one occasion I didn't even register that I was being dumped at all.

Even after I've accepted that a relationship is de facto terminated, it takes time for the reality to fully sink in. I must once more learn to be single, and that can be a challenge. It's like stepping off a ship and getting used to walking on land again. This time, I had to figure out how to sleep without my arm wrapped around another warm body. I'd pick up my phone to write a text, then realize the person it was meant for wouldn't be responding. In my brain I knew it was over, and it wasn't long before my heart knew it too, but the muscle memory associated with a relationship can take ages to fade. Phase Two of the Breakup Breakdown arises from this stubborn refusal to let go.

Phase Two: Bargaining

I believe relationships succeed for one of a couple of reasons. The first is because of stupidity. I believe when two stupid people fall in love, they're set for life. They'll live out their years in idiot bliss, eagerly awaiting new *Scary Movie* installments and never voting. The second reason a couple stays together is through pure determination. My personal philosophy is that if something is broken, I should make an effort to fix it rather than abandon it, and this somewhat naive notion becomes extreme post-breakup. I hole up in my room like a recluse and frantically concoct wild plans to remedy my dead relationship. Reenact the boom box scene from *Say Anything...*? No, too easy. Cut off my ear and send it to my ex? Bitch, *please*, that's been done to death. As the fantasies grow more and more outlandish in my head, I begin to lose my mind altogether, and I start having conversations with inanimate objects in my apartment.

After Riley dumped me, I briefly saw a therapist, and she told me my desire to fix things was because I'd feel like a failure if I let them stay broken. She told me that sometimes the braver thing to do is let go. I wish we could have explored that notion further but I ran out of money by session three and never went back. Still, it was helpful to gain that bit of understanding about myself, and I eventually accepted the fact that I couldn't beg, wish, or trick someone back into my life. With a heavy heart I sulked along into Phase Three of the Breakup Breakdown.

PHASE THREE: DEPRESSION

I don't know if there's a worse feeling than knowing the person you once loved doesn't need you anymore, to know they're out in the world, living their life. My breakup brought a pervasive sadness that caused me to power down like a robot in stasis. I spun a figurative cocoon around myself and entered a sort of personal emotional hibernation for two weeks. I felt too petrified to do much other than sleep and take walks by myself. I found I couldn't listen to music, as most of it would set me off. My appetite disappeared and I shed excessive weight from my already-skinny frame. Strangely, I stopped biting my fingernails, something I'd done since I was a kid. I can only imagine I did so in a psychological attempt to halt time, or delay dealing with my feelings. Most days I would lie in bed, watching comedies on Netflix, though never laughing. I let my work pile up, deadlines approaching, but couldn't bring myself to care. Offers for freelance jobs came and went with no reply on my part. I played through the first two seasons of *Parks and Recreation* so many times that it became routine and the characters' lines began to lose meaning. *Rushmore*, *The Big Lebowski*, and *Clueless* all received heavy rotation in my DVD player. I started to lose track of time and the days blurred into each other as I stared at the television, the jokes sounding flat and foreign to my ears.

My mom would call over Skype and I would try to act like nothing was wrong. She remarked once that I looked "like Jesus with a meth addiction," which I suppose was her way of telling me she was worried about me. I was too embarrassed to open up to her or anyone else about my depression because I felt guilty for *being* depressed. I knew some people had real, chronic depression that never went away, and here I was sniffling over a breakup. I imagined some starving African child

sitting on my couch, staring me down, and saying, "Really? *Really?* Eat a Hot Pocket and shut up, you diva."

When my depression finally let up, it was more because I was tired of being sad than anything else. At a certain point being miserable becomes work. It's easier than attempting recovery, so you actively bring up memories that will keep you depressed and you wallow in the pit of misery that you've dug for yourself. Eventually I acknowledged that I was purposefully prolonging my despair, so I turned off the TV and moved on to a different sort of destructive behavior.

PHASE FOUR: THE JENNIFER ANISTON JUNCTURE

Sorrow gave way to anger, and I began to rewrite the entire relationship in my head. It's destructive behavior, but typically Phase Four only lasts a few days. (I don't get enough protein to maintain the anger required to hate someone for long.) I rationalized everything I'd done to be a justifiable reaction to something Riley did. I imagined my life as a movie, myself as a jilted martyr, and Riley a fool relegated to an unfortunate footnote. The audience would sob over how poorly I'd been treated. Philip Glass would score the music. He'd be nominated for an Oscar, but he wouldn't win. He never wins.

Generally, it's during this phase that I act the most erratic and immature. Case in point: After a breakup in 2005, an ex called me asking to pick up some stuff that had been left at my house. I curtly obliged, but when collection time came, I threw everything out the window of my fourth-story dorm room, aiming directly for my ex's head. I'm not sure what was going through my own head to justify such an immature act. I figured it would make for a dramatic moment, but it just came off as childish.

Remembering the event, I could swear it happened in slow motion, like in an R. Kelly music video. I was nineteen; I'm not proud. Luckily, I managed to bypass that sort of behavior this time around. I suppose it's because I've matured, or maybe it's just that throwing sneakers and miniature TV sets out my window now would get me arrested.

After a few days of nasty thoughts projected in Riley's general direction, I came to terms with the fact that such behavior was destructive and only barely self-serving. It would be wonderful if I could leap to this conclusion sooner instead of enduring weeks of wallowing in bed, subsisting on little else besides peach Go-Gurt and revenge fantasies. After more than a month of gloom and doom, I emerged from my self-composed cocoon with one thought blazing in my mind: *I am fucking hungry as hell.*

PHASE FIVE: EAT EVERYTHING IN SIGHT

Stress always causes me to lose my appetite to the point of having to remind myself to eat, and my breakup with Riley was no exception. When I finally began to recover, I had lost about eight pounds, an alarming amount for my already-noodly body. Had I stayed depressed, I would have been a perfect fit for the Paris runways. I could clearly see my rib cage, and all of my extra-small T-shirts fit like muumuus. When my melancholy finally subsided, it gave way to rabid hunger and I became a human vacuum cleaner, inhaling every scrap of food I could find.

After that, Phase Six was an easy transition.

PHASE SIX: NO, SERIOUSLY, EAT FUCKING *EVERYTHING*

I don't know if it was the sudden influx of vitamins causing my system to reboot, but something seemed to click in

my brain and I just stopped caring about being upset. It's like when you're on an airplane and it's trying to descend through rough turbulence, and you clutch the armrests and pray it'll be over soon, and then the plane lands and you let out a sigh of relief, and then that's it. You turn on your cell phone and check your messages and forget the plane was bouncing around at all. My messy relationship and the difficult weeks following the split suddenly seemed so far in the past that I felt almost guilty for spending so much time indulging my anguish.

Carefully, I stepped back into my life. I turned on my iPod for the first time in weeks. I clipped off the mountain man beard that had overtaken my face. I ripped off each and every one of my fingernails with my teeth, and it felt incredible. I was ready for closure.

PHASE SEVEN: ACCEPTANCE AND RESOLUTION

Colors seemed brighter and the air smelled sweeter, though it was likely because my senses were dulled from eight straight weeks of staring at a television set, and I'm sure anything would smell sweeter than an unventilated room full of unwashed laundry. Regardless, I saw the world anew. Had a gaggle of forest animals joined me for a quaint musical number about how the heart can overcome, I wouldn't have been surprised (remember, I imagine my life as a movie more often than not).

I felt like I'd come out of the woods, so to speak—albeit sparsely populated woods close to civilization. My woods

were like the Central Park of wooded depression metaphors, but Central Park can be pretty scary at times (watch *Home Alone 2: Lost in New York* and tell me Central Park isn't scary). Semantics aside, I was feeling better. Still, something troubled me. I finally had a modicum of clarity, and with it came a disconcerting judgment about my past with Riley. In bits and pieces, the relationship played out in my mind. I saw the actions of us both for what they were: mostly childish, usually antagonistic. After everything that had gone down, all I really felt was ashamed for how I'd acted. Riley hadn't been blameless, but that was moot at this point. I knew I couldn't change anything about the past, but I *could* make an effort to better myself for whoever would turn out to be Riley's successor. That would become my driving force in the months that followed. I was aware I'd never know for sure if I'd improved until given a chance to test it with someone else, but realizing I needed to change was a small step in the right direction.

Step by step, I walked away from the memory of Riley and in the direction of a new, better me.

MAHALO, COME AGAIN

When sitcoms grow stale in their fifth or sixth seasons, the writers rely on a few tricks to reinvigorate the show and bring back viewers. Wedding episodes are always popular for some reason; or sometimes they'll add a cherubic youngster to make sassy quips at the adults, most often when the show's previous child actor has grown too old to still be cute. My personal favorite sitcom ruse is when the entire family decides to go on vacation. In the 1980s and '90s this meant the cast would be filming on location and a laugh track would be added later on in production, creating a surreal experience of canned ghost laughter following the characters around whatever new locale they were visiting. It was creepy and I loved it. Plus it generally meant a two-part episode, separated by a wacky cliffhanger. I'm a sucker for cliffhangers, even if the twist is no more exciting than Michelle Tanner going missing in Disney World after being a bitch to her sisters.

After my breakup with Riley, I found that Portland felt a

little claustrophobic. I was no longer pining for days gone by, yet I lingered in the midst of a funk I couldn't shake. I felt like I was in a fishbowl; I could see the city, but I didn't feel like I was really living in it. I was itching for a change of pace, to "clear my head," as Anglo-Saxon children of suburbia so often lament. I decided I would travel, ignoring the fact that my bank balance was hovering somewhere close to zero. Fortunately,

my credit card limit had just been inexplicably increased, so I set my sights on a trip. Uncertain of where to go, I opted to let the fates decide. I spun the plastic globe I keep on my desk.

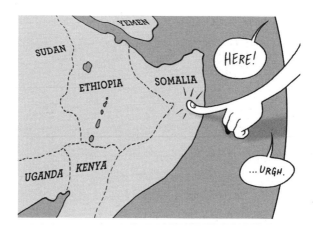

With Plan A an abject failure, I racked my memory banks of world geography. I'm the first to admit that my knowledge of the world is limited. In my brain, all of Europe is stuck in a prewar sepia-toned state of gloom. Asia is mysterious and dangerous and full of dragons. Africa is the same, minus the dragons. Feeling like I was at a loss, I considered the American sitcom, as I so often do when it comes to making decisions.

On *Friends* they went to London, but I didn't feel like leaving one rainy city for another. On *Roseanne* the Conners went to Las Vegas and Disney World. I thought, *I don't like to gamble and I'm a-scared of rides.* The cast of *Full House* similarly took trips to Vegas and Disney World, but they also vacationed in Hawaii. I considered this, and suddenly it seemed like such an obvious decision. *Hawaii.* It was sort of exotic, but not tremendously expensive, and I remembered I had a friend named Park who had moved from Boston to Hawaii for work. It had been years since we'd caught up, but I figured it would be worth a shot to ask him if I could crash on his couch. I emailed Park and told him I was considering a visit to the island, asking if he'd mind playing host. Being the laid-back guy he is, his reply was, "Yeah, sure, whatever." I booked a flight immediately.

The buyer's high wore off pretty quickly when I realized I was going to have to get on an airplane in a matter of weeks. I always overlook this horrifying little tidbit when I travel. I can't stand flying. Growing up it never bothered me, but several years ago on a flight from Boston to Montana I experienced some heinous turbulence that wrecked me for good. I remember it like it was yesterday. The flight had been smooth—almost suspiciously so. I was just about to bite into my twelve-dollar turkey sandwich and enjoy the in-flight presentation of *Beverly Hills Chihuahua* when the pilot chimed in over the intercom.

The rest of the flight was not unlike a roller-coaster ride. The flight attendants belted themselves into their seats at the front of the aircraft, and it's the only time I've ever seen a member of a flight crew look worried. The man sitting next to me began to hyperventilate and then *passed out*. When we landed, the pilot came back on the intercom and said, "Whew, we made it." He sounded shaken.

Since that flight, I've never been comfortable in the air. The slightest bit of turbulence sends me into a tailspin of panic. Once bitten, twice shy, three times a lady, et cetera. Now it's a struggle just to avoid having a nervous breakdown in

the airport, let alone on the airplane, so I try to keep calm by occupying myself with little games. My favorite is Airport Bingo. It's simple: Before I get to the terminal, I construct a Bingo card in my head of things one might see at an airport, and then spend the time before my flight seeing how many I can mark off. Sometimes I'll construct a physical grid on a napkin or a scrap of paper. It's like people-watching, only more judgmental.

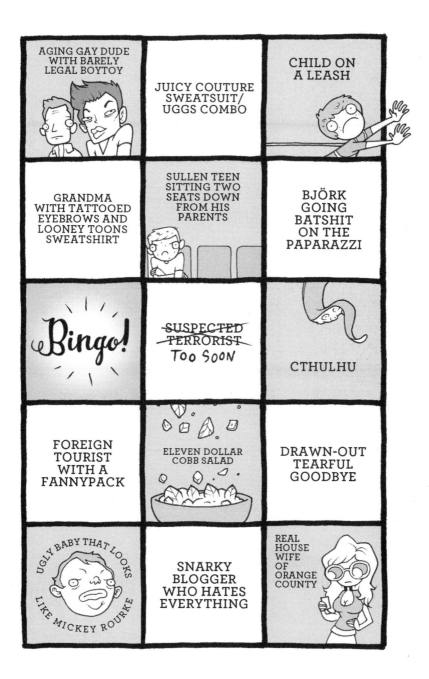

These kinds of mind games usually help keep my wild fantasies about flaming Boeing 757s crashing into the ocean at bay.

The day of my flight to Hawaii arrived, and as usual I waited till the last minute to pack, frantically tossing wrinkled clothes into my suitcase along with random toiletries and every pair of sunglasses I own, just to be safe. I arrived at the airport in typically late fashion and clamored through baggage check, arriving at my gate with precious moments to spare. As I waited to board, I gazed around at the crowd, mentally ticking off imaginary boxes on a made-up grid.

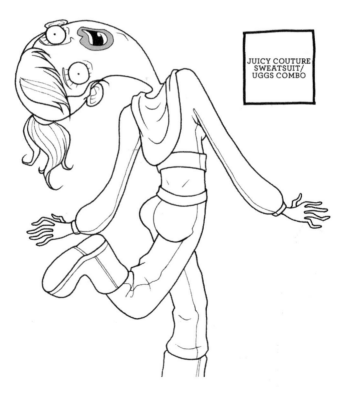

JUICY COUTURE
SWEATSUIT/
UGGS COMBO

184

GRANDMA
WITH TATTOOED
EYEBROWS AND
LOONEY TOONS
SWEATSHIRT

BACHELOR
DAD DECKED
OUT IN ED
HARDY

I was nearly on my way to a full Bingo blackout by the time I got on the plane. I closed my eyes, took a slow, deep breath, and prayed I wouldn't end up at the bottom of the Pacific. Mercifully, my flight was peaceful and uneventful, save for the woman I was seated next to, who insisted on gabbing incessantly to me about her planned "vision quest" to Oahu. I nodded politely, interjecting an "ah" here and an "oh?" there. I fell asleep sometime after her spiel chronicling how her bottle of "healing elixir" had been confiscated for being over the allowed volume. In recent years I've turned to prescription drugs when I fly, though none has sent me into slumber as effectively as being forced to listen to the assumed curative powers of crystals.

I'd never been to Hawaii before, and the first thing I noticed when I got off the plane was how warm and sunny it was— the exact opposite of the gloomy Portland winter I'd left mere hours before. I saw Park immediately: At six foot five he towered over everyone else. He greeted me with a lei, more as a joke than anything, and we took a taxi to his apartment. Along the way, I gazed out the window at the green mountains in the distance. My own vacation episode was off to a good start.

My first couple of days on the island were spent in typical tropical fashion: wandering around aimlessly, napping on the beach, and trying to avert my gaze from old dudes in Speedos. In the afternoons I walked around town with Park while he played tour guide, recounting the history of Hawaii; dutiful host was he. During the days he was at work, I meandered around the island on my own, looking for things to do. I briefly considered filming a better ending to *Lost* on my camera phone (starring myself as every character) but figured that might be too much work. Instead I opted for baking in the sun on the beach down the street from Park's home, waiting for the sweet, sweet melanoma to set in. I found it surprisingly easy to turn my brain off and languish on the warm sand like a beached sea lion.

My relaxing vacation hit a slight rough patch around day four. Park was, shall we say, *a connoisseur of the ganja.* That night he made us dinner and then went outside to get stoned, as was his general routine. I'd smoked plenty during college, but weed has always makes me ravenous, so I typically avoid it when offered. Having just eaten a hearty dinner of baked fish and fresh pineapple, however, I took Park up on his proposal when he offered to share. I joined him outside and we sat on his back porch, passing his glass pipe back and forth. When we were done, he wandered into the backyard to have a cigarette, following one vice with another. I sank into my chair and looked up at the sky. I waited for the high to set in. As I expected, not much happened at first except for the general relaxing mellowness I was accustomed to. But then *a lot happened.*

The stars in the sky began to move, slowly at first and then in more fluid spirals. The chair I was sitting in felt like it was melting backward into the concrete. I lost my balance even though I was seated, and caught myself in what felt like a fall. I felt panicky, paranoid. Without a word I moved inside and sat down on the couch. I stared at the wall, which seemed to move just like the stars had, undulating in and out. Tunnel vision set in and I became convinced my friend had drugged me in order to harvest my organs. I figured I should lie down. I went into Park's bedroom and curled up in the fetal position on his bed. I had no idea what was happening to me; the high I was experiencing was unlike any I'd ever felt before. For what seemed like eons I lay motionless, wide-eyed and stricken with terror. At one point I became convinced Park's bed was in fact a giant, sleeping animal, and if I moved it would awaken and carry me into the forest on its back and I'd never be seen again.

I'm going to die here in Hawaii, I thought to myself. *Nobody can help me. I need to call my mother and tell her goodbye. I need to tell everyone goodbye and that I love them.*

Park appeared in his doorway and asked if I was all right. From his point of view, I imagine the scene was unremarkable.

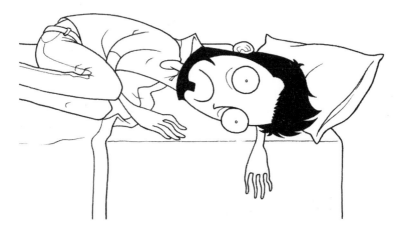

In my head, the severity of the situation was much more pronounced.

"Turn off the light," is all I said. Park did so. "It's too dark now, turn the lights back on," I responded. Park did so. Again I asked him to turn off the lights. We continued in this fashion for a few minutes, him flipping the light switch on and off, until I croaked, "I don't know what's happening to meeeee..." Park suggested that my blood pressure had dropped and triggered a panic attack, and told me I'd be fine in a little bit. I closed my eyes, focused on my breathing, and eventually somehow fell asleep. I awoke hours later in the dead of night, covered in sweat and convinced the sweat was actually blood. I searched my body for mortal wounds but found none. I collapsed back into bed, relieved, feeling slightly less anxious. The drugs were starting to wear off. *No more weed for a while*, I promised myself. *Strictly black tar heroin from now on.* I slipped back into slumber, thinking *I might be getting too old for this kind of thing.*

The next day I figured some relaxing beach time was in order to remedy the previous night's unbridled terror. I had come to Hawaii to relax and get centered, not have a heart attack. I located a bookstore on my phone and set off in search of something I could read in a day or two. *Something light and unchallenging*, I thought. *Perhaps some paranormal teen fiction featuring a love triangle...or maybe some Tolstoy.* In the bookstore, I meandered up and down the aisles, waiting for a book to catch my eye. I was about to reach for Danielewski's *House of Leaves* when suddenly, something far more appropriate caught my eye. There it was. *The perfect book.*

Could there be a more flawless choice than *Goosebumps: Ghost Beach*? Anything more divinely meta than reading *Ghost Beach* on the *fucking beach*? The bustling murmur of the bookstore seemed to fade away into silence; I felt the lights dim as I gazed upon the thin, hundred-page paperback, seeming to call out to me with a gentle whisper. *This is what I came to the islands for*, I thought. *I was meant to read this book, in this place, at this time. I am now a believer in fate.*

I spent the rest of the morning in utter bliss. I flipped through my new book, holding it gingerly in my hands as if it were a religious text. Though I'd figured out the twist ending by page 19 (everyone is a ghost, basically), it didn't matter. The trauma of the previous night slipped away, carried out to sea and forgotten.

LIKE A BOSS

By the time the sun was setting, I was all jazzed up on ghost stories and about fourteen shades darker than before. If I were a color swatch, it would have been Pantone 18-1242, otherwise known as "Brown Patina." Park would be getting off work soon, so I packed up my towel and headed back in the direction of his apartment.

That night I wanted to cut loose, and since the previous night's activity had not panned out, we decided to go out to a bar. It was dark, humid, and packed with people shouting over thumping club jams. I felt like a drunk ninja, my deep brown tan causing me to all but disappear into the shadows. At one point I caught a glimpse of myself in the mirror; I looked like a Cheshire cat, all floating white teeth and eyeballs.

Sometime after two, I found myself in a dance club, separated from my friend by a sea of people. The club's humidity made me feel clammy, like I was swimming through chowder. I caught sight of Park over the sea of people and attempted to wade through the crowd, but only succeeded in becoming caught in the middle of the bedlam. I was trapped. Next to me stood a wobbly, sleepy-eyed girl, and a middle-aged woman looking far worse for wear. Halfheartedly, I attempted to engage the girl in some friendly mutual footwork. She barely acknowledged me and instead motioned to the older woman next to her.

With that, the girl stumbled off the dance floor, either to ingest more alcohol or to purge it from her system. I found myself face-to-face with her mother, who seemed to barely register her surroundings. I shrugged and attempted to make the best of the situation.

It became apparent to me that my dance partner was entirely wasted, and I mean that in the most clinical sense. Her eyes were unfocused, her hair was a mess, and she had one boob in danger of flopping out of her cardigan. The woman was in rough shape, but I was hardly keeping my own balance, so I awkwardly shimmied away from her and left her alone. I was in no condition to take care of an old lady jacked up on appletinis. I made a beeline for the exit and texted Park once I was outside: *let's go home.* As I waited for him to show up, my eyes feeling heavy, I suddenly felt a little homesick for Portland. The prospect of getting back to the ease of the Northwest sounded pleasant. I was ready to go home, and it was then that I realized I actually considered Portland my home—not just some place I was trying to build a life in, but somewhere I actually had one. I belonged there.

A few days later, and with my vacation's end closing in, it occurred to me that I'd yet to actually go swimming. Since the ocean is on a short list of things that make me nervous (along with air travel, bees, meth scabs, and other people's feet, of course), I'd been avoiding the water. Still, I figured it would be a crime to visit Hawaii without swimming, so I traveled on foot from Park's apartment to the beach, my flip-flops slapping against my heels as I walked. I set my backpack and towel down on the sand and cautiously waded into the ocean. It was chilly but refreshing, and I quickly warmed up to it as I inched forward into the water. Eventually I felt my toes leave the bottom. Then I closed my eyes and went under. I realized that I hadn't been in the ocean since I was eight. When I broke the surface again, I was almost surprised to taste salt on my lips. I treaded water and gazed back toward land. I wasn't far out, but it was enough to take in the scenery. I noticed I was beaming and probably couldn't have stopped if I'd wanted to.

I could actively feel my batteries recharging and I was irrefutably happy for the first time in months. I thought about Riley briefly, but the moment was fleeting. Everything that had been bothering me in recent weeks suddenly felt trite and mundane. I felt silly because I could hear a future version of myself telling my friends back in Portland about my vacation. "It was so refreshing to just *get away*, you know? Such a boost to my psyche. My aura is probably, like, bright pink now." I remembered my flight partner, the lady who had yakked to me about her planned vision quest, and I regretted scoffing at her in my mind. Who was I to mock the prospect of feeling better? I decided to give in to it.

"I am healed!" I announced aloud to nobody.

The final charming surprise of my trip didn't occur until the next day. I was back at the airport, awaiting my boarding announcement, when a little girl approached me, unprovoked and unannounced, her brow furrowed with determination.

"*WATCH MY DANCE!*" she announced, and then proceeded to work it with such fierce purpose I was afraid she might have an aneurism right in front of me.

When she finished, her mom shook a bag of Teddy Grahams at her and she immediately lost interest in dancing and scampered off. My grandmother used to say, "This too shall pass," and it always seemed like Hallmark-card-style mumbo jumbo, but suddenly her words floated back to me. A few weeks ago, stricken with grief, I might've scowled at the little girl and found her obnoxious. Now, though, I couldn't do anything but smile at her exuberance. I could've gotten up and danced myself.

Back in Portland, with a complexion somewhere between chestnut and mahogany, I took a moment to reflect on my trip. I don't remember how the Hawaii episode of *Full House* ended, but I think there was a bit about being lost at sea, and then Uncle Jesse bizarrely played drums for the Beach Boys. Whatever the case, I'm sure someone learned a valuable lesson and there was some heartfelt string music. If I learned anything during my own Vacation Episode, it's that life is about experiences, good and bad. I had to take a step out of my own day-to-day life to realize it, but with some newfound perspective, I understood that it all balances out eventually. Sometimes you get lost at sea, but if you keep your head above water, there might just be something beautiful on the horizon.

IRON GODDESS OF MERCY

The legend goes like this:

In southeast China there was a run-down temple that housed an iron statue of the Bodhisattva Guanyin, the Goddess of Mercy. A poor farmer passed the temple each morning on his way to the tea fields. He would look upon the temple with a heavy heart, noting its crumbling condition.

Because the farmer was poor, he had not the means to restore the temple's glory. Still, he wanted to do something. He brought a broom from his home and swept the temple clean of debris, then lit some incense as an offering to Guanyin. He did this each day for many months. "It's the least I can do," he said.

One night, the goddess appeared to him in a dream and told him of a hidden cave behind the temple where great treasure awaited.

She told him to claim the treasure as a reward for his hard work and share it with the others in his village. The next day, the farmer

searched and found the cave the goddess spoke of, but upon entering it found no great treasure. Instead, he found only a tiny tea shoot poking up through the ground. He was disheartened.

The farmer took the tea shoot anyway and planted it on his farm. To his surprise, it grew into a hearty bush from which the finest tea was produced. He gave cuttings of it to his friends and family, and they began selling it. Before long the village prospered and grew famous for its delicious tea. The farmer's small act of kindness and his faith that something good would happen paid off. As thanks to the goddess, they named the tea after her: Tieguanyin. The Iron Goddess of Mercy.

I drink Tieguanyin most nights. Occasionally I'll switch up the tea I drink, but the Iron Goddess of Mercy is the one I continually return to. Making tea is a ritual I look forward to. My workload has a tendency to pile up and the routine of brewing tea offers momentary respite, during which time I can clear my head and recalibrate. I focus on the steps: filling the tea bag, boiling water, steeping the tea, then waiting for it to cool so I can drink it. It's a simple ceremony but a calming one, and the legend behind the tea's origin serves as a hopeful reminder that everything I do will one day amount to something more. It offers solace from the stress of my life, however fleeting.

Another little ritual I have is lying on the floor in the dark, panicking over the notion that I'm wasting my formative years on misguided endeavors.

In these ephemeral moments of despair, tea is of little help. While I'm comforted by the fact that almost everyone my age deals with the same ambiguities and insecurities, it doesn't negate those big moments of complete and all-consuming doubt that seem like they might cause my whole life to derail. Eventually I tell myself that everything is all right. I make some lists in my head, set some goals, and before long it's tomorrow and I'm fine.

Despite the pervasive uncertainty of life, I *am* gaining perspective. Here are some of the things I have learned so far:

1. I Can't Keep Dating Jerks, Hoping to Turn Them into Good People

This has taken me ages to learn, and I'm still not sure it's sunk in all the way. Barring one notable exception, I've dated pretty much exclusively garbage-people. For a while, it was fun to imagine that I could reform someone else, like a science project. A part of me still hopes I can find someone to mold into the perfect human specimen, as if I'm building a mate from carefully selected parts.

In reality, I have a hard enough time changing myself. There's no way I could possibly change another person.

2. I Can't Eat the Way I Used To

I will probably never be fat. Looking back at the men in my family, not a one of them was anything other than lean (and usually downright twiggy), and for this I am thankful. Still, I'm discovering that I can't continue to shovel food into my gullet and expect to maintain a figure like that of Christian Bale in *The Machinist*. Now when I eat loads of shitty food, I find myself feeling lazy and lethargic. I have to run longer on the treadmill to maintain my Voldemort-like physique. It would be so much easier if I could eat like I did when I was sixteen, but I fear that will lead to dark places.

3. I Can't Drink Like I Used To

I've always been a pretty responsible drinker (ahem, *sort of*), but I just can't keep up with my younger self any longer. A few months ago I went out for a friend's birthday and consumed what seemed like a perfectly reasonable number of vodka tonics. I went to bed and woke up the next morning with a crippling hangover. I spent the entire morning on the floor of my living room, my head pounding like Denver the Last Dinosaur was about to hatch from my skull.

In college I could spend the night partying, get three hours of sleep, wake up feeling buoyant and refreshed, and go to my 8 a.m. class without a care in the world. Now if I have too much to drink, I have to personally call FEMA to deliver me a bag of Egg McMuffins.

4. Money Vanishes

I try to keep an eye on my bank account, but it still feels like cash is being steadily funneled out of my possession and into a void. I feebly attempt to cling to my finances, yet frugality seems like a nonsense notion in my twenties.

It's almost sneaky the way it happens. A couple of visits to the Las Piedritas taco truck for $5 burritos, a night out at Wimpy's for $2.50 well drinks, a too-good-to-pass-up sale on Bonobos.com, then a couple of auto-payments hit my account for bills and my gym membership, and suddenly I have $500 less in checking than I did the week before. It's as if I'm tying hundred-dollar bills to a cat and sending her off into the wilderness, never to be seen again.

Before I realize what's happened, I'm destitute, with nothing to show for it except a burrito-induced tummy ache and orange chino shorts that don't even fit because of all the burritos I've been eating.

5. I Am Jealous of Everyone for Their Success, Be It Real or Imagined

I'm at that age where many of my friends are getting married and having little goblin offspring of their own. Every week I open my mailbox to find save-the-dates and wedding announcements, oftentimes from people I hardly remember. The barrage of invites is endless.

I remember being eight and adamantly claiming that I'd never get married (unless it was to Sailor Moon) and that I'd rather die than have children of my own. I've softened somewhat on the notion of children, though currently I can't imagine my life with a son or daughter present. I can fathom no

worse hell than having to pause my Skyrim game to change a diaper, and yet I somehow find myself jealous of all my friends who are getting married and becoming pregnant.

It shouldn't be a competition. I don't even *want* to get married and I certainly don't want kids right now, but I still stare at all the wedding announcements pinned to my fridge with a mixture of envy and loathing.

I try to remind myself that this is just a symptom of the Facebook age and that we all make unreasonable comparisons of ourselves and our peers. Then I brew a scalding-hot cup of Tieguanyin and casually pour it out the window onto some unwitting passerby.

Though my days are often filled with a vague sense of dread and foreboding, there are moments of profound insight, and I cling tightly to these, collecting them in my subconscious like precious jewels so that I may reference them later. These moments usually manifest in small and quiet ways—an electric, passionate discussion with a friend, or a walk through the city when the weather is perfect and the streets are buzzing with life. These moments are like little islands of positivity. Sometimes I get tired of swimming, but I trust there's another little island on the horizon.

I like to think that when my twenties come to a close, I will be at peace with myself and at one with the universe, wise and tranquil like a maharishi.

For now, I'll draw and I'll write, I'll try to learn new things, and I'll attempt to take something positive away from every experience I have, no matter how small. I'll try to keep my finances in check and be nice to people even when they're being insufferable. And I'll make Tieguanyin tea at night and imagine the Iron Goddess watching over me, telling me that someday the fruits of my labor will bear out and I will be happy and prosperous like the farmer.

ACKNOWLEDGMENTS

This book would not be possible without the abundant support I received throughout the process of creating it. I'd like to thank Kristin for reading everything I've ever written and giving me feedback, even though she probably had better things to do. I'm thankful to Trevor for being understanding when I periodically got frustrated with my work and subsequently became a spiteful monster. I'm grateful to my agent Monika and my editor Pippa, both of whom offered guidance during the very tricky process of crafting a book. And I have to thank my mother, who always made sure I had a book in my hands.